SISTER DEATH

SISTER DEATH

POLITICAL THEOLOGIES FOR LIVING AND DYING

BEATRICE MAROVICH

Columbia University Press   New York

Columbia University Press
Publishers Since 1893
New York   Chichester, West Sussex
cup.columbia.edu

Copyright © 2023 Columbia University Press
All rights reserved

Library of Congress Cataloging-in-Publication Data
Names: Marovich, Beatrice, author.
Title: Sister death : political theologies for living and dying / Beatrice Marovich.
Description: New York : Columbia University Press, 2023. | Includes bibliographical references and index.
Identifiers: LCCN 2022020339 | ISBN 9780231208369 (hardback) | ISBN 9780231208376 (trade paperback) | ISBN 9780231557399 (ebook)
Subjects: LCSH: Death—Religious aspects. | Death—Political aspects. | Political theology.
Classification: LCC BL504 .M283 2023 | DDC 202/.3—dc23/eng20220908
LC record available at https://lccn.loc.gov/2022020339

Cover design: Milenda Nan Ok Lee
Cover art: Krista Dragomer, *Binding for a Sanguine Shelter*, 2020.

CONTENTS

List of Works   vii
Preface   xiii
Acknowledgments   xxiii

Introduction: Sister Death   1
1 Life, Death, and Lifedeath   33
2 The War with Death   59
3 The Human-Above-Death   87
4 Constellated Negatives   123
5 Sisterhood and Enmity   159
6 Natal Disturbance   187
Conclusion: Into the Dirt   219

Notes   235
Bibliography   253
Index   261

LIST OF WORKS

All works included in this book are by the artist Krista Dragomer.

Frontispiece *Eden II*, 2013, 30 × 11 in.   x
0.1 *Synodic Portal 1*, 2020, 3.5 × 5.5 in.   xxx
0.2 *Signature*, 2013, 30 × 22 in.   12
0.3 *Silk Milk*, 2012, 30 × 22 in.   25
0.4 *Milk and Honey*, 2012, 14 × 22 in.   28
1.1 *Synodic Portal 2*, 2020, 3.5 × 5.5 in.   32
1.2 *Flutter of Fine Filaments*, 2013, 10 × 14 in.   35
1.3 *Held by a Blast in Unwritten Space*, 2017, 8.5 × 11 in.   52
2.1 *Synodic Portal 3*, 2020, 3.5 × 5.5 in.   58
2.2 *Enfleshed Transits*, 2014, 5 × 7 in.   73
2.3 *Reciprocal Community*, 2015, 11 × 13 in.   76
3.1 *Synodic Portal 5*, 2020, 3.5 × 5.5 in.   86
3.2 *Pure Soil*, 2020, 9.5 × 11 in.   99
4.1 *Synodic Portal 4*, 2020, 3.5 × 5.5 in.   122
4.2 *Made of Stars*, 2013, 30 × 12 in.   133
4.3 *A Planetary Cross Pollination Event*, 2013, 30 × 12 in.   155
5.1 *Synodic Portal 6*, 2020, 3.5 × 5.5 in.   158
5.2 *Untitled Sketch (cover/bind study)*, 2019, 9 × 12 in.   160
5.3 *Untitled Sketch (group movement)*, 2019, 9 × 12 in.   174

5.4 *Untitled Sketch (conversation companion)*, 2019, 9 × 12 in.   179
5.5 *Biopolitical Propositions*, 2019, 9 × 12 in.   182
6.1 *Synodic Portal 8*, 2020, 3.5 × 5.5 in.   186
6.2 *Untitled Sketch (growth)*, 2019, 9 × 12 in.   200
con.1 *Synodic Portal 7*, 2020, 3.5 × 5.5 in.   218
con.2 *Underlit Sky*, 2014, 10 × 10 in.   228
con.3 *The Forest Floor Is Always Busy*, 2016, 4 × 6 in.   232

PREFACE

Children are interested in death. For many American children today, their first brush with death comes as a message from the more than human world. Maybe they see a small bird that's fallen from a nest and is exposed, featherless, on the pavement. Or a dog, once perceived as an elder, has weakened and disappeared. Children hear this word, *dead*, and they become curious. Their interest does not preclude fear. But despite their fear, or perhaps because of it, many children are determined in their pursuit to understand whatever it is that the grown people call "death."

Small children are still so close to the moment of their own birth, even though they don't recall the traumatic event that tore them from the warm, dark waters where they gestated with a soft veil over their eyes. And it is unlikely they can still recall the way most of them cried, almost every afternoon, for the first several weeks of their life as the sun began to set. Do infants worry, in the witching hour that comes with evening, that the dark is returning to swallow them up for good this time? Is this why they continue to fear the dark, left alone to sleep as shadows dance menacingly on the wall?

Whatever the case may be, it does seem that small children must still feel incredibly close to the surging powers of life that pushed them into the world of dry air, bright light, and sharp sound. It still conducts them forward: a powerful stream, like water from a firehose. There must be some perceptual recall in children—some memory of the beauty and the horror of being drawn into singular life in an enfleshed body. This subtle, disappearing memory must make the often hushed and timid grown-up discourse on final endings sound naive and incomprehensible. When I try to imagine myself drawn back in time, toward that fresh pleasure and terror of first becoming alive, the idea that there is some grand and final ending when all sensation ceases (or when the earth itself, this home of sensation, is abandoned for a disembodied counter-dimension) does seem incredibly wrong.

As I type these words, I have not yet died. But I was born, and I have taken part in the birth event of another human. That second passage through birth has made me revisit everything that I think and perceive about life, and also about death. Birth events in the United States today are affectively dominated by advertising. A host of industries thrives on birth events; this commerce promises to soothe your anxieties and terrors with convenient products to address every possible infant or parent impulse, in soft pastels and charming prints. As a pregnant person, looking out onto the abyss of whatever mystery lies beyond this portal, you are confronted with the well-fed, happy faces of toothless smiling babies on countless product ads. And if you are anything like me, you might find yourself awash in resentment and disgust at the way that this joy has been packaged and commodified, at the expense of the raw honesty you are much hungrier for. When I first caught a glimpse of the sweet face I helped to usher into this life of flesh, I was captured by a rich joy that I experience again and again when I see this always changing wonder.

But when I reflect on the emergence into existence, it seems to me just as horrifying as the event of our exit from the flesh—more so, perhaps, given the intensity of sense perception in a small, brand-new body. Birth—that is, the beginning of embodied life—is an event full of power and beauty. But beauty and horror are not mutually exclusive. They live right up against one another in this event. Certainly, we must be able to say the same thing about death. Are children trying to remind us of this?

There is a story my mother tells about me as a child. When I was three or four, I apparently became very curious about death, and what happens when we leave this flesh behind. My mother, invested in the project of allowing me to become a free spirit, did not give a clear answer, and I was told that the perspective was mine to select. Unsatisfied by this lack of clarity, I began to outsource the question. When my grandmother told me with frank good humor that death means we are buried in a coffin below the ground, I told her flatly that she was wrong. When a stranger told me about a celestial heaven populated by angels, where we will reunite with those we love, I scoffed at this as well. My mother purchased picture books that had been written with the express purpose of explaining death to a child. I had no real interest in them. The question stayed with me. Then, one day, my mother was reading me an illustrated version of Oscar Wilde's *The Selfish Giant*, and I latched onto the word *paradise*. "That's it," I apparently said to her. "What?" she asked, confused. "That's what happens," I told her, "when you die. It's paradise."

When I think about this story now, I feel a little sting of shame for having been (if I was) a bit insufferable. But I also like to think that perhaps my intuition had simply found a sort of confirmation; I had stumbled upon the solution to a kind of problem. I had only just recently emerged from a potent something, and had torn forth into something else. Changes of state and form are limit exercises, of sorts, but they are not formal endings. I like to think that I was dissatisfied with the stories that would have me believe that death—one's departure from the flesh—was either some cold finality or something unearthly. I like to think that I could sense the flatness of these descriptions, and in *paradise* I heard something else. I want to believe that my little mind could perceive what etymologies of that beautiful word reveal: that it referred to an enclosed, secluded, secretive garden. That it was a figure not of annihilation nor of removal from this earthly terrain but instead a figure of what Jacques Derrida called *lifedeath*. Paradise was a word that could illuminate the way a garden brings together the stench of decay and the sweetness of blossoms—an illumination that blends beauty and horror.

Whatever peace I may have found in that word, at the age of three or four, it was not a lasting one. I had no sense of the history of this word *paradise*, of its many references, of its unsettled ideological proximities—in the present—to that other unearthly space-time that I found so unbelievable. But as I look back on the decades of my life, now, it becomes clear to me in hindsight that my obsessive dissatisfaction with flat or hollow explanations of death have been a centripetal animating force. I have been thinking about death for a long time, and I have been on a long quest for companions in beauty and horror: for others who will share this full reality with me as the currents pass through us. And I have found myself in theology—an ancient storehouse of apparently fixed positions on the nature of life and death—both in search of companions and in search of a method by which to unsettle these ancient forms. I am sometimes asked how I ended up as a scholar of theology, given that I was raised in a family of Marxist atheists, secular Jews, lapsed Latvian Lutherans, and witchy women. I can offer many rationalizations. But the image that most frequently pops into my mind's eye when I hear this question is the red balloon on the cover of the Routledge edition of Simone Weil's *Gravity and Grace*. I was an undergraduate at the University of Michigan, in Ann Arbor, when I found *Gravity and Grace* on the shelf of the now departed Shaman Drum bookstore on State Street. It was the single red balloon that drew me in, because it reminded me of the Albert Lamorisse film that I had loved, as a child. Like Pascal in the film, I grabbed ahold of the string on the red balloon and it took me on a very strange ride. Weil's work was brutal and unsettling in a way that can (still) make my lip curl in disgust. But at the same time it soothed me with a thing whose contours I could not grasp. As someone with absolutely no frame of reference for the word *God*, she drew me toward the term as a site of encounter, collision, or collusion between the beautiful and the horrific.

It took a little time and a number of adventures, but impulse and accident eventually landed me in a master's degree program in theology in Vancouver, British Columbia. I anticipated feelings of total alienation, so I was surprised to find a kindred spirit in my professor Sharon Betcher, whose work clearly inhabited that uncertain space where beauty and horror come into contact. And in Sallie McFague I found another lover of Simone Weil. Despite their companionship, I struggled to find my focus. It's not that I was uninterested in the power discourses that most people undertake when they talk about God. But I had trouble understanding what those conversations had to do with me. I had no real sense of the powers inherent in the word itself. I could not perceive them. They sounded abstract—simple power discourses that sought to validate or invalidate other gestures toward power. I had no idea through which portals or channels I was supposed to sense them. That was a question I needed to answer. And so I focused on the one classic theological figure that made sense to me: the creature who was created (by the creator) to die. I felt as if, in the philosophical fictions that I had been told about this limit figure—this mortal body—there were also some hidden secrets about the failures of these limits. I sought out those moments where acts of divine making had left little traces of breath and power on these mortal bodies. Or those moments when the creator could not help but lick his fleshy lips when he smelled the burning smoke of a sacrifice. I wanted to see if the limit conditions were liable to actively implode. Or perhaps those fleeting moments of transfer remained secretive because it was the secret that pretended to keep the lines in place.

It was at this time, early in my graduate school experience, that I met another kindred spirit. Krista Dragomer and I were both new to graduate school and met in the bathroom at a party in Vancouver. We quickly confessed to one another that, unlike all of the other people around us who seemed to love Vancouver, we both found it incredibly disappointing. This confession, and a kind of mutual contrarianism, made us immediate friends. But we also soon discovered that we were both drawn toward those difficult conceptual spaces where beauty and horror tend to bleed into one another. Our friendship became one of those that so changed my thinking that it has left its mark on everything I do. Krista was, and still is, a sound and visual artist whose art has always pursued the unsettled and the unsettling. From the very beginning, we shared new theories and ideas the way that other friends delightedly share gossip. During those Vancouver years, her interests in sensation and perception (which she was exploring deeply, at this time, through sound) helped to keep me grounded in the dense and veiny textures of embodiment. But she also, like me, had a wild and expansive form of thinking and was interested in the abstractions I was encountering in my discipline. Together we tested these ideas. We experimented with fusions that we would, in very different ways, performatively inhabit in our work. Mortal, creaturely, earthly bodies would collide and be reshaped by strange and wild forms of barely habitable power.

We both moved from Vancouver to the New York metro area after completing our master's degrees. Krista moved to Brooklyn, to make art. Initially, I was in New Jersey for my PhD program, though I later moved to Brooklyn. I had been drawn to study with Catherine Keller, whose wondrous *The Face of the Deep* had captured my imagination with its beautiful and unsettling interrogation of the relationship between God and nothingness. Krista would visit my place, in Jersey, for an escape from the city. And I would visit her frequently, in Brooklyn, to be immersed in it. I wrote words, and Krista experimented with works on paper. Together we investigated and discussed emerging work on multispecies encounters, work exploring our sensing and perceiving animal bodies, work interrogating historical relationships between the metaphysical human and the metaphysical animal, work that continued to speculatively reshape the way that people were catching glimpses of divine things on the ground, and dystopian apocalyptic scenarios. Many of the images that you will find in this book were created during this period. When I moved first to Grand Forks, North Dakota, and then to Louisville, Kentucky, for academic outposts, Krista and I remained actively in touch but our collaborations went on a hiatus of sorts and our work took off in different, though still resonant, directions.

In the wake of the COVID-19 pandemic, every dimension of life seemed to shift and reshape. My own work had taken a turn, even before the pandemic, away from the multispecies dimensions of creatureliness and further toward the death that stirred within this mortal figure. For more than five years, I had been teaching courses to undergraduates on death and the afterlife. But COVID-19 intensified my attention to this project. It is entirely possible that, had I not lived through this global crisis, I might not have written this book. Or I might not have written it so soon. The pandemic gave my thinking a new urgency. Death was, in a way that I had never experienced, intensely present. Working and teaching from home, my own time was also punctuated by the constant sound of meetings and phone calls coming from the other room. My husband—working for the Center for Health Equity in the Louisville Metro Health Department and reassigned to the planning section of the COVID-19 response for a year and a half—was constantly engaged in heated debates about the local vaccine rollout or fighting to stop the clearing of encampments where the housing insecure were seeking refuge. With these debates playing out in the background, it was clear to me just how protected I was, how protected my family was, from the pandemic. But at the end of our unchangingly routine days—in a home where work had (for lack of time) become the only form of play—we were heavy with sorrow and fear. At night, wrapped in the safety of the dark, we stared sleeplessly at the ceiling. We felt safe but also powerless and isolated. The shadows of death seemed to press ever more strangely against the windowpanes.

Meanwhile, Krista was weathering lockdown in her New York apartment and had begun to make art that was exploring the long and quiet nights that, like the shadows of death, made their strange presence known in the clearings of her windows. She also began to teach online drawing courses to help others experimentally explore dimensions of sensation and perception. Each lonely in very different ways, we began to exchange notes on what we saw illuminated in the dense shadows closing in on us. As all of our relations—family, work, and play—seemed to be relocated to the virtual, I took refuge and inspiration from what became almost daily text conversations with Krista. We shared photographs of passages of books we were reading, tarot card readings, and experimented with new ways of describing and engaging with our work. In the spring of 2021, when I was completely burnt out and disenchanted with online teaching, I struggled to think about how to teach an intensive virtual May term course. I wanted to do what Krista was doing: to invite students into their sensing bodies, even though we were gathered in the disembodied virtual. So I wrote a grant for us to co-teach a virtual course that we called Coming to Your Senses. We hosted drawing workshops, where Krista would send the students outside to gather rocks, or to observe their shadows and draw whatever appeared within their amorphous silhouette. We would discuss, with students, the multidimensional religious meanings of rocks, or how, if they were ants in the grass, they might perceive this human shadow.

Our work together reminded me of the way that being mortal is a perceptual condition. When we are told (when we believe) that we are creatures hurtling toward death, this idea shapes our sense of where we are and what we do. It shapes our view in a very particular way. But I suspect that we also recall, if only in some repressed dimension of our perception, that we were also born. We know that our time here is more than just a journey toward total dissolution. And in conversation with those who have lived before us, and died, we do this work that is more than—other than, even contrary to—death. This book does not venture to explain why this is. And it does not pretend to make any sort of real peace with the horrors of either life or death. But I wrote this book because I believe that there are real problems—failures—in the language that many of us have been given to make sense of this wild nexus where life and death collide and collude. What I seek to do, in this book, is to gesture toward other possible stories to tell, another sort of language to share, another form of perception. Krista's images model other forms of perception that are different, still, from the language that I offer as text on the page. In this sense, I hope her work will illuminate yet other possible stories.

In the writing of *Sister Death* there were passages that were so difficult for me to write that I cried as I wrote them. I grieved for those who are gone, and I grieved in an anticipatory way all that will soon be lost. There were also passages that were so cathartic they made me cry for entirely different reasons; they were a kind of discovery that shocked me into a chastened gratitude. Writing a book about death, in the midst of a pandemic, was an experience filled with beauty and horror. Each of us living through the pandemic has been remade by it in different ways. And what I think that life has showed me, as it has unfurled before my vantage point, are dimensions of its intimacy with death that were not visible to me before. It has become clearer than ever that death is neither a friend nor an enemy to us—or to life itself. As we have struggled to shelter one another from the claws of death, we have also sought to subject this virus to death. These acts, on the plane of lifedeath, are bound and are in relation. I have never been so aware of the pleasures and the terrors of being a livingdying being, floating and hurtling through space-time. And I am grateful for the soft hands of those who are traveling alongside me, even though some of them (both living and dead) are too far away for me to touch directly. I am indebted to these companions who travel with me, wide-eyed, in these spaces of beauty and horror. Without them, I would not have been able, in the first place, to open my eyes to it all.

ACKNOWLEDGMENTS

The seeds for this book were planted when I was invited to contribute a reading of Francis of Assisi's *Laudes Creaturarum* to a special issue of *Glossator: The Practice and Theory of the Commentary*, edited by Eugene Thacker and Nicola Masciandaro. This was the first time I considered, seriously and studiously, Christian theological positions on death itself. I am grateful to both Nicola and Eugene for this invitation that took off in its own direction, and especially grateful to Nicola for suggesting that I look at this particular text from Francis. This was where I met the figure of Sister Death and spent time thinking deeply about Francis's figuration of her. My commentary in this book on *Laudes Creaturarum* is pulled largely from this *Glossator* article, "When Death Became a Creature." Thanks also to Mårten Björk for translating this essay into Swedish, for publication in the journal *Subaltern*. Elements of my overview of Hannah Arendt's natality (in chapter 6 of this book) also appear in my essay "Death and the Negative in Agamben and Beauvoir" in *Agamben and the Existentialists*, edited by Marcos Antonio Norris and Colby Dickinson, published by Edinburgh University Press.

I began to further develop these ideas about death in a keynote address that I was invited to give at the DePaul University Graduate Student Conference, "Death, Decay, and Disgust," in January 2019. Many thanks to the warm welcome from the graduate students at this event and especially to Rachel Silverbloom and Eric Aldieri for their hospitality. I was honored to receive decisive early feedback on this project from Gil Anidjar, and am so very grateful for his consistent encouragement and willingness to give me feedback on this project at various stages. I am also grateful to my dear friend An Yountae for feedback on the manuscript at various stages and for the many hours of phone calls during which we dreamt, planned, and strategized about our mutual book projects. Thanks also to Todd Willison for his careful and gently critical feedback on the manuscript. Thanks to both Tommy Lynch and David Newheiser for their feedback on the manuscript offered at our panel "Theology & Catastrophe" at the 2021 annual meeting of the American Academy of Religion in San Antonio. And thanks to Anthony Paul Smith for his response to our projects on the catastrophic. I am also grateful to the Political Theology Network for the invitation to take part in the virtual 2021 Winter Workshop, where I was able to share (and receive feedback on) a chapter of the manuscript. Thanks to Kathy Chow and Mary Nickel for convening this workshop. And thanks to Emma Bilecky for offering a gracious and provocative response. Many thanks go to Catherine Keller for detailed feedback on the manuscript and for inviting me to share portions of the manuscript—virtually—with her collective of graduate students and alums on two separate occasions. Thanks to Hunter Bragg, JD Mechelke, and especially to Michael Anderson, who offered what would turn out to be crucial feedback on two separate occasions. Thanks, of course, to the gracious reviewers of this manuscript and to the advocacy and editorial support of Wendy Lochner and Lowell Frye at Columbia University Press, where I am grateful that this book found a home.

This work itself, and this particular project, would not have been possible without the broad network of scholars in the field whose work has inspired me, challenged me, and given me a sense of possibility. To Sharon Betcher, for inspiring me as a master's student and continuing to help me find my way as a PhD student. To colleagues from my graduate school cohort at Drew University who continue to be sources of inspiration: Karen Bray, Holly Hillgardner, Terra Rowe, Minta Fox, Christy Cobb, Jenny Barry, Anna Bladel, Lisa Gasson-Gardner, Lydia York, Luke Higgins, Sara Rosenau and Natalie Williams. And thanks to those many colleagues in the field whose work has inspired me to be bold and experimental (sometimes even a little fearless) with theological and philosophical and philosophical materials, such Adam Kotsko, Marika Rose, Anthony Paul Smith, Alex Dubilet, Amaryah Armstrong, Tommy Lynch, Sean Capener, Eric Meyer, Inese Radzins, Mary-Jane Rubenstein, Carol Wayne White, and Karmen MacKendrick. Thanks also to fellow members of the Constructive Theology Workgroup: John Thatamanil, Melanie Harris, Nikki Young, Pamela Lightsey, Shannon Craigo-Snell, Darby Ray, Benjamin Valentin, Jason Wyman, Bobby Rivera, Cynthia Rigby, Wendy Farley, Brian Bantum, Christine Helmer, Sharon Betcher, Ellen Armour, Brandon McCormack, Hannah Hofheinz, and Asante Todd. It was in conversation with members of this group that I finally decided to walk away from the dissertation that I'd long been attempting to revise and to pursue this project instead.

This project has benefitted, indirectly, from the advocacy and companionship of colleagues at the institutions where I've worked. I'm deeply grateful to Sara Patterson and Mike Duffy, my departmental colleagues at Hanover College, who not only mentored me as I learned (sometimes fumblingly) to really teach but also helped me find the time and space for my research. I'm grateful for all of my Hanover College colleagues who served on the Faculty Development Committee. Several generous grants from this committee helped to fund travel to conferences where I presented and developed ideas in this book. Thanks to Molly Winke and Melissa Eden for the moral and strategic support on those long commutes from Louisville. Thanks to support from Lucian Stone and Rebecca Rozelle-Stone at the University of North Dakota, where I had my first full-time academic position, and where I taught a course on death for the first time. And thanks to all of my colleagues at the University of North Dakota who helped to make that cold place more livable: Jack Weinstein and Kim Donehower-Weinstein, Sheila Liming and Dave Haeselin, Jesus Garcia Martin, Lauren Aldred, Kouhyar Tavakolian, and Arash Nejadpak. Thanks are also due to so many students at both the University of North Dakota and Hanover College. I have been regularly teaching a course on death and the afterlife since 2014, and every time I teach the course I learn new things and gain different perspectives from my students. I can't imagine having the drive to write this book without these conversations.

This book is also animated, in many invisible ways, by the stuff of life and the people who are closest to my little center of gravity. Thanks to Krista, for helping me see when I've guarded myself against the wildness of life and lost sight of its magic. Thanks to my mother, for somehow convincing me that a life really is a creative project. So many thanks to the grandparents—Harriet, Mom, Carl—whose presence (in many countless ways) helps our little world go round. Thanks to Ben for helping me create those many hours of solitude in which to write, for making both the daily coffee and the feasts to follow, for helping me laugh when it feels most difficult, and for those vaudevillian genes that help him play the optimist. Thanks to sweet Matilda the brave for all of the joy, for asking difficult questions that push me to think in new ways, and for her deep and serious appreciation of the first-edition picture books I've made just for her.

SISTER DEATH

FIGURE 0.1 Krista Dragomer, *Synodic Portal 1*, 2020

INTRODUCTION
Sister Death

Saint Francis of Assisi is one of the few figures in the long history of Christianity who has been lauded for his unapologetic embrace of the natural world. Others, perhaps, may have been concerned that declarations of love for the world would compete with the love of God. The harsh words of the apostle Paul, against those who appeared to worship God's creatures rather than the creator (Romans 1:25), are prominent in the New Testament epistles, after all. But for Francis there seemed to be no such competition between love of creatures and love of their creator. To show love for one was to show love for the other; this love was no zero-sum game. It was for this reason that the twentieth-century historian Lynn White Jr.—notorious for his broad and scathing critique of Christian views on the natural world—affectionately labeled Francis a "left wing" heretic.[1] And it was for this reason that Pope John Paul II declared Francis the "patron saint of ecology" in 1979, decades before the new pope chose Francis as his namesake, in recognition of a crisis in the fabric of creation.

This patron saint has been iconized as a lover of animals. But, especially given the ecological functions of death and decay, the earlier Francis might also be called a lover of death. One of the few texts attributed to him is the *Laudes Creaturarum*, commonly translated as "Praise of Creatures" or "Canticle of Brother Sun." The text itself is poetic—designed to be sung as a hymn of worship. In it, Francis does offer praise for creaturely life. But the creatures he addresses, with reverence, are not organisms. Instead, he addresses elements of the creation that are much bigger than humans. Indeed, these are facets of the natural world that have, in other religio-cultural contexts, been understood as forms of divinity in their own right, such as the sun. Francis praises the glory of the sun, the moon, the stars, the earth and its elements (wind, air, water, and fire). By way of finale, he offers praise for death. Each of these things, says Francis, is part of God's good creation. So each of these things, including death, is understood to be a praiseworthy creature. Caught up in his reverence for all of these good and glorious elements of creation, Francis names death "our sister." Death becomes Sister Death. "Praised be, my Lord," reads the hymn, "for our sister our bodily death, from which no living man can ever flee."[2] Praise be for this divinely created limitation on creaturely life.

This praise of death might—with only modest anachronism—be read as a frank recognition of the ecological function that death plays in the natural world. It might be read as an acknowledgment that life and death are entangled in a mutualistic process. There is no change or novelty in creaturely life without the decay and fermentation of death. Or it could be a nod to the fact that without this death and decay, without the soils that these processes produce, we would starve. It could be a realization that, in order to exist within a finite body, we need limitation as a framework for that finitude. The common name for that complex and impassable network of limitations is death. So it is that death acts as the foundation or root source of our finitude and mutual vulnerability. Death is not a simple destroyer or pure evil.

It would seem that for Francis death is not, as Paul suggested, the "last enemy" of God (1 Corinthians 15:26). Instead, Francis counters, there is something of the good or some form of kinship in death. Like water or air, death can nurture and sustain. So death—Sister Death—merits a kind of praise. Francis might, with all of this in mind, be called a lover of death. He refuses to make death an enemy. Rather, he charts another form of relation to death—one in which death is simply part of the fabric of things, part of the earthbound family.

Is it possible, however, to catch sight of some trace of enmity in Francis's figuration of death? Is it really the case that he has managed to compose such a radical counterfigure to that image of death as enemy? When we look with more careful attention at his figuration of death, we glimpse vestiges of another Christian sensibility playing out alongside it. Each of the creatures (or elements) that Francis praises in this hymn is gendered, either male or female. He plays with gender to make a commentary on power. Those creatures gendered male possess what might be deemed "active" traits or characteristics. The most potent of these elements is the one that Francis praises first: the sun (who he calls a "master brother"). This element, Francis suggests, most nearly resembles the creator himself. Fire is also gendered male and is deemed to be "fair and merry" as well as "vigorous and strong." Wind, air, and clouds are also deemed masculine. Francis suggests that their power is to provide God's creatures with nourishment. They channel the power of God and bring it closer to us. The moon, however, is a sister. She exists in a passive state, necessary only to be observed. Water, too, is a passive female element described as "useful" but also "humble." The earth (who is not a *mother* but is more diminutively described as a "sister mother") does some active work, providing humans with sustenance and even "governing" human life. But she, too, remains more passive than a masculine force like the sun. One could argue that, in feminizing dimensions of the natural world and rendering them passive, Francis reveals something about what he sees as the potency and impotence (the power) in and of these elements.

Death, also gendered female, appears to have more power than any of these other passive feminized elements. In this sense, death seems distinct. She possesses powers such that "no living man can ever flee [her]," Francis notes. And yet, there are clear limits to her power. Francis ends his hymn with praise for God—the most high—who welcomes the faithful into a "second death," a death stronger than Sister Death, allowing believers to be born into eternal life with God. The second death of believers is a miracle—an act of God—distinct from the work of Sister Death, who merely has power over our bodies (not our souls). The powers of Sister Death are ultimately transcended—rendered a kind of weakness—in the wake of the vital masculine power of the creator. Death, in this sense, is destined for a defeat even if it will never be possible for creatures to defeat her with their own limited powers. This is distinct, in interesting ways, from the power that Francis glimpses in Master Brother Sun, who, Francis suggests, is a purer channel for God's power. "You through him give light," Francis marvels. And in this way, Brother Sun "carries, O most High a glimpse of what You are." Brother Sun illuminates God's power, while Sister Death is ultimately a power that fails in divine illumination. One might argue that Francis, living in the thirteenth century, could not help but proffer the ultimate defeat of death. As modern readers who have enjoyed the privileges afforded by luxuries such as antibiotics and wastewater treatment plants, many of us are alienated from the kind of daily struggle against death that Francis and his contemporaries must have lived. And yet there are so many other ways of accounting for the presence and function of death in other ancient and indigenous traditions around the planet. Many generations of humans, in many different cultures and contexts, have struggled to survive in terrifying conditions and to shield one another from death. And not all of these cultures proffered the ultimate defeat of a death who is understood to be the enemy.

While it may be the case that, in some ways, Francis exhibits more curiosity about (and respect for) death than many other Christian theologians have historically done, some other proclamation nevertheless seeps through in the poetics of his hymn. Francis might name death a sister, but he also echoes an ancient and familiar theological pattern in Christianity: that of portraying death as the ultimate enemy. While there is a sense in which this hymn recognizes that death is part and parcel of life, there is also a sense in which it denigrates death, presenting death within a narrative framework that pits death against God. This theological point of view or framework—in which death serves as a permanent and ultimate enemy—is an incredibly powerful narrative. While it has never been the only Christian theology of death, it has arguably become the most powerful. This theology of death has left its traces on the work of generations of theologians and on saints like Francis. But it has also left clear marks on dimensions of culture we might otherwise deem nonreligious or secular. Because of its reach and scope, I describe it as a *political theology of death*. There are, perhaps, innumerable theological views on death. But because of the cultural and imaginative authority this political theology of death has garnered, in this book I often refer to it as *the* political theology of death. This is not to suggest that it is the only one, but to suggest that it is arguably the most dominant.

Political theology is a subfield, or conversation, with a contested set of meanings. The term itself is often linked to the work of Carl Schmitt, and many early conversations about political theology were sparked by Schmitt's claim that Western political concepts (such as, notably, sovereignty) are secularized theological concepts. Vincent Lloyd has described political theological projects oriented around the work of Schmitt as political theology in a "narrow" or restricted sense. Lloyd contrasts this with political theologies that are "broad." These would be projects in which the term *political theology* seems to function as almost interchangeable with *religion and politics*.[3] I would describe my own understanding of political theology as both broad and narrow. My reflections on political theology veer back and forth between well-worn themes from the work of Schmitt and wider-ranging reflections on the impact of theological history on dimensions of our political lives. For me, political theology is a term that describes both the erasures of, and the endurance of, theology within the secular. While it was long thought to be the case that the term *secular* marked a sharp distinction from the world of the religious, recent decades have seen a surge of publications from anthropologists, philosophers, political theorists, literary theorists, and religious thinkers who have gestured toward the enduring presence of—the relics and remains of—Christian thought within the secular. Indeed, the secular itself—as a space-time and a social sphere—is largely a product of Christian intellectual history. Political theology has become a conceptual tool for pointing out these complicities. For this reason, I see political theology as either critical work that illuminates these complicities, or constructive work that sources and transforms religious and theological figures, in order to make use of them in an intellectual realm not explicitly guided or structured by doctrinal authorities. Political theology points to the often hidden (sometimes intentionally obscured) entanglements between theology and the secular, between religion and politics. Sometimes this work is critical; other times it pulls from the theological as a poetic source. For my part, I seek to avoid restricting myself to either extreme. In this book I offer a critical perspective on this political theology of death with deep roots in the Christian tradition yet fully functional in secular contexts (political ideas, literary projects, popular discourses). On the other hand, I also work—with thinkers like Francis—to challenge this political theology with a set of counterpoetics. While I am certainly a critic of political theology, from another angle I am also arguably *doing* it. I remain caught up in these games of endurance and erasure.

I read Francis as a voice torn between positions and lured away from the political theology of death that I critique in this book. He does seem to understand that the fact of death, like a light breeze or the warm sunlight, is simply one of the elements that shapes the texture of life experience on the planet. In this sense, then, Francis's reading demands a kind of recognition of, or respect for, the work of death. Here, we might say, he pulls back from, or challenges, the Christian enmity toward death. But this old enmity proves to be powerful, even for him. Death, for Francis is *merely a creature*. As such, she will always be humbled by the divinized force of life itself. At best, perhaps, we might read Sister Death as a kind of friend. As our fellow creature, Francis seems to suggest, she is a companion to us. But this view of death, as a friend rather than an enemy, is still a product of the political theology of death that I will be critiquing. This political theology of death is not a simple hatred for death. Instead, it remains caught up in something more like a love-hate relationship, structured by the tensions of friendship and enmity. Death is the hated enemy of God, and yet it is also a precious gateway that illuminates God's power. In this sense, death remains a crucial interlocutor for Christian theology, not only because it is a force to do battle with but also because it is a good enemy to keep closer than any other friend. In figuring death as a sister, Francis offers a subtle poetic challenge to this political theology. But for him, Sister Death was an evocative figure, flickering forth in the lines of a poem. In this book, I seek to catch sight of her fuller contours.

Perhaps Francis was unable to read sisterhood as a powerful relation—one powerful enough that it might include life itself. Death, for him, is feminized. But he seems to understand this as, also, a way of limiting death's power. Simone de Beauvoir argued that a form of gendered violence is embedded in the fear of, the hatred of, or the desire to permanently transcend death. She argued that this fear of death was connected to our natality—our birth. Because we are born, we must suffer through death. So birth initiates us into the contingencies of flesh. The fear of death, Beauvoir argued, is also the fear, disgust, and dread of the contingent body's ripe, messy mortality revealed through our natality. Horrified by this mortality generated by our natality, men came to resent this "stain of childbirth," she argued, and to blame the bodies who birth babies for its production.[4] Through natality, women produce mortal beings. By this logic, women become the origins of death. Women are blamed for this natality that condemns the human "to finitude and death."[5] This is why, Beauvoir argued, death is often figured as a woman and why "women mourn the dead, because death is their work."[6] There is a form of misogyny operating in the fear of, and feminization of, death.

Perhaps it was simply the case that, for Francis, sisterhood was too weak a bond to attract life itself, and death was too passive a force to draw life into any sort of mutualistic relation.

What would it look like to think, more thoroughly, through this figure that Francis invoked? What would it look like to think Sister Death? I believe it would look quite different from the political theology that sets life and death in a relation of enmity (one that can, from time to time, venture into friendship). It would offer a perspective on living and dying that is outside of, other than, that of enmity. What I argue in this book is, in effect, that Francis offers a key figure in Sister Death. But I also offer a critique of Francis's presumption that death is a creature—*our* sister. Death is diffuse, extended, without containment or singularity. Death functions as a power or a force. Death is not our sister, I suggest, but instead a sister *to life*. To think of life and death as sisters, I suggest, is to see them as intimately connected. But it does not necessitate that we remove the antagonism or rivalry from this relation. Sisterhood is a bond. But it is not a bond without tension. "There must be some way to integrate death into living, neither ignoring it nor giving in to it," Audre Lorde reflected in her cancer journals.[7] Lorde wanted to resist the *embrace* of death. But she also reflected on death as something other than an enemy. "The acceptance of death as a fact," she wrote, "rather than a desire to die, can empower my energies with a forcefulness and vigor."[8] To think the sisterhood between life and death is, I argue, a gesture to acknowledge the fact of death, the fact of death's intimate relation with life, and yet also a recognition that death marks a form of otherness we continuously struggle with and against.

In this book I explore what I argue is a theological counter-figuration of death. Sister Death becomes a counterpoint to the figuration of death as the last and greatest enemy. Life and death are not bound in a relation of enmity but in a sisterhood. Because the figure of death as the enemy has been politicized—has become a powerful figure in political theological discourses—I argue that the figure of Sister Death can interrupt this political theology of death. I believe there are good reasons for such an interruption. While it may be the case that death serves as a powerful metaphorical marker for injustice, oppression, suffering, and trauma, I also argue that the political theology of death (when it amplifies this enmity between life and death) tends to collapse different forms of death into a singular paradigm, presenting a reductive vision of the relationship between life and death that would also seem to suggest that aging and decay are forces of evil. This is, in other words, a gross simplification of different processes and forces that are often labeled as "death." Even more problematic, when Christianity claims life itself to be in alignment with its own vision of God, those who Christianity holds to be enemies rather than friends (such as non-Christians) are conscripted to the realm of death—they become part of a constellated negative that pools together Western metaphysical dimensions of abjection such as privation, sin, evil, fleshiness, animality, and blackness.

In essence, then, I borrow the figure of Sister Death from Francis. But in doing so, I reinvent it. In order to assure that death becomes something entirely other than God, Francis offers an assurance that life itself triumphs over death. But what he then seems to forget is that, even in Christian thought, the life of God (eternal life) is alleged to be other than biological life. This life we lead on earth, biological life, is creaturely life. And the life of God, as well as the form of life of those who are thought to walk with God after death, is alleged to be a form of life bound to creaturely or biological life through a connective distinction. That is to say, it is connected to, but ultimately other than, the life of the body as we live it presently. This other form of life is a resurrected form of life, which is a life that is not this life. Which is not to say that it is nonlife. But it is also not to say that it isn't.

I argue that this dominant political theology—*the* political theology of death—presents a bifurcated view of life and death. It intimates that one can have a death that is disconnected from life, and a life that is disconnected from death. Life is on the side of God, and death is not. But this view would also contradict passages in the biblical texts that indicate the presence of God not only with the dying but in the worlds (such as Sheol) where the dead reside. Instead, I suggest, in conversation with feminist thinkers (especially Black feminists), that the sisterhood of life and death acknowledges that life and death are bound in an integrated and inextricable relation—a "lifedeath" relation. Borrowing the term *lifedeath* from Jacques Derrida, this book explores this sisterhood. I do not suggest that this is a relation of peace and bliss. In sisterhood there can be mutual support. But there can also be antagonism, agonism, and rivalry. It is possible, even if life and death are bound together, to weaponize one against the other. What has been called, with simplicity, death, is deeply complex. Irreducibly so. And to think that all phenomena connected with death bear within them some form of enmity is a tragic and fatalistic fiction. Without a doubt, we live in a world where death is politically weaponized, where death is dealt with impunity, and where those with power gain and exercise this power by dealing death to those who are vulnerable or who appear to pose some threat to power. And we live in a time of extinctions, in which we are hounded by more visions of death, more facts of death, than any of us can metabolize or even comprehend. Extinctions are playing out, regularly, in more than human worlds. And our political discourse in places like the United States is haunted by the many possible avenues that might lead to human extinction. So death is something to struggle against. Indeed, to shield one another against death is the heart

FIGURE 0.2 Krista Dragomer, *Signature*, 2013

of tenderness. And yet, it is also the case that the ability to ripen and grow old is a privilege rather than an evil. We are deeply dependent upon forms of death (viral, bacterial) for the very life of our bodies. There are, in other words, dimensions of nurture within death as well.

I am not claiming that death is good, or beautiful. Neither am I claiming that it is not worth struggling against death and protecting one another from death (of course it is!) Nor am I arguing that death is a *friend* rather than an enemy (a claim that I find still problematically bound up in the paradigm of enmity between life and death). Instead, as I elaborate over the course of this book, thinking the lifedeath relation as one of sisterhood offers another paradigm for contemplating this relation. I would, ultimately, describe this perspective as "death positive." But I will also offer some caveats and complications of what that might mean.

A DEATH POSITIVE ICON

As I write, we are living through a pandemic. The dead cast their shadows over us and these shadows hang over our shared or communal spaces. Some cower in fear, avoiding these shadows, and others aggressively proclaim the need to bring the vitalizing bright light of capital and commerce back into those abandoned spaces, as if this would scatter the shadows of death. In the midst of the pandemic, we live in a time that is conditioned by more than the specter of individual death. Death, as we face it, is also collective. We live, moreover, in the shadows of another form of mass death. Within and beyond our human collective, we are haunted by extinction events—either the predicted, prophesied extinction of our own species or the many extinction events that are playing out in more than human worlds. Take your pick. The shadows are everywhere, and death lurks within them all. For the time being, and for the foreseeable future, the evasion of death in its individual and collective forms becomes less and less possible all the time.

I concur with Donna Haraway when she suggests that the task for living now is "learning to live and die well with each other in a thick present." Against the idea that we must stop what we imagine the future has in store for us, Haraway calls for a different relation to time and the future. The task, in responding to these times of trouble, is "to make trouble" to "stir up potent response to devastating events, as well as to settle troubled waters and rebuild quiet places."[9] In that spirit, what I pursue in this book is not only (or simply) a form of critique.

It is also an attempt to, as Haraway puts it, "create, to fabulate, in order not to despair."[10] It is an attempt to tell a different sort of story about life and death. About lifedeath.

Those who have not been so captured (as I once felt myself to be) by the political theology of death might find the stories that I am telling here familiar old stories. But those who have been so captured may, begin to see (as I have) what it might look like to refuse to cast death in the position of absolute enemy. It is this approach—a refusal to transcend, discount, deflect, erase, or make an absolute enemy of death—that I am calling *death positive*. Sister Death, then, might be described as a death positive icon, and in the sisterly tensions of lifedeath we may find the nascent conditions for death positivity.

Death positivity, a term I have borrowed, is a disposition associated with a grassroots movement that—at its core—seeks to change the way that we (as Americans or inheritors of Western cultural traditions) think and talk about death. Death positivity is at the heart of the founding tenets of The Order of the Good Death—a network of thinkers, artists, and activists dedicated to death work. The group describes death positivity as a refusal to ignore the reality of death, or the fact that death shapes life itself. The Order articulates eight fundamental propositions such as, "I believe that the dead body is not dangerous, and that everyone should be empowered (should they wish to be) to be involved in care for their own dead."[11] The staff of the Order includes one of the most high-profile members of the death positive movement, Caitlin Doughty, who is a mortician and author of the best-selling *Smoke Gets in Your Eyes and Other Lessons from the Crematory*, as well as host of the popular YouTube channel Ask a Mortician. Also on staff is Sarah Chavez, a podcaster and activist who reflects on the issues that adversely impact the way marginalized communities experience death. Founding members of the movement come from a wide range of fields and disciplines and include people like Katrina Spade (founder and CEO of Recompose, which promotes composting as an alternative to human burial in urban settings), Jae Rhim Lee (an artist who created a mushroom burial suit that facilitates rapid decomposition), Sarah Fornace (a puppeteer), Melissa Cooper (a forensic artist), Cassandra Yoder (a death midwife), and Nancy Caciola (a medieval historian). Through diverse and multiple perspectives, the Order raises a host of new questions about what it means to do death work, today.

The sex positive movement has worked to foster attitudes toward human sexuality that regard it as a normal and healthy part of our embodied experience. The death positive movement borrows from this frank acknowledgment of our biological, embodied realities. While sex and death are often discursively and conceptually co-implicated, the death positive movement is ultimately pushing for something distinct. Affects typically celebrated and embraced as central to the sex positive movement—such as pleasure—are not dominant or central in discourses about death positivity. Nevertheless, as Chavez clarifies, the death positive movement is (like the sex positive movement) a feminist movement oriented around embodiment. "The future of death," Chavez has quipped, "is a feminist one."[12]

The death positive movement is, to date, driven largely by women, as Chavez notes, offering a critical perspective on why this is the case, as well as an affirmation of how women and nonbinary people can challenge dominant cultural discourses on death. Some have speculated, as Chavez points out, that death work requires a "caring factor" and that woman are, archetypally nurturing, sensitive, and "in touch with their emotions." Chavez finds speculations like this reductive; they reiterate familiar and harmful stereotypes about women, and confine the movement itself to a "narrow lens." But Chavez, like Beauvoir, does not deny the cultural resonances between women and death. "As women and non-binary folks many of us are often forced to confront death in ways that most men are not," Chavez writes, listing patterns of non-positive death that have been deemed "epidemics": the murder of trans women of color, the murder of indigenous women in Canada, and the death of women "at the hands of our domestic partners." One might also mention maternal mortality in childbirth, which is especially death-ridden for women in marginalized communities. The relationship between women and death, Chavez observes, "is too often forced upon us." And so, "our very existence demands that we acknowledge it. We cannot be unconcerned with death—that privilege is not ours." To be death positive is to recognize that this frank acknowledgment of our embodied realities does not have to be faced with resignation. Instead, Chavez says, "working with death is an act of resistance. It is a way of reclaiming our spaces, our bodies, our lives and ourselves."[13] This form of resistance is also a form of care. It acknowledges that death is an inevitable part of our embodied mortal experience, yet it also pushes back against the systematic realities that would seek to seize or exploit the powers of death in order to render some bodies more mortal—more vulnerable to death—than others.

In an interview with anthropologists Cymene Howe, Susanna Zaraysky, and Lois Ann Lorentzen, a transgender Mexican sex worker named Jajaira describes her relationship with Santa Muerte—the Mexican folk saint, depicted as a skeleton in a cloak lined with colorful flowers. Santa Muerte (Saint Death or Holy Death) is a feminized figuration of the divine, and the work that she does is death work. The popularity of this folk saint has been on the rise in Mexico and the United States, particularly among people like Jajaira who live in marginalized and vulnerable conditions. Jajaira's connection with Santa Muerte underscores this dimension of resistance, in working with death. "Some people are homophobic," Jajaira tells her interviewers. "Some people are claustrophobic, others are afraid of spiders, closed rooms, darkness, et cetera." The nature of fear is plural and indeterminate. But, Jajaira argues, "all of humanity is afraid of death." To be a devotee of Santa Muerte, Jajaira suggests, is also a quest to inhabit a form of courage. This form of worship is "about *not* being afraid of death," or more realistically, "about not being so attached to the fear of death."[14] As a manifestation or iconization of death, the saint appears to give devotees the ability to inhabit their fear of death and transform it.

For trans sex workers like Jajaira, marginalized working conditions leave them disproportionately vulnerable to a violent form of death. Santa Muerte, as a figure, extends not only the offer of protection but—more—the transformation of their fear. She extends the invitation to inhabit one's own finitude and contingency in order to find within it not a source of dread but, instead, a source of courage and power. Here, Santa Muerte does not erase vulnerability or finitude with a power that exceeds it. Nor does she offer an inoculation against the fear of death. Rather, she seems to open a door that leads deeper into vulnerability. The fog of this space contains something to help mortals rise up. This is not a transcendence of death but, perhaps instead, the awareness of a potent lifedeath intimacy. The worship of Santa Muerte (in honoring the fact of death) opens onto a deeper and more powerful dimension of life—one that is entangled with, and enabled by, death. It is a recognition, we might say, of the sisterly dimensions of lifedeath.

This enabling but also contentious lifedeath intimacy in a figure like Santa Muerte illustrates what I have suggested is a sisterhood dynamic. To see this lifedeath sisterhood at work, and to understand the powers of resistance and courage within it, is to inhabit what I am describing as a death positive perspective. This is not a suggestion that death is *good*, or that we should be *happy* about the fact that we will die. Rather, it is simply to acknowledge the presence of death and to understand that there are protective, nurturing, and enabling powers embedded in this acknowledgment.

Sisterhood can nurture. But it would be inaccurate to call it inherently nurturing. Sisterhood—the idea of sisterhood itself—has a long and complicated relationship with women's lives and with feminism. The idea of sisterhood structures the nun's convent—an institution that has nurtured the minds and spirits of women, giving them a space to live free of the burdens of reproduction while also subjecting them to effectively immobile structures of patriarchal authority. The idea of sisterhood was rife in a second-wave feminist movement in which many white women advanced their personal affairs as universal issues and effectively silenced the political agendas of some they called sisters. Perhaps not coincidentally, sisterhood in American culture today is often more immediately understood as a bond between Black women.

Perhaps because I am an only child, the idea of sisterhood has always been very abstract to me. My only real exposure to it was through my mother—one of seven children in an immigrant family that struggled to find its footing in the United States. My mother's relationship with her four sisters was racked with painful emotions: jealousy, envy, resentment, contempt. And yet, despite that, I also saw how powerful and sustaining those bonds nevertheless remained. Her sisters were at the core of that vibrant network of beautiful, powerful women who inspired and nurtured the powers that I later came to think of as my own. Sisterhood, in other words, is a potentially fraught name to give the lifedeath relation. And yet, or perhaps for this very reason, I think it apt. Among other things, it retains that subtle invocation of the ancient and contentious relationship between women and death.

Chavez and Beauvoir are far from the only people to make note of the ancient and integral relationship between women and death. Many commentaries—from disciplines such as literary studies, philosophy, anthropology, and sociology—explore the ancient cultural associations between women and death.[15] And it is useful, perhaps, to note that high-profile figures of the death awareness movement that developed in the mid to late twentieth century were often women, such as the psychologist of death Elisabeth Kübler-Ross and the founder of the hospice movement, Cicely Sanders. But this is not an argument in favor of naturalizing such associations. There are, to be sure, problems with these stereotypical assumptions about the so-called nature of women. But I concur with Chavez, who sees a social benefit in recovering dimensions of women's death work from earlier generations. A century ago, says Chavez, "our bodies were lovingly washed and dressed for burial by our kin." Funerals were part of a communal process, "and women were typically at the helm."[16] Like the birthing process, the dying process has been increasingly medicalized and professionalized. While this is protective in many cases (helping to mitigate, for instance, the spread of disease in our communities), there are also socially destructive consequences of this transition. The embrace of practices such as embalming (described after the Civil War as a more "scientific" method of burial) has facilitated the development of a funeral industry that makes death and burial incredibly expensive for contemporary Americans. This industry also helps to sustain life insurance industries, designed to protect the living from being financially exploited upon the death of a loved one, but which often end up exploiting the living in order to do so. The result of the professionalization of death, Chavez argues, is also a "commodification of death" that has "resulted in one of the most profound and transformational events of our lives being mediated and staged through two industries—medical and funeral—that were initially created to financially and socially benefit men."[17] To resist this history of commodification is also to reclaim the powers that inhere within "the sacred space surrounding the corpse."[18] The death positive movement, in other words, has deep ties to a feminist politics that resists the co-implication of women and death yet also seeks to more actively inhabit and embody the intersections between life and death. This is why I have suggested that Sister Death is an icon of a death positive form of thought.

A death positive standpoint does not call for happiness in the face of death; it does not counsel happiness about the fact that we die. It does, however, challenge us to take part in rituals and forms of thinking that weave life and death back together, without resentment or revulsion. Death is a fact. But so is life. As facts, they are related but distinct. Death is folding into life, right now, and it will not stop. This knowledge can generate both terror and gratitude. *When* there is death, and *where* there is death, a death positive standpoint seeks to make dying well together (witnessing the ripples of death as they move through our own bodies, finding ways to grieve ritually and emotionally, opening up the caverns of feeling and sensation that tap into the powers of mourning, finding ways to listen to the dead, or commit the dead to memory, or to remember the dead) part of the way that we live. Staying with the trouble means, in this sense, having the courage to do death work, to sit with the dead, and to do palliative care when this is what is called for. Yet this courage to stay with the trouble also feeds into dimensions of resistance.

A death positive perspective does not catch a glimpse of death in order to surrender to it. Death positivity is not simply about the powers of death but about the powers within and for life. It is about how we find ever new ways of posing vital resistance to death. It is about the dimensions of resistance that surge up in, around, and in spite of, death. It is about the weaving patterns, themselves, that bring life and death closer together—the patterns that illuminate lifedeath. In order to keep these dimensions of resistance to death alive, it is crucial to conceive of the enduring distinctions between life and death, even when they act in complicity. Death positivity is a posture that lives into a life that is shadowed by death, and yet is not confined or conscripted by it.

A HAPPY DEATH?

As is the case with all movements, perhaps, the death positive movement has its critics. However, not all of them target the death positive movement specifically. Instead, many such critiques are directed against a more generically framed "death awareness" movement, with roots in the mid-twentieth century. Scholars such as the sociologist Lyn Lofland trace this movement back to figures such as Kübler-Ross, who promoted open conversations about death, and conversations with the dying. Another frequently cited progenitor of this movement is the cultural anthropologist Ernest Becker, whose 1973 Pulitzer Prize–winning *The Denial of Death* used the work of psychoanalysts and philosophers to argue that humans are caught up in elaborate refusals to deny their own mortality.

Some scholars, such as the criminologist and sociologist Ruth Penfold-Mounce, simply argue that Becker's term *death denial* is meaningless, as it does not point to a specific form of denial and instead gestures toward a widespread cultural tendency that may not actually exist.[19] Lofland explains one reason for the vagueness of such references by describing the movement as a "general social movement," which is to say that it is characterized by "uncoordinated efforts, lacking established leadership and recognizable membership and with a literature as varied and ill-defined as the movement itself."[20] Somewhat caustically, perhaps, Lofland labels this movement the "happy death" movement—as if the aim were to challenge people to be happy about the fact that they will die.[21] I find such descriptions reductive, dismissive, and out of touch with what thinkers such as Kübler-Ross and Becker are actually claiming about our mortality. As I have already mentioned, my understanding of the term *death positive*—informed by others who are actively engaged in the movement today—is *not* that it encourages us to face death with happiness, let alone to desire it. Death positive thinkers and activists leave plenty of space open for sorrow, mourning, grief, and lament. Indeed, they often argue that these are the very affects that death denial suffocates. But they also suggest that these affects are a dimension of our human experience that need not be sublimated into something else. They can be acknowledged, lived into, processed, and shared.

There are other, more nuanced critiques, however. Benjamin Noys, for instance, has argued that death awareness, or what he calls "death liberation," movements rest on the claim that death has become taboo, in the modern West. These movements seek to liberate death from its condition as taboo. This notion—that death is a taboo—has become "entrenched in popular understandings," he argues. But Noys finds the notion lacking, if not deceptive. "If death is so taboo," he poses, "then how do we account for the fact that the media continues to give us increasingly explicit representations of death?"[22] Popular culture does not *deny* death so much as it saturates our imaginative landscapes with so many images of death that we are effectively inundated with it. Even more troubling, he says, is the fact that over the course of modernity increasing numbers of people have become more and more subject to forces and structures that expose us to death rendering us, essentially, what Giorgio Agamben has called bare life—a merely biological form of life, relentlessly exposed to the powers of death. "After the Holocaust and during a century of genocides and mass exterminations, from Cambodia to Rwanda, it is difficult to claim that death is now 'invisible,'" Noys writes.

Perhaps it would be more accurate, Noys suggests, to say that we live death-conditioned lives, in which our constant exposure to death-dealing social and political structures makes death mundane. We live, increasingly, in a biopolitical frame that is necropolitically driven. And death seems to be at the beating heart of our violent, modern, political structures. "Our exposure to death," he argues, "takes the form of being exposed to the possibility of death organized politically, through bureaucratic planning and government intervention."[23] Noys raises an important question for the death positive movement: How is it possible to simply acknowledge the fact of death, in a political context in which death has become part of a set of biopolitical management systems that seek to manage specific lives by exposing them to death, or the threat of it? What does it mean to do death work, or to be a death positive activist, in conditions like this? How is it possible to be death positive in a necropolitical time of extinctions?

This is precisely where I read death positive voices, like Chavez's, as intervening in an important way. Death happens, whether social and political structures make political use of it, or not. Death is not simply or reductively a condition of biopolitical or necropolitical management. Death itself is part of, and yet still not reducible to, necropolitics. Death can be politicized and made use of politically. But to imagine that this is all there is to death is reductionistic. Death is complex, plural, and multiple. Death itself can be defined in any number of ways and remain recognizable. No death is ever the same. Different bodies, different communities, and different species die differently. Some deaths generate relief; others are painful sites of tragedy. More than that, many bodies are more exposed (made more vulnerable) to death than others. As Chavez notes, part of the death positive movement is to build solidarity with others, in order to resist those social and political structures that make room for some bodies to die well, while other bodies are left to die traumatically. For those of us less viscerally exposed to the threat of death, what right do we have to claim this privilege—the privilege to seal ourselves off from the presence of death?

In her analysis of what she called the "happy death" movement, Lofland argues that the movement (at least as it was constituted in the 1970s when she did her fieldwork) was primarily composed of "presumably secular upper-middle-class professionals."[24] It would seem, then, that death awareness or death positivity is something that educated people, who enjoy access to wealth and privilege, are more concerned with. But perhaps this is precisely because those who are most likely to deny, or ignore, death are those who have the privilege to do so. "Death denial is a privilege," writes Brandy Schillace in a historical analysis of the medicalization of death. "It's a privilege of the young, healthy, and wealthy, and has come about largely thanks to Western advances in medicine." In other words, if a person denies death, it is because she *can*.[25] No mortal, of course, is actually privileged enough to deny death for long. The day and manner of our

FIGURE 0.3 Krista Dragomer, *Silk Milk*, 2012

own death is, mercifully, concealed from us. It may be closer at hand than we presume. Nevertheless, it is undeniably the case that some bodies sense the presence of death much more acutely than others. Some bodies, as Noys has observed, are subjected to the threat of death by the bureaucratic structures of daily life in the modern world. And perhaps it is the case that many people drawn to death awareness movements, or death positive movements, are people who enjoy the privilege of contemplating death at a distance. But to think death into your life, to acknowledge the intimacies of lifedeath, can be a fundamentally different approach to this privilege. To face death, even when we do not sense that she has come calling for us, can also be a way of critiquing the privilege of death denial. There is a dimension of solidarity, and resistance, in the act of facing death. This is not merely true of our relations with other humans, but our relations with the more than human world as well.

MULTISPECIES MORTALITY

If it is indeed the case that we are currently undergoing a sixth extinction event, most Americans still enjoy the privilege of living with a dim awareness of the mass extinction events playing out in more than human lifeworlds. If extinction events are a sign of a decimation of the commons,[26] then these commons are common to both human and more than human worlds. The destruction of these lifeworlds will have dramatic consequences on human worlds, even if they do not give way to extinction events within all human communities. To imagine that extinction is simply a problem faced, in the present, by other species or communities is a denial of what Jessica Weir has described as our "co-produced" reality.[27] It is a form of death denial writ large. "Coexistential thinking," as Sam Mickey describes it, is an acknowledgement of the fact that—in our current condition of environmental crisis—we become vulnerable to the devastation of more than human lifeworlds. To live, coexistentially, in a time of extinctions is to recognize that mortality is not simply an individual existential problem. Nor is it merely a problem for the human collective. Rather, to reflect on our mortality in a time of extinctions is to reflect on the mortality of multispecies collectives.

Acknowledging the finite and vulnerable "conditions of planetary coexistence" is an act of solidarity, argues Mickey: an exercise in "becoming-with."[28] To face the ongoing reality, and the hovering possibility, of extinction is to reflect on collective vulnerability and collective death. To refuse to see this, or to evade it, is also to surrender a form of solidarity and resistance. As Deborah Bird Rose, Thom Van Dooren, and Matthew Chrulew have put it in a collaboratively written project, "by *staying with* the lives and deaths of particular, precious beings" we also open space "for a reflective gathering of energies *against* extinction, but also *creative* new modes of survival and fragile flourishing, of solidarity and respectful separation, new earthly webs of biocultural prosperity among the wounded and unloved, the precarious and ruined."[29] Resisting extinction, then, is not a matter of denying that it can happen and *is* happening. Rather, it is a matter of facing the fact of extinction (the fact of multispecies collective death), of seeing it, and engaging with it—without losing the creative tension that seeks to counteract it, or to wrest some mode of thriving from its grasp. There are life-giving powers embedded in the engagement with death, as well as the engagement with the collective death we call extinction.

To be death positive in a time of extinctions—in a time and a place dominated by the shadows of death and discourses on actual and possible extinctions—is to find forms of solidarity and resistance in facing or engaging with lifedeath. It is to wrest from this solidarity and resistance some creative form of thriving as a multispecies collective. We are not required to feel any form of happiness about death or about the fact that we die. It does not erase the grief, sorrow, lament, or even terror that we might experience in the presence of death. Instead, it opens spaces for grief, mourning, and lament. It refuses to silence or suffocate or mute these dimensions of feeling. It accepts the fact that these fibers of affective experience comprise the tissues that shape us and connect us to one another (as humans) and to the more than human world. And it accepts the fact that while some deaths are painful and horrific, others are experienced as a form of relief or release. In this recognition—the acknowledgment of these intimacies of lifedeath—there is also something vivifying. These tissues of connection, these fibers that tear and stretch and threaten to break us, are also where we find a responsive sort of courage. It is here that we live into the textures of experience that others

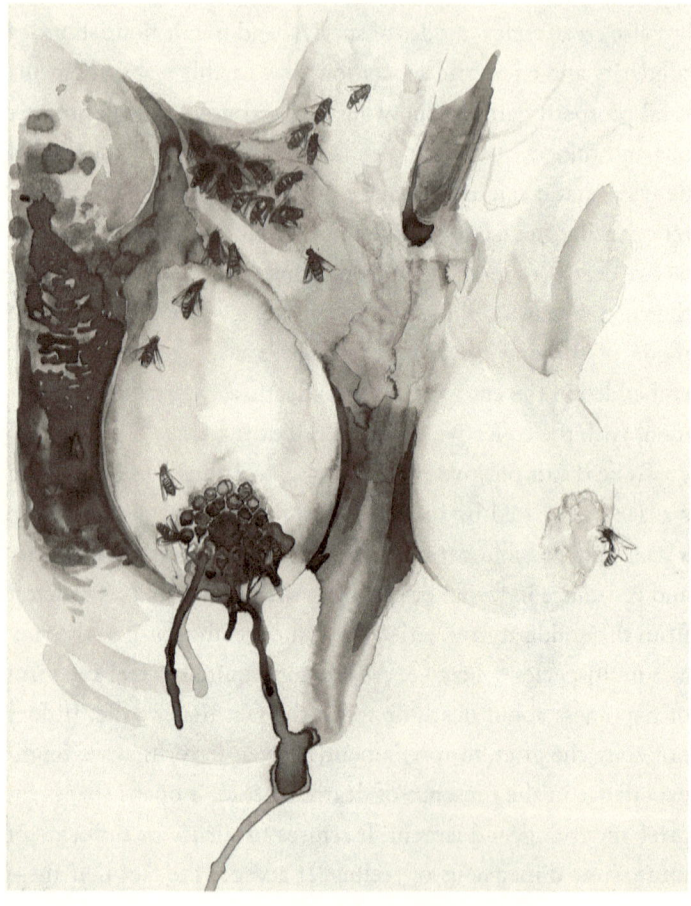

FIGURE 0.4 Krista Dragomer, *Milk and Honey*, 2012

have woven for us—the textures that bring life and death back together, incessantly.

To be death positive in a time of extinctions is to refuse to ignore the deaths of others—human and otherwise. It is also a refusal to let those deaths be the end of a story. To refuse to ignore the deaths of others is also, at least in part, to question and challenge the privilege that some have to merely *contemplate* mortality, rather than to fight (every day) for its preservation. It is a refusal to forget that there is no justice in the uneven distribution of mortal vulnerability among earthlings. To approach this injustice from a death positive perspective is not to suggest that, somehow, these deaths are "good." Instead, it is to acknowledge that all mortals are fundamentally vulnerable. If we find ourselves among those mortals who have been allowed—by the sheer accident of our natal conditions—to forget this, then perhaps we should become more responsive to the presence and work of lifedeath around us. Perhaps this kind of responsiveness is part of what will allow us to stay with the trouble. Perhaps it can help to lift us up, and help us lift one another up, even in the wake of death.

I am no more deserving of the privilege to contemplate death in the abstract than any other living creature. I can commit my mortal time to questioning and dismantling those structures that give me the leisure of contemplation, while others fight to preserve their mortality. I acknowledge the fact of death, in solidarity with those who have died, or who face death right now. I have no more (or no less) a right to rise above my mortality than they have had. I die because this is the way of life on this planet. I *can* die because I am fully alive (even as I am already tipping into death). In this condition of lifedeath I want to, in some way, honor the courage and beauty of all those many people who have lived and died before me. I seek them, somehow, in my vital and living memory as I walk forward toward the uncertain future to join them—in fear and bravery. I do not pretend to offer solutions to what are, in essence, a set of ruinous political and psychic phenomena that surround us in a time of extinctions. I remain, however, stubbornly subject to that ancient flight of fancy that has infected many storytellers, artists, poets, and philosophers:

the fantasy that the adventure of ideas that is thinking itself can help us create other modes of experiencing life in a body.

There are moments when I wonder if this is, perhaps, nothing but a gesture of self-soothing—an attempt to install a different kind of symbolic imaginary that might allow me to understand living and dying a bit differently. But this act of self-soothing has been conducted in active conversation with so many others that I cannot help but think of it as an act of web-weaving that I am not doing alone but instead am joining. What this book offers, then, is both a critique of the long war with death as well as a small gesture to think about how to exit the form of life that drives this militancy. It is a small gesture toward thinking otherwise.

FIGURE 1.1 Krista Dragomer, *Synodic Portal 2*, 2020

1

LIFE, DEATH, AND LIFEDEATH

The antagonism toward death that the Apostle Paul expressed, in his letters to the early Christian community, has hung like a thick cloud over the history of Western thought. Death, as Paul wrote in his Epistle to the Corinthians, is *the last enemy*, the most formidable and ultimate enemy to conquer (1 Corinthians 15:26). The idea that God is the victor over the malevolent powers of death has contributed, over the course of Christian history, to a political theology that continues to shape the most mundane forms of Western religious and secular thought. Indeed, the idea that death is fundamentally bad—even evil—has become almost an object of common sense, beyond and outside strictly religious discourse. The philosopher Thomas Nagel exemplifies this, in his claim that death essentially functions to destroy "whatever good there is in living."[1] Death is a deprivation, or a privation. Of course, sin, in the history of Christian thought, has been considered a privation—the simple "privation of good," as Thomas Aquinas described it. Indeed, for Aquinas privation itself is a kind of nothingness that—in its state of lack—is simply the absence of all that is created and good.[2] Death and sin, bound in a state of evil, are linked as conditions of lack and nothingness in Christian theology.

So death remains bound, in Christian imaginations, to the original sin of the first woman: she who introduced the painful necessity of childbirth (natality) and so the reality of finitude (mortality). The original woman (in this reading) is she who condemned us to be born into this privative state of lack and nothingness—lost in the mortal world, threatened by death and evil. Death, in the West, has a long and deep relationship with evil. And this relationship has often been twisted into a weapon to punish and condemn others.

To think of death as Sister Death—a sister to life—is to think otherwise. It is not, as I have already clarified (and will continue to do), to love death, to desire it, to become intimate friends with it, or to claim that it bears any inherent justice. But it is to understand that death, in its way, is integral to and supportive of life. Death enables life and the living. Life is supported and nurtured, invisibly and obviously, by dying, decay, and death work. Life and death are bound, temporally. I do not mean that the sisterly tensions of lifedeath call for a simple embrace of temporal limitation or absolute finitude. The claim that the fact of death calls for a robust embrace of pure finitude (even a rejection of divinized eternities and infinities) offers a kind of logical counterpoint to Paul's declaration. If, historically, Christian theologies have claimed that death is the ultimate enemy of God's infinite life-giving power, then perhaps the most proper challenge would be an embrace of death and the finitude or nothingness it brings— to become reconciled, in other words, with the form of limitation that creates finitude. Or, if death has been presented as the enemy, then another logical counterpoint would be to claim death as a friend.

In what follows, I explain why I distance the sisterly tensions of lifedeath from either of these logical counterpoints or conceptual alternatives. In essence, I find both of these alternatives

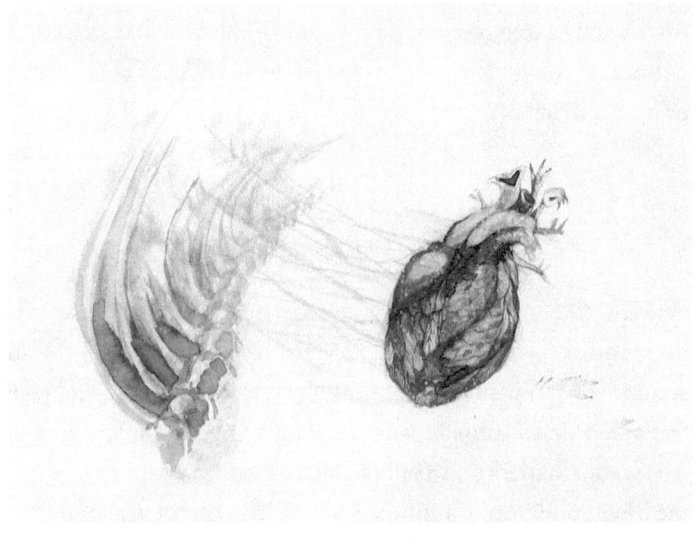

FIGURE 1.2 Krista Dragomer, *Flutter of Fine Filaments*, 2013

to be, still, too bound up in the metaphysical dynamics that are shaped by the political theology of death. This view of death—as the enemy of life—presents death as a power or force that is separable from life. This conceptual bifurcation of life and death, I think, continues to be reiterated in the call to embrace finitude as if it were absolute. While it might, at first, appear that befriending death would neutralize the violent antagonisms of enmity, I argue that the politics of friendship is also integrally bound to the political theology of death animated by enmity. In this chapter I explore what it might mean to think the sisterly tensions of lifedeath by way of explaining what lifedeath is not. In other words, I seek to better illuminate the figure of Sister Death by exploring what Sister Death is *not*. Sister Death is not a figure of absolute finitude. Neither is Sister Death an intimate friend *to us*. Rather, I suggest, the figure of Sister Death invokes the tensions of what Jacques Derrida called lifedeath—an intimate bond of difference and nonidentity between forces that the political theology of death has taught us to think of as separable or non-relational.

ABSOLUTE FINITUDE

Perhaps the most common way to neutralize or defuse this antagonism toward death, in Western thought, is to call for an embrace or acceptance of our finitude. If we can learn to embrace and accept it, this line of thinking tends to go, we might finally release our hatred and fear of death. Accepting or embracing the limit condition of finitude unfolds into acceptance of death. It is almost as if becoming grateful for the limit condition of finitude is to give thanks to the death that produces it. While I find dimensions of this argument helpful, what I am ultimately pushing for—in the argument that there is a kind of sisterly tension in lifedeath—is something a little different. Given that this embrace of death as the origin of finitude is so philosophically and conceptually commonplace, however, I want to walk through a discussion of it. I want to indicate both why I find these arguments compelling and where I see my own lines of analysis departing from them.

One such argument that I've read with appreciation is Jeff Noonan's description of death as a *frame of finitude*. In reading death this way, Noonan finds (in death) a potentially positive form of limitation. Death is part of a living process; death captures this process in a frame. In Noonan's characterization, death is not simply a form of oppression or violation (though he acknowledges that the powers of death are often conscripted for oppressive and violating ends). Rather, death can also be a frame that enables a kind of focus. It sets the flow of life experiences into sharper relief, intensifying or illuminating them.

Frames of finitude are sites of limitation. As mortals who occupy somewhat singular bodies that will, at some point, cease to function in the manner they do now, the life I refer to as "mine" is shaped by both intrinsic and extrinsic limitations. Intrinsic limits, Noonan writes, "stem from our embodied, finite nature. They are intrinsic not only insofar as they are constitutive elements of our human organism, but also because they shape our expectations, goals, and goods."[3] What I call my body, or my condition of embodiment, is an intrinsic limit. Because of this intrinsic limit I am able to sense and feel: sensation requires a boundary to brush against. This limit condition, and its periodic erosion or eruption, facilitates any pleasure we experience in life, or any state of joy. Intrinsic limitations are tactile and mobile boundaries against which sense and sensation can play. On the other hand, intrinsic limitations introduce affects like pain and suffering. It is because of embodiment that I feel pain. Intrinsic limits are ambivalent: the source of positive affects like pleasure and negative affects like pain.

Extrinsic limits are those that press in against our bodies from an outside that is other than our immediate sense of embodiment. Extrinsic limits can be nurturing (such as a caring relationship with other embodied beings). But extrinsic limitation is also where Noonan locates forces such as social oppression and violence. Like intrinsic limits, these extrinsic limits are ambivalent. They can be sources of positive or negative affects, or those that refuse to be either. There is, naturally, some degree of overlap between these forms of limitation. A caring relationship between parent and child imposes extrinsic limits on both beings, in many ways. But these limits can also foster multiple forms of intrinsic growth and development. Illness or disease might be understood as a form of intrinsic limitation, brought about as a condition of embodiment. Yet many diseases are caused by extrinsic limitations (such as air pollution in urban neighborhoods generated and exacerbated by racist zoning policies). These illnesses are structural impositions and external in this sense. But Noonan argues that it is useful to attempt to distinguish—to the greatest extent possible—between intrinsic and extrinsic forms of limitation.

The reason for such distinction is that an intrinsic limit, for him, functions as categorically positive. Intrinsic limits serve a kind of aesthetic function. They are *frames* that set something apart or call attention to it. When we see a frame, it narrows, sharpens, or intensifies our attention. A frame placed around a mundane object can set this object apart as a form of art. This is a different form of limit than a fence, which serves as a border to protect private property. A frame, says Noonan, "is not part of the *content* of the art work, but it gives it coherence."[4] A frame is somewhat synthetic but never fully external to what has been framed. He suggests that a frame can be a positive limitation in that it marks something off, protects it, draws attention to it, or distinguishes it.[5] Frames of finitude are never singular. Indeed, the frames themselves are complex, and they knit together many dimensions of experience. Notably, the positive limitations of embodied experience also generate pain and suffering. Our embodiment, our frames of finitude, introduce causes of suffering: disease, old age, and death. What would it mean, then, to include these causes of suffering in a frame that is deemed, in some fundamental way, "positive"? It is through the recognition of these causes of suffering that we begin to sharpen our attention, to awaken affects such as gratitude and compassion. Disease, old age, and death can be experienced as painful and yet they also drive us to turn toward others with an awareness of the pain their limitations might cause them, and to extend our hand. They can make us compassionate and companionable. Intrinsic limits give our life experience coherence; they mark out lines and vectors of attention. It is only within such limited frames that we can experience affects such as pleasure and joy in the first place.

Death, for Noonan, is an intrinsic limit. He argues that pessimism is a failure to distinguish between intrinsic and extrinsic forms of limitation. He contends that the pessimistic claim that death is an oppressive extrinsic form of limitation often leads to a vision for liberation that would, ironically, sever or separate us from what generates meaning, well-being, or value in the first place. Noonan points, for instance, to techno-utopian arguments that seem to read our intrinsic limits (disease, aging, and death) as if they were extrinsic limits we will soon be capable of manipulating, managing, or even doing away with. He gestures toward thinkers such as Nick Srnicek and Alex Williams, who argue that "human liberation should not fear technological development, but democratize it and let it flower to the fullest." Noonan's critique is that a logic like this "rests on a basic principle that life is the mechanical execution of a program that is separable from its biological embodiment." This is a hope, in essence, that our technologies have put us on the verge of executing total human wellness and immortality.[6] Noonan is less concerned with whether or not such plans are feasible and more concerned with whether or not they are desirable. This vision of the future, he argues, is a kind of replacement theory—a liberation *from* our biology and a philosophical view that "conceives of the good as unconstrained realization of human desires." Given that such a vision is dependent upon technological forces, the animating force behind such visions is ultimately the unconstrained "money-value that drives the capitalist economy."[7]

What would it mean to think of Sister Death as a frame of finitude? In such a view, perhaps, Sister Death would emerge as a positive, or blessed, limit condition. She would not mark a site where death is used as a political tool to do damage to the vulnerable. Instead, Sister Death would name a limit condition that shapes our life in such a way that—without her—we would not value our relationships. Sister Death might become the blessed source of our finitude. She would limit, and particularize, each of us in just such a way that we are rendered finite and vulnerable enough to depend on others. In this dependence, we become rooted in relationships. Sister Death would name a temporal limit that drives us to mark our time differently—to seize back our time from the structures of extrinsic limitation and to engage in forms of work and play organized around our intrinsic limits. There are, clearly, benefits to thinking about death as a frame of finitude. For one thing, it wears away the resentment we might otherwise feel toward life processes such as aging or sickness. It would also deflate any irresolvable enmity toward the fact of death.

My concern, however, is that this logic continues to maintain a problematic bifurcation or boundary condition. For Noonan the sharp distinction between intrinsic and extrinsic limits remains fundamental, even if it may not ultimately be possible to distinguish between them. But limit conditions are malleable. Extrinsic forms of limitation bleed into intrinsic ones. Extrinsic forces weaponize our own intrinsic limits against us. Political oppression causes disease, premature aging, and death. Systematic oppression has a clear impact on embodied realities that is not easy to isolate. Similarly, the line between the finite and the infinite remains fundamental for Noonan, even though the infinite seems to have been pushed out of the conversation entirely. Where has the infinite gone? Is death, as the frame of all finitude, the new infinite or absolute? My ultimate discomfort with the call to embrace death as a frame of finitude rests on a hunch that this sort of embrace continues to drive problematic divisions or bifurcations. Lifting death up as the ultimate positive frame on our finitude seems to risk the assertion that death is, in some way, more crucial, primal, or foundational than life. Given the ancient Western philosophical bifurcation of life and death, it is easy—it feels almost "natural"—to repeat and reiterate this bifurcation. It seems as if the choice is either to embrace life or to claim instead that death is more potent or powerful. But this, it seems to me, is to remain trapped within an oppositional form of thinking. There is a deep ambivalence in death, in the wake of death, that I do not want to deflect or erase. There is a kind of tension that is evaded—perhaps even a dimension of resistance that is lost—if we try to turn the ambivalence of death into a pure positive.

DEATH THE FRIEND

Another strategic approach toward deflating the theologically driven enmity between life and death is to suggest that death is a friend rather than an enemy. If the critical problem is a fundamental enmity between life and death, then a friendship between life and death seems to offer a necessary critical counterpoint. But casting the relation between life and death as one of friendship, rather than enmity, keeps these processes embroiled within the same political theological problem. Friendship and enmity are counterpoised against one another in a relational continuum. While their relationship may be oppositional, it can also be integral and mutually dependent. The friendship between life and death remains caught up within the same political theological complex as enmity. That is to say, the idea that death is a friend maintains a kind of capture of life and death within what Carl Schmitt called the *friend-enemy distinction*.

The concept of enmity is at the core of Schmitt's analysis of the political. He claimed that the unity of a political group was established and maintained through the friend-enemy antithesis. Schmitt argued that the figure of the friend, in political thought, denoted an intense form of union or association while the enemy was a site of dissociation.[8] The enemy is, politically speaking, the other, the stranger—an alien.[9] The enemy is a public figure that serves as an antagonist against which political collectives push, bonding and grouping themselves together as friends. But enemies create friendships. In finding a common enemy, a political group creates friendly alliances. This rendered political what Schmitt called "the most intense and extreme antagonism."[10] And yet, these antagonisms of enmity also support friendship. Schmitt's claim is that this friend-enemy antithesis is universal: the foundation of the political itself. In Schmitt's analysis, "every concrete antagonism" becomes more political as it approaches or approximates the friend-enemy antithesis.[11] But what the friend-enemy distinction can also—more intriguingly—illuminate is the strange bond of intimacy between friendship and enmity. The friend-enemy distinction locates these forms of relation on a tense continuum of affiliation and disaffiliation. While it may be the case that specific figures are labeled as one or the other, friendship and enmity are not entirely other to one another. Rather, I would argue, the distinction itself presents a range of different relational compromises between pure friendship and pure enmity. The continuum itself creates a kind of false choice (between friend or enemy), as well as a kind of feedback loop that continues to bind friendship and enmity in a connective distinction. I want to think about the relation between life and death outside of this continuum.

It is clear that the theological declaration of death as enemy feeds into a form of political alliance. Those who make enemies of death become, themselves, friends of a sort. What is less clear, however, is the extent to which friendship itself—even love—can remain bound up in this antithesis rather than providing for an exit from it. Gil Anidjar, gesturing toward the Christian commandment to love one's enemies, notes that "the theological enemy" is not simply *other* but instead is "at once enemy and beloved."[12] The command to love the enemy functions, says Anidjar, to deny the distinction between oneself and the enemy. "The irrelevance of distinction," he writes, is "at the core of the commandment to love one's enemies." Which is to say, "to love the enemy would thus mean not to distinguish, not to separate."[13] In the wake of this indistinguishing love, the enemy is not an other but instead appears to vanish, withdraw, or go into hiding.[14] To fold the enemy into love is, perhaps, a particular sort of evisceration of the enemy: a quest to take the enemy into oneself, to digest and metabolize it. It is in precisely this sense, perhaps, that Christian theology loves its friend, the last enemy who is death. Love facilitates a particular sort of destruction of the last enemy.

This is not a commentary on love and friendship *as such*, which is certainly far more complex than my analysis here. Rather, this is a commentary on political theologies of love and enmity. Not all friendships conform to this political theology, but within political theology friendships and enmities are often rendered inextricable. In political theologies derived from the Christian tradition, hatred and love often remain bound in a complex relational distinction that draws from the tense mutual dependence between enmity and friendship. For this reason, I resist the argument that death is a *friend* rather than an *enemy*.

To set up this sort of opposition, I think, is to keep life and death bound up in the structures of enmity—destined for a new form of capture, within enmity, when the friendship has worn thin. More than that, the reduction of death to *either* friend or enemy relies on a simplification of death itself. It is a reduction of the complex textures of experience related to the phenomena that go by the name of death. If the name "death" points, for instance, to both biological phenomena (decay, fermentation, germination) as well as dimensions of social exploitation (suffering, injustice, oppression), then to label death as an enemy allows for a clear condemnation of the forms of injustice associated with death. To oppose this, by naming death a friend, would also seem to neutralize this clear opposition to injustice and oppression. It goes without saying, perhaps, that much of the process of living is a struggle against the work of decay in our own bodies. These modes of critical antagonism, in relation to death, are essential to both care and survival. The risk of arguing that death is a friend is that it defuses this critical antagonism and reduces our understanding of death to a simple shell that shows us nothing of the complex, moving, and embodied textures through which we encounter death in its many guises.

It is also the case that, in a culture for which death has long been a great and powerful enemy, the act of making friends with death—befriending death—can become the capture of a form of power that is easily weaponized. The friendship with death can be militant. It is as if the enemy might be captured, and made into a friend, in order to fight alongside oneself in a new and different battle—a powerful solider recruited from the other side. Michel Foucault has described a process of transition, in early modern medicine and clinical practice, in which death was befriended so that its secrets might be appropriated. For doctors into the eighteenth century, he suggests, death represented a kind of absolute—a transcendent dimension, pointing beyond knowledge or comprehension. Death was "that absolute beyond which there was neither life nor disease."[15] But the end of the eighteenth century, and the beginning of the Enlightenment, also marked a shift in relation to death.

The expanding reach of the clinical eye brought the doctor's gaze closer to a series of signs and symptoms that had once been considered impenetrable. In this new clinical environment, "death, too, was entitled to the clear light of reason, and became for the philosophical mind an object and source of knowledge." The corpse itself became, for clinical practice, "the brightest moment in the figures of truth."[16] Through autopsy, and the anatomical practice of opening a corpse, death was no longer transcendent and absolute but instead became immanent to the clinician. Death became a "moving" phenomenon that worked in "stages." Death came to be seen as "multiple, and dispersed in time" rather than "that absolute, privileged point at which time stops and moves back."[17] As death became a phenomenon immanent to (rather than transcendent over) the clinician, Foucault argues that it became possible for physicians themselves to occupy "the height of death." They took on a form of seeing—a gaze from the powerful point of view of death—that would offer new perspectives on disease and the body. Instead of being "the night in which life disappeared" death instead became "endowed with that great power of elucidation that dominates and reveals both the space of the organism and the time of the disease." The pathologist Marie François Xavier Bichat was, for Foucault, especially instrumental in this process of relativizing death, of "bringing it down from that absolute in which it appeared as an indivisible, decisive, and irrecoverable event."[18] Bichat, in effect, pivoted toward death and demanded of it "an account of life and disease." Foucault argues that for physicians like Bichat, the opening of corpses was also a way of brightening, animating, and amplifying the clinical gaze, dissipating the darkness in which death once stood, allowing medicine instead to be founded "in the brightness of death."[19]

What Foucault highlights here is, in essence, what I would describe as the emergence of a form of friendship. Early modern medicine steps back, in at least one sense, from the enmity long maintained toward this godlike absolute that went by the name of death. Pathologists such as Bichat, particularly those engaged in the anatomical analysis of corpses, developed a strategic friendship with death. They glimpsed secrets buried within death. In death there was also knowledge about life: knowledge of its destruction and potential extension. Death was befriended in order to learn, to appropriate, these secrets. Death, in this friendship, becomes a form of brightness, the site of a kind of truth. Foucault describes the process through which this view of death in early modern medicine filtered into European philosophy—into the work of thinkers such as Holderlin, Nietzsche, and Freud. Through this friend that is death, philosophers suggest, we can learn and appropriate the truth of our being. If, for classical forms of thought, the finitude (made by death) was meaningful only in that it pointed to a negation of, or opposition to the infinite, mortality and finitude began to take on their own form of powerful meaning. Death becomes the way that we appropriate our own source of truth, especially in secularizing forms of thought that resist the theological. In these discourses, death "opens up the source of language that unfolds endlessly in the void left by the absence of the gods."[20] The individual in this emerging intellectual environment, says Foucault, "owes to death a meaning that does not belong to him."[21] Yet one can demand, from death, one's own truth with little regard to whether one has acted out of place. Death's power (unlike God's) is not paternal or redemptive. But it is both clarifying and illuminating.

Foucault illustrates how the process of befriending death generates new postures of relation toward death itself. Rather than serve as the great antagonist of life (the enemy), death becomes the friend who can structure the meaning of life in the absence of God, or in the void left by God. But Foucault also points to a militancy that structures the relation to death, even in this reversal. Death helps to arm the physician and to enable the penetrating powers of the clinical gaze. In a real sense, then, this flip or opposition (in which death moves from being the enemy to being, instead, a friend) continues to keep dimensions of militancy and enmity at play. This act of befriending death arms medicine itself—the clinician's gaze—with new forms of technological power. Having turned toward death, having befriended it, death then helps to authorize "a scientific discourse in a rational form."[22] The world of medicine, and of health, offers new promises of salvation. This health is secured by the knowledge provided by the point of view of death, which gives rise to what Foucault describes as a "technical world" that is also "the armed, positive" and "full form of (man's) finitude."[23] This possession of the point of view of death, this befriending of death, continues to create and recreate a form of life that is armed with technological power, knowledge, and its own truth. This modern form of life is now armed with knowledge of death and seeks its truth within death (rather than God). But this friendship with death remains laced with a kind of militancy. Death has been recruited from across enemy lines. Yet this friendship nevertheless remains captured and structured, in subtle ways, by the friend-enemy continuum. It is not fully detached from the militant legacies of the political theology of death.

This militant legacy is barely visible in modern Western philosophical projects that source forms of truth and meaning within death itself. Indeed, in the context of modern European philosophical projects such as Heidegger's, death arguably comes to seem like something of a benefactor. Death as a source of immanent subjective truth (one that remains stable in the wake of God's own death) creates an almost subversive but also beneficent bond between modern subjectivity and the negativity of death. But in these modern continental discourses on death, the figure of death comes linked to the individualistic human subject of these discourses. These are discourses not simply on the role that death plays in subjectivity but on the relationship between *man and death*. In these philosophical conversations death is a singular problem, or a problem of singularity. Death is either *mine*, or it is the death of the other. But death is not collective, in the manner of an extinction. It is a singular event or an event of singularity. All men go alone into their death. Even in the work of Jacques Derrida, who has interrogated philosophical discourses on death in (especially) the work of Heidegger, death remains an event of singularity.[24] Death, suggests Derrida in conversation with Heidegger, "names the very irreplaceability of absolute singularity" in that, "no one can die in my place or in the place of the other."[25] When it comes to awaiting one another at the border called death, "the one and the other never arrive there together, at this rendezvous."[26] Death, in its singularity, remains linked to individual experience and so is a matter of what might be called the self.

This firm link between death and subjectivity—this position that death is the inexhaustible source revealing a kind of human truth—has been interrogated and critiqued by feminist thinkers in the continental tradition. I am in conversation with these critiques in this book and will not develop them here. But, for the time being, I would make note of Simone de Beauvoir's critique in *The Second Sex* of her male colleagues' failure to understand that their obsession with death is at times indistinguishable from an obsession with the womb. Hannah Arendt famously reversed the Heideggerian aim of subjectivity, critiquing a form of being that was oriented toward death and presenting instead a natal subjectivity that is rooted in birth. I have my sympathies with this turn—against what Grace Jantzen argued was the morbid "necrophilia" of Western philosophy. I sympathize with this critique of death as the source and origin point of a singular subjective truth. But I also think that this focus on natality betrays the tendency to turn into a simple reversal: a focus on birth *rather than* death. It is as if birth presents a dimension of positivity that can be rescued from the abject negativity of death. This excludes the many complex relations of entanglement between birth and death. Inevitably birth itself, and so the conceptual discourses on natality that may abstract it, can be death-dealing. As Black feminist thinkers such as Saidiya Hartman have noted, reproduction in the context of slavery has been a tool of domination. Natality remains, in this sense, implicated in death-dealing. But what I think critiques such as Jantzen's can help us see is that attempts to unseat the pure positivity of life, in order to replace it with the negativity of death, are not as separable from the theological and metaphysical histories of death as they might otherwise appear to be. They remain trapped in a similar struggle. This is where I believe that the figure of lifedeath can make a crucial intervention. To think of the relation between life and death as *lifedeath* offers a figure of difference that is not dialectical and yet still remains ambivalent—potentially structured by both nurture and antagonism.

LIFEDEATH

Derrida's seminars on life and death (given in 1975–1976 and recently published as *La vie la mort*) highlight the way that Western philosophical habits of thought freeze life and death into patterns of opposition, contradiction, and juxtaposition. Such positionality, he notes, comes embedded in European grammar. To connect the two terms with an "and" is to conjoin them, but such a conjunction also implies opposition or contradiction. To even introduce a different form of conjunction (life/death or life-death) seems to maintain this latent relationship of opposition. Derrida does not wish to suggest that life and death are simply congruent, let alone the same thing (to erase forms of difference that exist between them.) But he is critical of the "driving scheme" that keeps this relation of opposition or contradiction at play.[27] Derrida does note that dialectical thought presents a more complex relationship between life and death. Indeed, in Hegel's *Logic*, Derrida notes that death is necessary to, and for, life. But, for Hegel, it is also the case that death remains purely natural. So it is that when natural life dies its natural death, this end provides the conditions for the dialectical emergence of Life itself. Imperishable and absolute Life stands above a natural life. In this dialectical relation, Derrida notes that "life no longer has any opposition." Life has reappropriated both (natural) life and (natural) death so that life no longer has "any other facing it." Death, thus, "becomes unthinkable as something that is."[28] Life, in the end, still transcends, neutralizes, and effectively erases the powers of death. Death, for Hegel, remains a conceptual necessity. But only so that she can be transcended by a Life force that is more absolute and sovereign. This is, I think, a rearticulation or secularization of the transcendence of the God of life over death.

In these seminars on lifedeath, Derrida seeks another way of thinking about death. He is clear, however, that he is not seeking another *logic* for thinking about this conjunction of forces or terms. If Western thought has traditionally placed life and death in a relation of opposition, contradiction, or juxtaposition (in order to either set them at odds or in a dialectic), then Derrida is not interested in finding another logic for this relation. What he illuminates, instead, might better be called another grammar or another poetics. His use of the term *lifedeath* strategically removes the space between these forces. It does so, however, without rendering them one and the same. The logic of position is strangely suspended, yet the forces remain distinct. The question, then, is no longer which force predominates. Instead, other patterns of relation, other forms of betweenness, emerge: new tensions and collaborations. What lifedeath illuminates is neither opposition nor sameness but a form of difference.

In his final seminar on the topic (XIV), Derrida reflects on Freud's *Beyond the Pleasure Principle*. There are passages in the book, I would note, in which Freud seems to be falling into the ancient habit of setting life and death in a relation of opposition. For instance, Freud's claim that "the goal of all life is death,"[29] or that all organic instincts are driven to return to their initial condition as inanimate and inorganic, risks reduction to the argument that death (as opposed to life) is the absolute origin and that death, rather than life, is the omnipotent and the eternal. But Freud is also quite clear about the fact that *Beyond the Pleasure Principle* is a deeply speculative and provisional project.[30] Indeed, he even betrays his own confusion over how to make sense of the death drive. He is especially uncertain about how to address the relation that he calls the death instinct (bound to what he calls the ego-drive) and the vitalizing of inanimate matter that he ties—with an admitted speculative leap—to the

FIGURE 1.3 Krista Dragomer, *Held by a Blast in Unwritten Space*, 2017

sexual instinct. Freud admits that his speculations have begun to resemble Schopenhauer's "incarnation of the will to live."[31] And it would seem, in his mind, that this is a point against his own project. It is almost as if he is struggling to recognize that the bifurcation of life and death, in grammar and thought, is itself the problem that must be tackled. But he lacks the language with which to interrogate this problem directly. So he remains confined—on the surface of his speculations—to reflect on drives that seek more life versus the drives that seek to be extinguished. It is almost as if these drives were simply in opposition, while the underlying point of the pleasure principle is—in fact—to illuminate their entanglements and strange collaborations.

What Freud does not articulate explicitly is what Derrida picks up on. Derrida is not interested in claiming, with Freud, that death and the inorganic are the source and origin point of all life. Rather, Derrida is especially interested in a sense of rhythm that emerges in the tension between the death instinct and the sexual instinct—in, we might say, the lifedeath of the text. Freud describes what he calls "an oscillating rhythm in the life of all organisms" in which "the one group of instincts presses forward to reach the final goal of life" whereas "the other flies back" only to "traverse the same stretch once more from a given spot and thus to prolong the duration of the journey."[32] This rhythm is incessant and unsettles Freud's speculations throughout the text. Freud ends the book on a note of what Derrida calls "irresolution" or even "insolvency."[33] Freud ends with uncertainty, coming up empty. The sense of irresolution with which Freud closes his speculations is, Derrida suggests, a tension. That tension is a bond (*bindung*) "that extends, unresolved, to an extreme degree, without conclusion, without solution."[34] This bond is stretched between differentiated tendencies, and it oscillates with a kind of loping uncertain rhythm between them. This irresolute tension is pulled toward pleasure (animacy), back toward the extinction of pleasure (inanimacy), and then back again. The pleasure principle is, itself, this tension, this bonding, this connection; it is "caught between two limits," between "the preparation and the end; desire, if you will, and its ultimate fulfillment."[35] Neither of these functions is ever completed. Instead, the pleasure principle captures them within a tension or state of irresolution that limits each of these potentialities. And, indeed, the tension (which is also a limiting structure) is what makes pleasure and non-pleasure possible. In their limitation, they become accessible rather than purely destructive. The limit—the tensive irresolution—is itself a bonding structure that produces through its acts of limitation. It "is played out between two infinities." If there were absolute limitation, the whole game would disappear. But if there were (conversely) an absolute release, we would be left with a similar outcome.[36] There is, instead, an irresolution. It is not a smooth and stable oscillation. It does not equalize. It does not end in a pure state of either annihilation or satisfaction. And it does not bring these two states harmoniously together. Instead, Derrida suggests, it works "badly" in order to work at all; "it very well limps along."[37] This is, perhaps, why Derrida finds it so unsurprising that Freud ends *Beyond the Pleasure Principle* with a poetic allusion to limping. He is referring to Freud's closing citation of the poet Friedrich Rückert: "What we cannot reach flying we must reach limping. . . . The Book tells us it is no sin to limp."[38] The irresolution is a limping and loping bond. But it is one, notably, done in the absence of flight and yet as soundless as an owl's wing beat. It lopes, but it does so elegantly. This limping, loping tension is of the order of necessity and in that sense it is paradoxically both graceless and full of grace.

Derrida ends his own seminars on lifedeath with his own loping comparison—one that seeks to amplify the limping, binding rhythm he discerns in Freud's pleasure principle. If the central bond, or connection between drives, in *Beyond the Pleasure Principle* is an irresolution that manifests as a rhythm, Freud likens it to an insight in Nietzsche's *Will to Power*. These two texts might, on the surface, be set at odds. Freud has been accused of a kind of nihilism, with his focus on the death drive. Nietzsche, on the other hand, has been deemed a vitalist for his interest in the powers of life. But Derrida discerns a resonance between them in their mutual interest in this tensive irresolution. Nietzsche, notes Derrida, speaks of pleasure as "a sort of rhythm in the succession of minor pains."[39] Pain, Nietzsche suggests, "is the feeling of being faced with an impediment." And yet power and pleasure become self-aware only in the face of obstacle. So it is that pain becomes "an *integral part of every activity*." The will to power thus "*aspires* to find resistance, pain." There is, says Nietzsche, "a will to suffer at the root of all organic life."[40] This is not, quite, a desire to return to inanimacy or the inorganic. But, like Freud, Nietzsche highlights a rhythm that oscillates between pleasure and its extinction. The point is neither pleasure nor pain, pleasure or its extinction, but instead the irresolute rhythm between these things.

Derrida calls this bond, this tension or central irresolution, something in the "lexical register of speculation" rather than a logic.[41] Derrida suggests that "the ultimate concept or value is that of a certain *rhythmos*," which is not a logic.[42] If the critique that Derrida stages in these seminars is an interrogation of the Western philosophical logic that endlessly opposes life and death, then this bond does not present an alternative logic. Instead it is simply another speculative structure for framing the terms. So we might say that lifedeath is a grammatical intervention into a logical structure, one that introduces a speculative framework, without offering up another logic. To see this irresolution functioning between the tensive positions of life and death is, perhaps, to discern a kind of bond between them—one that does not function smoothly but limps and lopes. In the grammatical and speculative structure of lifedeath, a bond or connection throws them into relation with one another. They become counterpoints, or points of opposition, that generate relations of feedback. In their relation, each becomes limited. They serve to limit one another. And in this mutual limitation, they each become present or manifest. What emerges between them is a rhythm that plays between two infinites. What emerges, more concretely, are the livingdying entities, the natalmortals who fly, creep, crawl, roll, limp, and leap back and forth in this incessant irresolute connection. Birthing and dying play out as phases in this rhythm and in the pauses between its beats—in the rest.

To think of Sister Death as a death positive icon is not to turn death into a new absolute or to cultivate a love of or desire for death. Instead, it is to become attuned to the rhythms in which death is caught up. It is to imagine a form of sisterhood in the limping, loping lifedeath bond. This sisterhood is the differential pulse, the loping and limping rhythms of lifedeath—the survival strategies that are wrested from the tension between these forces or infinities. To be death positive is to resist the impulse in the political theology of death that generates enmity between life and death, so that death becomes something to eviscerate. This ancient political theology envisions death as a kind of false infinite—a devil's trick, in disguise. The political theology of death incites a constant war between life and death, enlisting those who crave life as soldiers in the battle. The lifedeath sisterhood is not a harmony or a smooth compression. It does not remove antagonism between these forces. But neither does it mute their resonance.

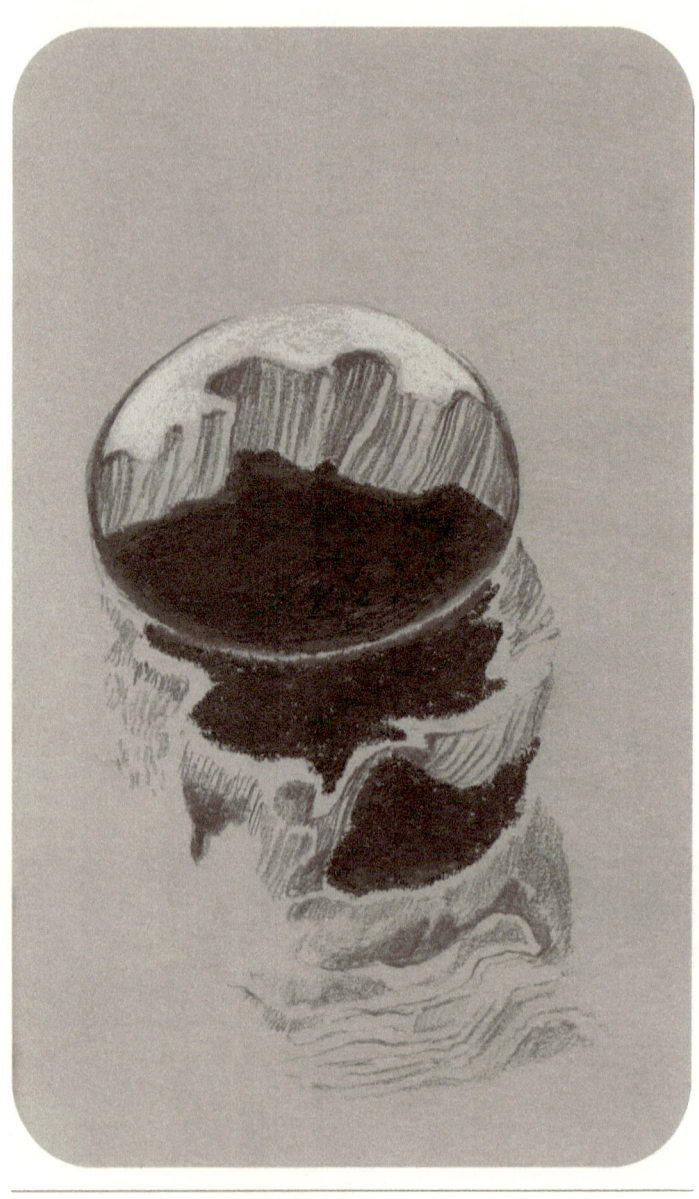

FIGURE 2.1 Krista Dragomer, *Synodic Portal 3*, 2020

2

THE WAR WITH DEATH

There are as many ways of describing the phenomena we glibly label "death" as there are bodies that live and breathe. In practice and in effect the relationships between life and death, and the processes of living and dying, are irreducibly complex. I have no desire to reduce this complexity. In fact, it is my hope to amplify it, or at least to remember it. But in this book I am interested in critically interrogating what I argue has become, over the evolutionary history of "Western" forms of thought, a dominant and powerful method for articulating and describing the relationship between life and death. My critical target is the narrative of a fundamental enmity between life and death that, I argue, has been aided and abetted by a political theology informed by Christianity. I seek to disrupt and destabilize the narrative that the basic relation between life and death is an irresolvable relation of enmity. It is not because I believe that enmity itself is inherently bad or even avoidable. Nor is it because I want to argue that death is the opposite of an enemy—a friend. Rather, I want to explore what it might mean to think about life and death, living and dying, from outside of the militancy that this enmity feeds, this state of war.

I do not want to close my eyes for the last time feeling as if I have lost a war. And yet I also feel like I have been set up or conditioned for this sensibility, as if there is a symbolic regime etched just behind my eyelids that I haven't quite been able to scrape out. Perhaps if I were one of those who had already proclaimed victory over death, if I were confident that I would die "in Christ" (and so, as the apostle Paul promised, with death underfoot), the whole scenario would look different to me. But as I see it, this vision of death—as an enemy to do battle with—is part of a symbolic regime that was itself spread (necropolitically or necrotheologically, we might say) through the sword. It remains difficult for me not to feel this sharp point still cutting—softly, as if only a half-threat, or in jest—against my own skin.

I have made this narrative of enmity a critical target because I have felt more than this sharp point against my own skin. I have also felt the militancy behind it both intimately and internally. I have learned to struggle against it. But my struggles have also, often, been ineffectual. This militancy is in the water, you might say. Growing up in the United States, I learned to believe that death might not be coming for me. That is to say, growing up in economically privileged conditions, growing up white in a racialized lifeworld crafted by and for whiteness, I learned to believe that death might not be coming for me. I do not mean that I misunderstood the fact that I am mortal, like all other living beings. This data has always been available. But the fact of death seemed always, somehow, assuredly postponed. It was always possible, at the very least, to put it out of sight and, so, out of mind. In this way, it felt distant, abstract, alien. And if I felt myself in its shadows I could feel my defenses rise and my blood course through me until I believed I'd scared away the phantom.

"White Americans do not believe in death," James Baldwin argued.[1] He was not referring to the moment of shock and stupefaction that can accompany a death—an inability to comprehend or make sense of someone's disappearance from the world of the living. Baldwin spoke, instead, of a form of denial or repudiation. Death, for white Americans, is a condition of the negative, a symbolic collapse, a state of terror, a nothingness that is also a darkness. And so for them, he said, death becomes an "unspeakable" fear that conflates these dimensions of the negative and projects them onto blackness, "onto the Negro."[2] In the midst of this disbelief in death, one might (as I often have) choose to *contemplate* one's own death—to meditate on what it might look like, or feel like, to become a corpse. Or one might reflect on what gifts come bound up in the limit conditions of being mortal. But these are spiritual exercises undertaken in a peaceful state of contemplative abstraction and remove. This sort of exercise is, itself, the sign of a form of privilege; it is something we do when we are not in the throes of mourning and grief. Abstracted from grief, mourning, or terror, the contemplative reminder of their possibility gives us the control to turn these affects on and off. This is different from what Christina Sharpe has called the wake work that happens in the afterlives of American slavery. In the wake of slavery, she says, "the ongoing state-sanctioned legal and extralegal murders of Black people are normative and, for this so-called democracy, necessary; it is the ground we walk on." Death, when it is normative and state-sanctioned, is outside the domain of personal control and less likely to blend easily with a sense of peace and contemplative silence. So it is that Black life is lived "in relation to this requirement for our death," Sharpe writes. Black life is lived "near death" and yet also, when stripped of rituals through which to grieve, to mourn, and so to celebrate life, is also "deathless" in "the wake of slavery."[3]

In this kind of America, racial lines are policed through the activation of particular narratives about living and dying—about who lives, survives, thrives, and dies. White Americans have told, and continue to tell, stories about who is meant for life and who is walking toward death. In this kind of America, the militancy that feeds the war against death becomes part of a spiritual apparatus that maintains divisions and boundary lines that also become racialized. From one angle, this story is a tragedy or a tragic narrative about the poverties and deprivations of whiteness. It is tragic, we might say, that white Americans fail to catch a glimpse of destiny. Destiny, as Carol Wayne White has described it, is finitude. But this is not finitude as a simple limit condition. Instead, it is finitude as a contingent actualization of the past and finitude as the transformation of this past into a future. This is finitude as a "partial actualization" that is also a crucial aspect of "the evolving, unfolding stream of life."[4] Death, in destiny so understood, is not "an experience of oppositional otherness," says White, but instead a necessary and foundational condition for the unfolding of a destiny in the first place.[5] It is tragic that in this kind of America, whiteness occludes what Baldwin calls the ability to "rejoice in the *fact* of death" because this fact reveals the luminous power of a human who is also a "small beacon in that terrifying darkness from which we come and to which we shall return."[6] It is tragic, we might even say, that in this kind of America whiteness occludes what Sharpe illuminates in the wake: that there is an irreplaceable form of power in wake work, "the power of sitting with someone as they die, the important work of sitting (together) in the pain and sorrow of death as a way of marking, remembering, and celebrating a life."[7]

This book is not about this tragedy, however. While I make note of it, I worry that to amplify it would also lead to misplaced narratives of victimhood. Instead, it is about the war with death that—I argue—has helped to create the conditions in which this tragedy takes place. It is about the war with death that is, in part, an act of seizure—a gesture that seeks (in putting death to death) to isolate, ally with, and capture the powers of life in order to unify them with the powers of light. I argue that this understanding of oneself as a warrior for life, in the great battle against death and its powers, can also create a set of subjective conditions and so a mode of self-understanding. In these conditions, what Baldwin calls the fact of death is often actively repressed. In these conditions, the intimate forms of connection and mutual support between processes that make live and processes that make die, between forms of emergence and forms of decay, are repressed.

REALMS OF DEATH

Although my critical target in this book is a political theology derived from Christianity, biblical texts themselves often illuminate complex textures of lifedeath. Kathryn Tanner, arguing against the theological perspective that death is merely or simply a force to be overcome, points out that Old Testament figurations of death affirm that there is a form of "bad death" that must be struggled against: "premature, painful, community-rending death."[8] What Tanner also refers to as a *realm of death* becomes a "catch-all for such things as suffering, poverty, barrenness, oppression, social divisiveness, and isolation." And it is contrasted with a *realm of life* that serves as a cognate for "fruitfulness and abundance, longevity, communal flourishing, and individual well-being." In this contrast life and death serve largely poetic and metaphorical functions.[9] This metaphoricity is illustrated, for Tanner, in the fact that in the biblical texts "one can be dead while alive." And "one can also enjoy a death that imitates life—in old age, surrounded by one's posterity."[10]

Life and death also describe patterns of relation to God, Tanner notes. "To die is to break with this life-giving, blessing-bestowing relationship with God" and to live "is to place oneself joyfully and willingly within it."[11] Additionally, claims such as the Psalmist's observance, "If I make my bed in Sheol, you are there" (Psalms 139:7–8), indicate that death is a realm that remains within God's reach.[12] Which also means that "death does not have the power to separate one from God."[13] So while biblical texts, especially Hebrew scriptures, may affirm that this form of bad death may be struggled against, they do acknowledge the fact of death. Tanner points, for instance, to the plea to "teach us to number our days that we may get a heart of wisdom" (Psalms 90: 12) or the affirmation that we are dust into dust (Genesis 3:19). This is a simple recognition, says Tanner, of "temporal cessation" or "limited duration." Echoing Francis of Assisi, she notes that "as a natural fact about the created world, death could indeed be considered one of the goods of creation."[14] The crucial distinction in these ancient discourses, of course, is between different forms or dimensions of death. This creates a more complex texture in biblical lifedeath. Death is not reduced to either a biological function or a mythical one. The fact of death appears, we might say, as a biomythical dimension of a complex social and spiritual ecology.

With this idea in mind, it is possible to give a more nuanced and generous reading to Paul's claim that death is the last and greatest enemy. If we understand Paul to make an enemy of bad death, or the realm of death that is suffering due to poverty, oppression, or isolation, then Paul's claim could be read as a proclamation of the victory of justice over injustice. We might understand Paul to be struggling not against biology, or the processes of decay that nourish the soil, but instead against the violence of (for instance) a necropolitical order. I make no claim to understand Paul's own true intentions. Nor do I intend to prevent this sort of reading of Paul's declaration of war with death. I am less interested in what he hoped to say and more interested in the interpretive legacies of his many billions of readers. And the collapse of the realm of death (of bad death) into the fact of death has been enduring and commonplace in Christian theology throughout the centuries. The result is a biomythical discourse on death that collapses various forms of death into the same frame and amplifies the most terrifying emotional potencies that might be harbored within them.

This collapse has maintained its hold over contemporary Christian imaginations. Take, for instance, the once popular claims of the twentieth-century German Lutheran theologian Oscar Cullmann, who argued for the radical distinction between Greek and Christian views of death. Contrasting the death of Socrates with the death of Jesus, Cullmann argues that the death of Socrates is presented as a "beautiful death" that sets him free from his body. For Cullmann this perfectly illustrates the Greek view that death is the "great liberator" that "leads the soul out of the prison of the body."[15] Cullman argued for the inappropriateness of this Greek view, for those who follow Jesus. For the Christian, he said, death "is something dreadful."[16] To die "means to be utterly forsaken."[17] Death for Christians, he said, "is not something natural, willed by God as in the thought of the Greek philosophers; it is rather something unnatural, abnormal, opposed to God."[18] Erasing the textures of complexity that Tanner illuminates in the discourse on death in Hebrew texts, Cullmann argues that the view of death as unnatural, or an enemy, is filtered into Christianity through Judaism—more specifically, "the Jewish connexion between death and *sin*." This is what the Genesis narratives teach, he says: that death is "a curse" that "came into the world only by the sin of man."[19]

Cullmann's figuration of death is a gross simplification that serves primarily to uphold a clear dimension of enmity in the relation between life and death. God is placed on the side of life, and death becomes a negative receptacle for all that is opposed to God. Not only does this view erase the complex textures of lifedeath that a theologian like Tanner illuminates, but it infuses enmity into the form of life that arises—against death, fleeing from death—within Christian subjectivity.

The figure of Jesus Christ creates immense complications in and for Christian discourses on death. The resurrection of Jesus, the story of Jesus rising from the dead, clearly indicates that for Christians, death is not the absolute. Because death is not the end of the story of Jesus, the fact of death is placed within a narrative frame in which his life story continues after the death event. The story itself does not characterize death in a formulaic way. But it does raise significant questions about how to make sense of death, within the frame of the narrative. Is the endurance of life, after the event of death, a metaphor that expresses the interlacing folds of lifedeath? Or is this a message that life triumphs, always and eternally, over any form of death? Is the story of Jesus about the divine triumph over injustice and the realm of death? Or is it a story about the evisceration of all forms of death and decay? It would seem that, theologically, all of these questions might be answered in the affirmative. Some theologians have read death as a kind of necessary passage, suggesting that the form of life that is resurrected can only unfold or take place after a mortal or creaturely life has reached its limit or completion. But it has also been commonplace to understand the resurrection of Jesus as something like a military victory that defeats mortality itself. Thus the figure of Jesus seems, for some theologians, to make mortality a sacred necessity, while for others Jesus promises the militant defeat of mortality itself. It is often in the figure of Jesus that we see Christians stage this war between life and death. The figure of Jesus models, for some Christians, a militant subjectivity that does violence to death. Jesus models, in these contexts, a martial form of life.

MARTIAL FORMS OF LIFE

The language of battle, embedded and fixed into the relation between life and death, resounds with traces of the ransom theory of atonement. In this theology, following Gustaf Aulén, Jesus Christ becomes the key player in a story of "divine conflict and victory." Jesus becomes the "Christus Victor" who "fights and triumphs over the evil powers of the world."[20] Such a theological viewpoint, in which Jesus and those who worship him are warriors for the God of life, is at ease in imperial and colonial conceptual frameworks. The fight for the ultimate glory of divine life, after all, does not always call for tenderness toward the living. The living may be, in effect, on the side of evil and sin: allies with death. Indeed, this has been a common accusation leveled against the non-Christian world over the course of Christian history. The non-Christian is effectively against God and so is complicit with evil, sin, and death. Christians have dealt death with impunity, in other words, to those destined for death. And they have done this in the name of eternal life. The figure of Jesus Christ does not generate a necessary enmity between life and death. But it has been commonplace, over the course of Christian history, to understand Jesus as doing just that. Jesus is read as a warrior against death in the great battle between life and death. The implication for Christians is that they, too, are warriors in this great battle. So it is that the defeat of the enemies of a Christendom established in the name of Jesus has been considered part of the grander defeat of the greatest enemy of all.

This language of battle, and this understanding of a subjectivity forged in the violent enmities between life and death, reads easily into what Jairus Victor Grove calls the "martial genealogy" of the Eurocene.[21] The figure of the Eurocene, for Grove, is a critical counterpoint to the concept of the Anthropocene, a term that Grove has found to be stripped of its geopolitical dimensions. Examining the formation of the concept of the Anthropocene, specifically in the research of Paul Crutzen, Grove argues that the Anthropocene is presented as a "universal concern" that ultimately demands or requires a "depoliticization of the causes of that concern."[22] The figure of the Anthropocene places the blame for mass extinction events, climate change, and accompanying forms of planetary crisis on the shoulders of Anthropos—a generalized figure of humanity. Grove finds the generalization of this figure to be the heart of the problem with the category of the Anthropocene as such. "As a philosophical and political crisis," says Grove, many have "been too quick to forget the geopolitical arrangements of power and violence that have brought us to this point. Not all of 'us' have played an equal part in the making of either the Anthropos or the Anthropocene."[23] The risk, argues Grove, of a figure like the Anthropocene is that its universal generality seems to demand a global, hegemonic response through methods of statecraft enacted by "the power politics of the same states and the same practices of statecraft that made the Anthropocene."[24]

What Grove names, instead, the Eurocene describes not a universal phenomenon generated by human activity as such but instead a "practical problem not captured by the Anthropocene."

The Eurocene is (more specifically) "a five-hundred-year project of violent terraforming and atmospheric engineering."[25] It connects the political and environmental devastation frequently attached to the Anthropocene to a more particular historical genealogy, rooted in Euro-American politics, a "five-hundred-year geopolitical tradition of conquest, colonization, extraction, and the martial forms of life that made them all possible through war and through more subtle and languid forms of organized killing."[26] The Eurocene also gives rise, he argues, to a particular form of subjectivity—what he calls a martial form of life.

A form of life, for Grove, is "not quite race" but is also "more than culture or style." It is a term that describes "ways of being in the world—always lived collectively—without which one would no longer be who or what one is." A form of life is both biological and cultural. A form of life inhabits biomythical dimensions. And forms of life, among humans, can vary in potentially infinite ways. Additionally, "the interruption of a form of life kills people and frequently cascades into genocides and extinctions."[27] The Eurocene, argues Grove, has given rise to at least one form of life. In the wake of a geopolitical order in which warfare has become "an ordinary practice," Grove argues that this becomes written "into the very musculature of our bodies, practices, and communities."[28] This form of life, born and crafted in the Eurocene, is conditioned within a savage ecology that is awash in militarization and security politics.[29] This martial form of life, crafted by the geopolitics of the Eurocene, "displays an obsession with warfare and order—part technological hubris, part ecological sabotage." And the martial forms of life animated by this geopolitical order "have ripped their way through every continent on this planet, making a geological mark."[30] To be an American, Grove writes, "is not merely to be a citizen of the United States." Rather, it is "to be part of a precarious mixture of

European industrial and demographic expansion, a homegrown sense of Christian providence, liberal institutional development, and a ruthless martial art of extermination and settlement that has continued unabated since its founding."[31] Through the geopolitics of the Eurocene, this form of life has been spreading across the globe and the biodiversity of forms of life in human communities is itself collapsing at accelerating rates.[32] One fundamental problem of the Eurocene, in other words, is the martial form of life that sustains it.

The Christian sensibility that pits life against death in a permanent state of enmity and battle sustains this martial form of life. When Christians imagine themselves to be, like Jesus, warriors against the death that is integral to all life, this militancy of a martial form of life is amplified. The view that life and death are enemies in a great cosmic battle plants a seed of hostility at the heart of lived experience. This hostility cannot but be felt at some level in the affects, postures, and musculature of those whose own embodied lives are shaped by this form of life. One of the key issues with the political theology that pits life against death in a form of fundamental enmity is that it helps to create and recreate the conditions in which this martial form of life can be born, flourish, and give rise to progeny.

This martial form of life is not *all forms of human life* as they exist on the planet today. But it is a powerful one. Numerous critical projects have already illuminated, in many different ways, how this martial form of (human) life has aided and abetted various projects of conquest and domination. Grove's analysis places this martial form of life in a position of ascendant power, which suggestively indicates that it may be destined or doomed to overtake all other forms of life on the planet. He also recognizes that the savage ecology created by, and for, this martial form of life is creating the conditions for mass extinction events, including the possibility (though not the inevitability) of its own extinction. This martial form of life—aided by the political theology of death—is generating the conditions of man-made mass death in a time of extinctions.

MAN-MADE MASS DEATH

The realms of death described in biblical texts gesture toward ancient sensibilities. They point us toward ancient forms of experience. But these ancient affective dispositions also give shape to the phenomena that we consider, today, life and death. While we can clearly sense a resonance between these ancient sensibilities and our own, there is also a dissonance that is crucial to illuminate. One of the primary distinctions we might draw between the view of a thinker like Paul and the views that we might harbor toward death today is the fact that we are living in a time of extinctions. This can mean many different things, but one of the things that it clearly indicates is that we are living in a world conditioned and created by what Edith Wyschogrod called *man-made mass death*.

Reflecting on death in the 1980s (in the wake of Auschwitz and Hiroshima more specifically), Wyschogrod argued that the philosophical meaning of death had been radically altered in the face of "the obliteration of cultures" and "the possible extinction of human life."[33] The "mass annihilation of untold numbers of persons" that we have been witnessing since the twentieth century, she said, embeds death into life in a way that completely evades rational contemplation. There is no meaning to be made of this kind of death. And no form of understanding can make sense of it. While it was once the case, says Wyschogrod, that Western philosophers would contemplate death as a truth of subjectivity that might give meaning to their existence, death can no longer reveal such truth. Instead, we are confronted with the horror of death worlds, "mini-cosmoi made of the living dead embedded in larger societies."[34] In these death worlds, "vast numbers of persons are simply marked for annihilation as part of an impersonal process of destruction."[35] Life and death have become too closely integrated. In the increasing sense of intimacy, in their entanglement, martial forms of life that seek to master or defeat death also bring violence to life.

Wyschogrod's own analysis was, to her mind, prompted by events of the mid-twentieth century—more specifically, Auschwitz and Hiroshima. But, I would argue, the phenomenon of technologically enabled man-made mass death she refers to extends into both the past and the future of these twentieth-century events. Man-made mass death was an epiphenomenon of both settler colonialism and the Atlantic slave trade and many people are still, as Sharpe has put it, living in the afterlife of these events. And man-made mass death is another way of describing the mass extinction events that are currently playing out (and will inevitably continue to play out) across the globe. Man-made mass death has rescaled death until it has ruptured what Deborah Bird Rose has described as the "twist" that mortuary rituals developed to perform—setting up a "recursive looping between life and death." Man-made mass death, through annihilations and extinctions, produces instead what Rose called "double death."[36] This double death, write Eben Kirksey and Julieta Aranda, "reverberates through ecosystems as living creatures feed on poisoned carrion for sustenance. As the poison moves through generations and across species, life becomes non-life." Life on the planet is full of non-life, which fails to be woven back into a form of death that can reintegrate the dying and the living.[37]

FIGURE 2.2 Krista Dragomer, *Enfleshed Transits*, 2014

Man-made mass death, in other words, is a product or side effect of what Grove has called the Eurocene.[38] So it is that the war with death continues, without the promise of providing an exit from the double death of these proliferating death worlds. In these planetary conditions, surrounded by man-made mass death and the death worlds it has produced, the war with death that seeks its own evisceration seems destined to merely perform more militancy. Militant forms of life are at war with more than death—they are at war with lifedeath. While I don't know what will bring an end to this war with death—this war with lifedeath—I do think it is necessary to stage a critique of Christian repressions of death, flights from death, or biomythical theories (political theologies) that charge death itself with evil and enmity.

THE WINGLESS FLIGHT FROM DEATH

For a glimpse at the structures of repression, it is only natural to turn to psychoanalysis. Norman O. Brown argued that psychoanalysis was, itself, a biomythical theory. Brown admits that psychoanalysis (especially Freud's theory of the instincts) bears what he calls a kind of "mythic" dimension,[39] but he also argues that the Freudian instincts are informed by biology. Fundamentally, the psychoanalytic instincts are oriented around Freud's observations on the biological processes of living and dying, of life and death.[40] The instincts are, in this sense, a kind of biomythical theory.

Brown argues that Freud's claim in *Beyond the Pleasure Principle*—that all living entities seek to return to the inorganic state—is simply a claim that "death is an intrinsic part of life." It is an argument that death is not an "external accident."[41] In this sense, then, there is no materially fixed or irreducible conflict between life and death. Rather, the conflict arises as a dimension of culture. It is at the level of human culture and through the construction of history, Brown argued, that life and death are poised as "conflicting opposites." It is through cultural discourses that the relation between life and death takes on a more mythical cast, infusing life and death with broadly sweeping biomythical narratives. So it is in this way, through grand biomythical narratives, that death assumes an accidental or unnatural character or is presented as less inevitable (at least for some). And yet, Brown argues, what these stories also do is facilitate a repression. In their flight from death, certain biomythical narratives function to repress the fact of death.

Repression, argued Brown, is most fundamentally a repression of the body. So it is that, when the fact of death is repressed, it is also a repression of the body. It plays out within the body and has consequences for embodied realities. It is a repression that, impacts the *life* of the body. To repress the fact of death also involves, then, a repression of life. "If death is a part of life," Brown argues, "if there is a death instinct as well as a life (or sexual) instinct," then a repression of one dimension of this instinct is met by a repression of embodied complexes of instinct. The human in Brown's view is in flight from sexuality, eros, or pleasure at the same time as he flees death.[42] It is not the case, in other words, that in fleeing death (or Thanatos) one runs into the arms of life and pleasure (Eros). Instead, the flight from death (which creates an irresolvable biomythical conflict between life and death) is a flight from the complex interactions between Eros and Thanatos in lifedeath. The flight from death is a repression of the fact of death, so a repression of lifedeath, which is also a repression of the body (and its life).

The function of repression, Brown argues, is not simply to deny or negate. And while it may be the case that repressions, such as the repression of death, are simply repeated (neurotically) over and over again, culture also makes productive use of these repressions and their resulting neuroses. In this sense, repression serves as a transformation or a production. Repression, he argues, "turns the timeless instinctual compulsion to repeat into the forward-moving dialectic of neurosis which is history."[43] Repression produces the biomythical narrative that we call history. Brown sees, in the distinction (endlessly revisited in Western thought) between what is considered human and what is considered animal, a permanent state of flight— a flight from death, as well as a flight from sexuality. And this flight from instinct (from death, from sexuality) becomes the foundation of history. "Man aggressively builds immortal cultures and makes history in order to fight death," as Brown puts it.[44] The erection of culture out of this flight from death is what

FIGURE 2.3 Krista Dragomer, *Reciprocal Community*, 2015

he calls an "extroversion" of the death instinct. This "extroverted" form of death—the death instinct pushed outward, directed outwardly—functions as aggression. In the flight from death, as death becomes the greatest enemy, aggression is aroused and accordant forms of desire are born. This extroversion of the death instinct is "the drive to master nature" and also "the drive to master man." In essence, it is the fact of death, repressed and "transformed into the desire to kill, destroy, or dominate."[45]

In keeping with numerous intellectual predecessors, Brown believed that psychoanalysis, like other intellectual byproducts of American and European culture, was articulating universal truths about human nature. For him, the flight from death was a universal symptom of civilization as such. He understood his own diagnosis of culture to be shared by much, if not all, of humankind. But formulations of the relationship between life and death are resistant to this kind of simplification or reductionism. The irreducible enmity between life and death is not a pure cultural universal, nor are there any enduring patterns in lifedeath that repeat themselves identically in all contexts. Instead, I read Brown's diagnosis as a critique of the cultural context in which he lived and thought—a cultural context that I, at a slightly different point in its history (writing six decades after he first published these thoughts), now share. I think he provides a critical take on especially American reenactments of Western legacies of thought.

Over the course of many centuries, philosophical dispositions inherited from Europe, and informed by Western Christianity, have generated particular conceptual formulas for the naming or recognition of a human. A distinct form of the human—a distinct form of life, a martial form of life—has taken shape over and against the amorphous, shifting, fluid, and highly abstract figure of the animal. While the human was understood to be connected to the animal, often in problematic or degenerative ways, the formation of the human as such was understood to be that key or crucial moment of departure—his[46] flight from animality. The beginning of the human was that moment when the creature who is human makes the critical cut or distinction that severs him from the animal. Rather than a creation *ex nihilio* this is something more like a creation *ex animalis*.

There has never been universal agreement on where, exactly, this cut is or should be made. Is it the development of language? Is it a certain dimension of cognition? Is it a form of conscious awareness? Brown himself notes that the distinction is often drawn near death. That is to say, there is a conceptual tendency to distinguish between what is human and what is animal by making the argument that the human differs from the animal because it is conscious, or aware, of the fact of death. The beginning of the human is the awareness of animal mortality—the realization that the animal dies. This recognition becomes the dream that, perhaps, the human does not have to. Brown, arguing for the insufficiency of this formula, charges that the human differs from the animal in its (wingless) flight from death. In other words, what is significant is not the *awareness* of animal mortality but the belief that this mortality might be escapable. That, in becoming human, one might shake off that mortality like an old coat and fly away. Because of this flight, Brown argues, the human is distinguished through a particular form of sickness or neurosis—the human is the animal who represses the fact of death, its own body, its nature. To be human is to be sick in a particular kind of way.

Brown, I think, was making a diagnosis of this conceptual figuration of the human when its symptoms would have been considered a bit more subclinical than they are today. He was intuiting what has become increasingly clear to inheritors of the legacy this human left behind. Brown's argument is not that the human is a grand achievement but that to be human is to suffer from a particular form of illness. He recognized that this particular form of life was aggressive, alienated, problematic. He also understood this human to be universal—present in any dimension of culture that would call itself "civilized." He did not recognize it as a particular form of life: a martial form of life. But it is often difficult to understand how much our own vision is crafted by the water we drink. Brown was describing the human as he knew it—as he had come to live and understand it. Today it has become clear that this allegedly universal formation of the human (inherited from European thought, performed, dissected, and examined in the academic and cultured recesses of the United States of America) was designed, specifically, to exclude forms of the human that did not fit within its contours. It was, in its incipient dimensions, normatively male. More than that, it was white (or perhaps more to the point, anti-Black). And the figure of the animal on which this particular form of the human so critically depends enacts and facilitates a reductionist erasure of animate lives; it is a subjective erasure or systemic collapse of biodiverse forms and figurations. It is, we might say, a martial form of life that has flowered in the Eurocene.

The formation of the human that Brown was diagnosing and critiquing—in his time—was beginning to show its cracks. It had become subject to too much wear and tear. Today, it is more clearly imploding. This imploding figure is approached, reflected on, and picked apart from any number of critical angles today: the posthumanities, animal studies and the environmental humanities, Black studies, African diaspora studies, decolonial thought, feminist theory, and queer theory (to name but a few). Here, I am interested in this figuration of the human primarily for how it models a particular relational configuration between life and death. To follow Brown and others, this figuration of the human takes shape against the generic, abstract, figure of the animal. If the animal comes to represent, for this human, the world of nature, then part of what the animal succumbs to is the pattern of death that works within and upon nature. To take flight away from animality, for this form of the human, is also a flight away from death. It is to live—to try to live—above death. Death becomes the enemy to flee because death knows that this human has no wings and cannot fly far. Death threatens, always, to pull the human back into the confines of his own two-legged animality. One of the implications of the implosion of this figuration of the human (and the lifeworlds it has created, to nurture and sustain its progeny) is that it is now being faced with the death it was designed to repress—the possibility of its own extinction.

In the end, Brown believed that it was possible to redeem this form of the human, and the purpose of his diagnosis was to understand the cure. He believed that there was a kind of redemption in the return to animality, which was, of course, also a return to nature—what Spinoza called God-or-nature. What Brown called the "abolition of repression"[47] would also mark a return to what he called the "polymorphous perversity" of childhood—an experience of the erotic potentialities of the body that refuse to be restricted to the genital organs.[48] He argued that this polymorphous perversity was, in essence, identical to what Spinoza called the intellectual love of God,[49] which is also the love of Nature. It was with all of this in mind that Brown made the argument that psychoanalysis is fundamentally a part of what Alfred North Whitehead called the Romantic Reaction.[50] It harbored a redemptive potency in the return to nature and animality. I am not interested, in this particular project, in either cultivating or stifling romance. Ultimately, I do not entirely trust myself to traffic in redemption narratives. Perhaps I am too skeptical of them and yet also too curious about the possibilities they might harbor. But what I have observed, from my own critical context, is that the figure of the human I have been speaking of is imploding in ways that may ultimately render it beyond redemption.

I am not speaking here of the extinction of human life on earth, although I realize that this is one of the possibilities that circulates in the many discourses on extinction that cloud us, today. We live in a time of extinctions. Mass extinction events in the more than human world underscore the multiple nature of the figure of extinction, and extinction events in their full plurality cloud and haunt our conversations about living and dying. The fact of extinction has become as inescapable as the fact of death, and it renders the fact of death a collective (rather than simply an individual) reality. In this conceptual climate there is not just one form of extinction that seems to threaten but many. I am speaking here about a specific, contingent, and particular formation or figuration of the human that has presented itself as universal. It is becoming increasingly clear just how contingent this martial form of life is. It is becoming increasingly clear just how racialized this form of life is, and just how much the line between this form of the human (on the one hand) and the animal (on the other) serves as another racialized distinction to secure Western superiority, to rearticulate whiteness. And it is becoming increasingly clear just how much the weapons, tools, and technologies developed by those who lived fully into this form of the human harbor the potential to decimate planetary life as such. It is becoming increasingly clear that the hunger for capital appropriation that pulses in the belly of this form of the human is driving species extinctions in more than human lifeworlds. And it is becoming increasingly clear just how intimately our own fate (as humans) is bound to and dependent upon the fates of these earth others. This particular form of the human is hovering in a kind of indeterminate zone, and it is not yet clear whether it will burn to the ground only to rise up from its ashes into a richer militancy or whether it will—instead—find itself in bed with its own mortality. Will this form of the human, this particular human story, continue to repress the fact of death more militantly than ever before? Or will it allow us to sit with it, as it takes its final breaths—to do a kind of palliative care?

What I find most useful, or relevant, in Brown's idiosyncratic psychoanalytic theory is not his promise of redemption. Rather, I find his illumination of the flight from death as a problem of repression to be clarifying. Death, or lifedeath, is never uniform or singular (even if we name these complex processes as if they were one phenomenon). There are more than a billion avenues that lead into, and out of, death. Forms of death and decay play out on the surfaces and interstices of our own bodies every day. Without the death and decay that add nutrients to the soil in which plant life grows, we would starve. Without the death of viruses that have the potential to decimate the functions of a human body, our own human lives would be terminated. We literally depend on death in order to stay alive. And yet, of course, this does not mean that we are not also in a constant struggle against its inevitability; to shelter forms of life against death is the heart of tenderness. To be in both a relation of dependence and struggle with death sounds like a contradiction or a paradox only because of the fact that Western thought has sought to configure a crude, rudimentary, and singular form of death to occupy our imaginative and symbolic attention. What the flight from death represses is the radical complexity of living bodies and systems. What the flight from death produces is a figure of death that inspires terror and becomes associated with dimensions of the negative in Western moral and philosophical thought, such as sin, evil, and privation. This flight from death, this repression that Brown describes, may be—more than anything—a diagnostic of the mid-twentieth century American culture that surrounded him. This culture was informed deeply (as it continues to be) by a particular European intellectual history and, so, a particular form of Christianity. This form of life who is at war with death is symptomatic of the Eurocene. This flight from, or repression of, death configures death as a site of enmity—life's greatest enemy. In effect, the flight from death models a subjective posture that obscures complex functional relations in lifedeath and amplifies affective dimensions of enmity that arise in the repression of the singular, reductive, figure of death.

This is worth remembering when we think, for instance, about discourses of death as they relate to what Achille Mbembe calls necropolitics. The nature of necropolitical power is, says Mbembe, "a sort of inversion between life and death, as if life were merely death's medium."[51] In essence, then, the central function of necropolitics is "subjugating life to the power of death."[52] Necropolitics turns life into death's tool. Racism drives the necropolitical order, argues Mbembe, "insofar as [racism] stands for organized destruction, for a sacrificial economy, the functioning of which requires, on the one hand, a generalized cheapening of the price of life and, on the other, a habituation to loss."[53] Racism, then, motivates the subjugation of life to the power of death. And this subjugation, this necropolitical order, is rapidly spreading across the globe, he argues. "Almost everywhere the law of blood, the law of the talion, and the duty to one's race—the two supplements of atavistic nationalism—are resurfacing."[54] In this way, "nearly everywhere the political order is reconstituting itself as a form of organization for death."[55] Mbembe also notes that this spreading necropolitical order can be thought of as a "planetary scale renewal of the relation of enmity and its multiple configurations."[56]

Mbembe's critical target, here, is the necropolitical order itself. He is not making metaphysical pronouncements or speculations.

And, yet, in this critique of the subjection of life to the powers of death it would be easy to argue that for him, death itself is the problem. What political response is called for, in the face of the militarization or weaponization of death? One might argue that the only proper response is to become a warrior for life, in this great battle. Lift up the powers of life. Let life fight for its rightful dominance over death. Mbembe, however, is not simply reiterating the argument that death itself is the true enemy. Rather, his analysis reveals the ways in which the weaponization of life—in order to deal death—is also a "renewal of the relation of enmity."[57] In this renewal of enmity, brought about by the amplification of enmity between life and death, I hear echoes of Brown's claim that the result of the repression of death, the war with death, the flight from death, is an extroversion of the death instinct that flowers into aggression. Necropolitics, we might say, is linked to the power of aggression and dominance that occupies the enmity-riddled gulf between life and death. Necropolitics capitalizes on this enmity to weaponize the force of death on behalf of particular forms of life.

Those of us who have been taught to speak (and, so, think) about lifedeath according to this pattern of relation need another language, another way of speaking about and making sense of lifedeath. Rather than a radical bifurcation of life and death that posits enmity in the spaces between, I argue for a language that can both critically illuminate the necropolitical weaponization of death and accept the fact that death is a process at work in our bodies and the soils that we depend upon. Our relationship to the phenomena called death is both dependent and antagonistic. What is often named, with a single stroke, as death presents something to resist and struggle against and also a set of processes that nourish the planet in ways that allow earthlings to thrive. The discourse of enmity between life and death fails to provide that sort of language or conditions for thought. It is for this reason that, I explore what it might look like to try to shake loose from this form of understanding death, which also calls for a critique of the form of life that drives and amplifies this war with death. Before we explore these alternative dimensions, however, we will need to interrogate—even more deeply—the form of life created and sustained by the political theology of death.

FIGURE 3.1 Krista Dragomer, *Synodic Portal 5*, 2020

3

THE HUMAN-ABOVE-DEATH

Death occupies a place at the heart of Christian interiority. Christian affects and sensibilities have long been forged in conversation with death. How could it have been otherwise, with the figure of a crucified god as a central icon for worship? For this reason, Christianity has often been described as a morbid, death-obsessed tradition. Few have argued this so vociferously as Friedrich Nietzsche, who declared that Christianity tilled the soil for a social life that was "thoroughly morbid." No one, he wrote, "gets 'converted' to Christianity." Instead, he argued, "you have to be sick enough for it." Christianity, for him, was a force against life or a practice of anti-vitalism that was based on "the instinct *against* the healthy, *against* health."[1] Christianity was oriented toward death. We see this anti-vitalism most clearly in figurations of the emaciated corpse of Jesus, slumped and lifeless on the cross. This figure is, of course, an icon for contemplation and worship. But what Nietzsche conveniently failed to observe is the fact that historically, in Christian theology, the cross itself is a site of transformation. On the cross death becomes life. As the God who died lives again, life and death are woven back together.

We might even argue that the cross—made of wood—is an organic icon that figures the divine powers of decay. The cross is a site where lifedeath plays out, where God elegantly weaves life and death back together again after a tragic rupture. But Christianity is complex and lacks uniformity. There is no singular Christian way to make sense of lifedeath. Indeed, Christian theologians have often disagreed over how to articulate the lifedeath relation, especially when it comes to the death and resurrection of Jesus. While it may be the case that some theological thinkers, such as Francis of Assisi, have understood death and decay to play a crucial role in the fabric of divine creation, others have sought to write death out of the story of God. In this narrative, the Christian is not (as Nietzsche argued) a lover of death. To be Christian is to be on the side of life—against death. Death, in this story, can be taken up, digested, metabolized, and eliminated by life. This metabolization functions as a form of dissolution that also works as a kind of destruction. This destruction is divine resurrection. In this form of resurrection, the divine performs an act of transcendence above and beyond death. In resurrection, death is effectively laid low as life lives on, eternally. Christ on the cross might call death to mind. But the cross itself becomes a paradoxical and mysterious reminder of the ultimate triumph of life over death.

The political theology of death, fueled by the idea that life and death are enemies, feeds on the triumph of the resurrection. That is to say, the political theology of death is fueled and amplified by a reading of divine resurrection as a power of life that metabolizes and eliminates death. I am not suggesting that the concept of resurrection, in itself, can simply be *reduced* to a life-triumphant supersession of death and mortality. But I do suggest that theologies of the cross, visions of resurrection, and the christologies they feed are especially susceptible to amplifying destructive tendencies that have long fed political theological enmities toward death. In this chapter I reflect on a subjectivity generated by the triumph of life over death, or the subordination of death to life. I argue that long-dominant Christian sensibilities have fed the enmities that structure a political theology of death and these theological and political theological sensibilities have generated and amplified a particular form of subjectivity: what I call, here, the human-above-death.

I seek to describe this human-above-death as what Sylvia Wynter calls a "genre of the human." I call attention to this particular genre of the human in order to critique it. The intent behind my critique is not to demand an embrace of pure finitude, without reservation. As I have already argued, what I think of as death positivity does not call for an embrace of pure finitude without reserve, one that surrenders any sense of antagonism toward death. Rather, I want to offer a critical perspective on how the transcendence of the human-above-death is founded and predicated on a fundamental subordination. The transcendence of the human-above-death relies not only on the subordination of death itself but also upon the perceived subordination of others to death. The power of death is made real when others are subjected to it. The human-above-death seeks to rise above death by both subjecting it to life and subjecting other forms of life (including other forms of human life) to apparent certain death. The transcendence of the human-above-death seeks to turn death into a kind of magnet that attracts dimensions of the negative (i.e., sin, disbelief), drawing them away from the positive force of life. The transcendence of the human-above-death depends upon the certain death of others. This death is attributed to factors such as their intractable sinfulness or their disbelief. The human-above-death gains freedom from death because others are thought to be enslaved to it. Their enslavement illuminates his freedom.

In this sense we might say that the human-above-death turns death itself (drawing on Achille Mbembe's necropolitics) into a kind of necrotheological tool. Those "in Christ" can use the tool to distinguish themselves from non-Christians, and against it they can develop a subjective model for being human that exceeds the condition of mere mortality. The figure who seeks to hold death as a tool or a weapon seems to imagine that this gives him the control he needs to become somehow exempt from the finitude that death facilitates. This figure of the human seeks to leave death to others—those who are thought to be less human, further from the divine, and *more creaturely*.

This subjectivity of the human-above-death is not static. I argue, in this chapter, that a key development in the formation of this subjectivity was the Christology eventually formalized after the Council at Nicaea (325 CE). But I also concede that the aspirational image of the human-above-death changes over time and is transformed; it undergoes mutations. Nor is it the only way in which Christian theology has figured death or made sense of lifedeath relations. Nevertheless, I suggest that we can hear the enduring pulse of this human-above-death across time. It is beginning to seem, however, as if his breath is becoming raspy and his grip on life is loosening. Perhaps it is time to do palliative care for this ancient and idealized genre of the human. Perhaps it is time for its otherwise future descendents to think with, learn from, and help to cultivate the other modes, genres, or practices of humanness that the human-above-death sought to render less visible or to actively subordinate. What other dimensions of human lives become more visible and vital when those of us who have inherited dimensions of this subjectivity understand lifedeath as something other than a condition of pure enmity? What other modes of human living become more visible and vital when we read lifedeath as, perhaps, something more like a form of sisterhood?

ILLUMINATION AND DECAY

Christian texts and iconographies code many relations to death into Christian subjectivity. At times, death illuminates the work of God. At other times, God appears to consume and eliminate death. At still other times, it seems as if both things occur. Take, for instance, the hagiography of the fourth-century desert mother Amma Syncletica of Alexandria. In the story of her life, death takes center stage. It occupies her, quite literally. She becomes a living-dead icon. Syncletica had been, it was said, a beautiful woman with a full crown of *cosmos*, or hair, marking her with a kind of worldly glory. But in taking up the monastic path, her hair was one of the first things to go. It was not that Syncletica sought to make herself undesirable. Rather, her body just seemed preternaturally primed to reject the things that made it vital and lovely to the world.[2] As her late ancient hagiographer Pseudo-Athanasius describes, Syncletica had no need to undertake typical monastic austerities such as fasting. Although she reportedly had the appetite of any other grown woman, her body became miraculously emaciated anyhow—as if her spiritual distaste for corporeal sustenance discouraged her body from taking in nourishment as food passed through her.[3]

The self-denial and austerity of asceticism came easily to her. Because of this, the devil was said to be deeply drawn to her. Syncletica was a woman who denied her own worldly riches and the powers of her sexuality—her sensual body of beauty. Humility is apparently one virtue that the devil cannot imitate, which makes it an especially delicious lure for the forces of evil.[4] As Pseudo-Athanasius tells it, Syncletica was afflicted with a number of maladies, including a terrible toothache. When her tooth finally fell out, it left a hole in her gums that caused her jawbone to rot and putrefy. The decay spread through the rest of her bones and, in less than two months, she had become worm-eaten. As a host to these more than human creatures, Syncletica apparently stank so much that her aroma was "inhuman."[5] But there is something in this inhumanity that lifts her up, ennobles her, or renders her a figure of wonder. Even (or especially) in her living-dead condition, she generates the praise of her hagiographer and that of centuries of mystified readers. In her body, Syncletica illuminates lifedeath. In her saintly body, she illuminates the proximities, the strange rhythms and sisterly tensions of lifedeath. In a sense, we might say, she actively weaves life and death together.

This is not, however, the end of Syncletica's story. Pseudo-Athanasius's hagiography goes on to inform the reader that the closer Syncletica was to death—the more visible death became in and on her body—the more she was lifted above it. As the cloak of her mortal body fell away, the power of her spirit was illuminated—exposing her mortal frame as a weak artifice, illuminating the power of the spirit that stirred within her. Syncletica was sustained, in her time of suffering, by visions of angels, holy virgins, and ineffable forms of light. Fed by these visions, she became such a vision herself.[6] It is here, in this transfiguration, that she defeats the devil and his mortalizing powers. In dying while still alive, Syncletica is transfigured in order to indicate that our mortal body is but a farce—merely a rusting channel, or a portal to something much greater, something more pure and divine. In the ancient text that narrates her life, her rotting and gruesome animal body (invaded by other animals) becomes inhuman in the most disgusting and deathly way in order that it might illuminate what most clearly opposes it—the pure, bright, divine powers of an eternal form of life.

As a reader, I am moved by this story that does not shy away from describing a mortal body. I am moved by this in the same way that I am moved by the finger bone of a saint. I'm moved not because it belonged to a saint, but because it is a relic from an animal body that has endured across the ravages of time. I am moved by the refusal to let the powers of her animal body be extinguished—how we hold a kind of vigil for one another, across the centuries. There is bravery and courage woven into the vulnerable mortality of this text. And yet I also see, in Syncletica's hagiography, a reemergence of enmity toward death. Her story is also about the triumph of life over death—a triumph that becomes visible when mortality and the processes of decay become more visible. When we fully see and embrace mortality, perhaps, we are in a position to love the enemy into total dissolution. Syncletica's body becomes a frame for the triumph that Paul proclaimed, in his pronouncement to the church in Corinth. Syncletica is steeped in death so that we can witness her transcending it, so we can be assured that God will always do away with death. In this sense, her story might also be read as a performative rupture in lifedeath—one that subjects the powers of death to the superior powers of life. It is a story of the human-above-death.

THE HUMAN WHO WOULD NOT THINK HIS FINITUDE

The subjective figure of the human-above-death is, I am suggesting, something like what Wynter calls a "genre" of the human. I am using her term a bit anachronistically, perhaps. Wynter's description of the genres of the human actually emerges from her interrogation of the modern Western figure of the human, which she refers to as Universal Man. Her critique of Universal Man addresses the genealogy of two figures, which she calls Man1 and Man2. As modern figures, both are postbiblical. They are understood to be secular in that they are not subject to the absolute authority of an extra human divine or to forms of theological knowledge. These differentiated figures of Man pull authority from science and economics rather than religion. In this sense, the universalizing figure of modern Man is formed through a rejection or extrication of theology rather than a deep continuity with it. But both of these figures nevertheless work to subject humanity to a universalist model that is haunted by rejections of human difference that pull from more ancient antagonisms.

Deeper in the genealogies of Man are the contours of other genres of the human. Tiffany Lethabo King suggests that Wynter's "surgical" analysis of the "schematic of humanism" can also help to expose the "epistemic ruptures" within humanism itself, as well as those places where secular humanism overlaps with or becomes a transmutation of Christian humanism. King describes, for instance, a form of "conquistador humanism" exhibited in figures such as Columbus, which transformed Christian rejections of the "heathen (evil, unbaptized)" into the rejection of "secular forms of human otherness" including lack (what theologians called privation) and "symbolic death." This conquistador humanism transformed the demonization of "heathens" into a social ranking system that sought to place Black and Indigenous people at its "bottom rungs."[7] What remains true for both ancient Christians and conquistador humanists is that these rejected human others are understood to be chained to death—they are the ones who are bound for death.

Wynter resists the reduction of humanness to any singular genre, such as *Homo sapiens, homo politicus,* or *homo economicus.* Even in her critique of Universal Man, she exposes more than one genealogy that has shaped this figure's narrative. So Wynter offers a critical perspective not only on the universal narrative of the human but of a set of other genres that have essentially colluded or congealed in order to serve as an "overrepresentation of the being of being human itself." Instead, she describes the many "genres of being human."[8] Universal Man in various incarnations (even in the biologized figure of *Homo sapiens*) is what Wynter calls a genre-specific creation of Western modernity. There is not one singular or absolute ontology that all human lives must subject themselves to or model themselves after. She argues that the "praxis of humanness" (a verb and also a performance that can be contrasted with the rigid ontology of *human being*) is autopoietic, or self-organizing. The praxis of humanness is "storytellingly chartered, symbolically encoded" and "thereby self-organizing."[9] As a self-organized phenomenon, this narrative mode is not universal but, instead, determined by multitudes of entities and collectives living out myriad narratives.

As Wynter's work stresses, the universalist narratives of human living are not the script according to which the majority of humans on earth perform, practice, and actualize their humanness. She argues that, against this supposed universalism of Man, we need another "origin narrative possibility."[10] Wynter offers, in essence, a parochialization of the Western figure of the human that exposes the colonial and racializing dimensions that support its universalizing aims. In unsettling and reflecting critically on the human-above-death who is animated by the political theology of death, I aim to support this emergence of different scripts. I believe that this human-above-death serves as a kind of ancestor of Universal Man, feeding both enmities and perceived capacities into this modern subjectivity. I believe it is useful to think about the story of the human that emerges, especially in the wake of the Nicene Creed, as a specific and parochial genre of the human that is later revised and adapted in other "storytellingly chartered" descriptions of being human. These later adaptations will feed into and influence the modern Western forms that Wynter critiques.

My primary critique of the human-above-death will be directed at the enmity that develops between life and death in the figure itself. But I also argue that the human-above-death feeds into the racializing, colonizing, and misogynistic dimensions of Universal Man. We see this most acutely, perhaps, in the way that the human-above-death seeks to make use of death as a kind of necrotheological tool, illuminating the necropolitical dimensions of this subjectivity. Mbembe has described political life, as it has been constructed, developed, and maintained in the West, as necropolitical. Western politics performs "a sort of inversion between life and death, as if life were merely death's medium." Racism, as I have noted, drives this version of the political in that racism serves as a form of "organized destruction," a "sacrificial economy" that demands both "a general cheapening of the price of life" and also "a habituation to loss."[11] Necropolitics, in the modern West, asserts and deploys the powers of death as if they were sovereign. And the powers of death function in the service of the organized destruction that is racism. Yet, ironically, Mbembe also notes that the Western subject has not been so death-oriented as to contemplate or reckon with its own finitude. Western thought, perhaps, has left death for the (racial, colonial) others. "It can be argued," Mbembe writes, "that the West has never properly thought through its own finitude."[12] Instead, it has been fixated on its own sovereignty. This quest for sovereignty is also a quest to exert "control over mortality,"[13] not a quest to cope with it or work through the facts of its pain. This inability to cope with mortality, the fantasy of remaining in control of it, or master over it, is arguably illuminated in the racializing dimensions of Western subjectivity.

It is with all of this in mind that I am interested in parochializing the human-above-death, in order to think about its complicity in Christianity's racializing, colonizing impulses. As the human-above-death asserts its alliance with life, and seeks to mortalize the other, it performs a necropolitical function. The human-above-death misrecognizes and dissociates from death (including the death embedded within itself), instead seeking to make use of death as a political tool to wield against others. Emerging from the soil seeded by an ancient Christian theological doctrine is a shifting subjectivity that maintains, at its heart, a deep sense of enmity for death and those who are left to die. The human-above-death lives into the hope of extricating death from his own personal humanity. The Western figure of the human that Mbembe critiques has flickers and traces of this political theological enmity seeded within it. It is no wonder, then, that the West has not considered its own finitude. It has considered the finitude of others. It has considered finitude as a property of others. Indeed, the structure of necropolitics is to subject life to the powers of death. It is a wielding of lifedeath that aims to use death as a political tool to render the other even more finite, to mortalize. Necropolitics offers us a glimpse of lifedeath—partially, at least. But necropolitics, I argue, is itself aided by a political theology of death that understands death as a site or condition of enmity. What I offer, here, is an attempt to reflect on this conundrum of a necropolitical culture that configures itself through lifedeath yet nevertheless obscures the sisterhood dynamics of lifedeath with a myth of enmity. In essence, the necropolitical utilizes death as political tool and in so doing, it fails to cope with what James

Baldwin called "the fact of death." In necropolitics the mutually supportive dimensions of lifedeath are severed, while the antagonisms within lifedeath are amplified.

Who is the human-above-death? And from where does this figure emerge? I argue that the human-above-death takes on a clear shape when theological anthropology configures a mode of being human that is said to be divine, *without being creaturely*. Excised from this figure of the divine human, the creaturely becomes pure mortality while the human becomes something else. Those humans who refuse to live into (or are rejected by) the human-above-death are ascribed with this more creaturely, death-bound subjectivity. They are said to be bound to the more than human world, whose divinity (and bonds with the divine) are muted and suffocated, while the human's own nascent divinity is—increasingly—amplified. For the human-above-death, who aspires to a story of being human that is itself modeled after a post-Nicene Christology, finitude is very real and very true. But the human-above-death aims to become exempt from it. In this exemption, he seeks to make use of death. For those with fierce faith, who exert great effort to be or become Christian and sever themselves violently from those who are not, death is for the sinners or the disbelievers—those who have not taken the figure of Christ into themselves, letting this purify and vitiate them like an antiseptic that bubbles up in a wound. The human-above-death seeks to use death like a secret or precious tool to facilitate his own ascension above creaturely mortality.

GOD AND DEATH

Death divides the living and the dead, performing what is effectively a social reorganization; the dead become the ancestors, or

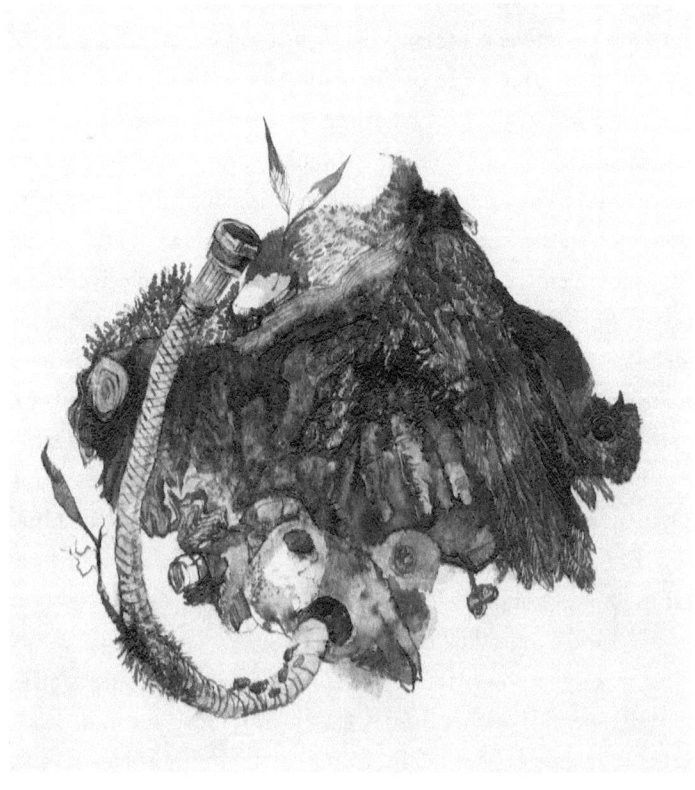

FIGURE 3.2 Krista Dragomer, *Pure Soil*, 2020

ghosts, of the living. One of the most powerful ways to reorganize relations among the living is to change how they relate to their dead: to reshape their ancestral lineages, to change who they turn to when they seek strength (and how), and to reshape their sense of community and their social ecology. Altering relations between the living and the dead shifts the center of gravity; it reshapes the mythological dynamics of a people. Theology itself, and political theology, is altered by (and reveals the marks of) these shifts in sociality and the subsequent mythologies that emerge.

Rosemary Radford Reuther has argued that the theological enmity between life and death is a natural consequence of monotheism. The origin of the lifedeath enmity, in other words, can be found in the advent of monotheism. In Ruether's reading the divine life of God (the singular form, the proper noun) is constituted by an uncomfortable relationship with the immanent powers of sex and death. The reform movements of the ninth to seventh centuries BCE demanded more exclusive forms of worship, Ruether notes, and as petitions to other divinities were increasingly prohibited, this ancient deity was challenged to usurp the functions not only of the ancient gods of war, storm, and battle (often gendered male) but functions such as fertility and reproduction (often the responsibility of goddesses). This singular monotheistic deity, increasingly, has to do it all himself. But Ruether argues that sex and death seem to somehow escape his oversight or control. When it comes to the creation of life, God's reproduction is asexual. When it comes to battle, God cedes the power to kill to representatives (humans or natural disasters). Ruether argues that in this way, "sex and death become realms of the unholy, from which God is separated and from which those who worship him must separate themselves."[14] This monotheistic divine, in other words, abjects sex and death. So sex and death become unholy enemies to the traditions that follow in his wake. God, in monotheistic form, creates the enmity in lifedeath.

What Ruether seeks to do, it seems to me, is to explain God's enmity toward death as a consequence of the symbolism and metaphysics of God. Because God rejects death, traditions emerging in the wake of this divinity reject death in kind. What an analysis like this does not illuminate, however, is the way that the enmity in lifedeath (an enmity in which God is implicated) is itself a consequence of political tensions between human communities and a consequence of human forms of self-understanding and communal, political division. Ruether thus intimates that the figure of God establishes a kind of social and political mandate when it comes to death. But I would suggest that the enmity in lifedeath emerges more concretely in the quest to shift the way that people—the social and political communities they inhabit—relate to the dead. I am not saying that the figure of God doesn't provide symbolic fuel to feed the enmities in lifedeath. But I do suggest that these enmities do not find their origin point in the metaphysical shapes of the divine. In other words, it is not the *concept* of God that marks the crucial difference but instead how particular communities weave (or do not weave) life and death back together again. God, we might say, could allow for a number of different weaving practices. But the particular weave a community creates results in political and communal distinctions.

When we examine what archaeology reveals about the burial customs of ancient Israelites, we see a different story emerge about God's relationship with death. What becomes clear is that emerging political tensions between human communities shaped the nature of the deity they worshipped. Rachel Hallote argues that in social and political tensions between the ancient southern kingdom of Judah and the northern kingdom of Israel, the matter of death (more particularly, how to bury and memorialize the dead, or how to understand the powers of the dead) became a significant political tension. The northern Israelites often faced accusations from the southern Judahites that they were "backsliding" into a form of worship that resembled their Canaanite neighbors. One key way in which Israelites approximated their neighbors was in the continuation of Canaanite rituals associated with the Cult of the Dead.[15] This cult was family oriented. Small family units preserved family tombs but also contributed to the maintenance of clan tombs. Several clans formed a tribe. So, says Hallote, the Cult of the Dead was a central method through which to uphold the structure of a tribe.[16] The goal of a United Monarchy of Israel, which would bring together both the northern and southern kingdoms, was to unite the people as a nation, "in spite of their tendency to revert to tribal divisions in hard times." This cult strengthened tribal bonds at the expense of national unity.[17] What I would underscore here is the extent to which the cult's rejection was a consequence of political divisions among communities of people who took part in the worship of a collective vision of the divine. God's relationship to death, in other words, was shaped by political tensions and not by any essential qualities of death itself. Indeed, one might argue that through burial rites such as *tahara*—ritually cleansing the dead for burial—Judaism retains a sacred space around the corpse that might still resonate in crucial ways with the Cult of the Dead.

This is not to say that rituals of the Cult of the Dead created no theological distinctions whatsoever. It is possible, for instance, that those who practiced it may have understood the dead to possess certain powers. In the Cult of the Dead, ancestors were sometimes understood to have healing powers and the ability to know the future. This may have been considered a form of idolatry by those who advocated a stricter form of monotheism. Nevertheless, some who followed the divine figure shared by the northern and southern kingdoms may have understood this divinity to coexist in some form of reciprocity with these powerful ancestors. In other words, perhaps for some this figure of the divine did not rule exhaustively over death. This was not because death was inimical to God but because this divinity was understood to cede some powers to the dead themselves. Hallote also points to archaeological evidence that the Israelites sealed their tombs with capping stones, preventing anything from entering or exiting. There is also evidence that they left food offerings for the dead. This indicates, she notes, a lack of belief in resurrection. "Had the Israelites believed that their bodies were going anywhere, they would have made provisions for them to do so."[18] This, too, could have emerged as a theological tension with others who believed that this form of the divine would ultimately resurrect the bodies of the dead. But, of course, resurrection itself would remain a theologically divisive matter among Jews for centuries.

These theological distinctions could have had an impact on emerging political theologies. Indeed, they left a mark on canonized texts (where Saul, by contacting the dead, breaks a law that he himself enacted)[19] and in the writings of the prophets (where Isaiah equates sitting in tombs with "the worst kinds of sins.")[20] But these are tensions borne through changing political circumstances and not necessarily inspired by key features of death itself. This form of the divine, singular though it may be, bears no essential or necessary relation to death and the dead. And death, while contact with it might (according to ritual law) render a person temporarily impure, does not itself bear an essentially or irredeemably unholy status. It may have been the case that the political insistence on worship of a singular national deity—against the worship of any tribally oriented figures, including ancestors—fed a kind of political tension between this divinity and death. But it would not be accurate to say that death has always been alien or unholy to this ancient deity.

When *did* death become the enemy of God? This question is difficult (if not impossible) to answer, as the formation of ancient thought patterns is nothing if not obscure to us now. There are some moments in the intellectual history of theology that serve as touchstones, offering the illumination of an intensifying enmity. I will highlight what I believe are some crucial touchstones. Nevertheless, I acknowledge that this enmity between God and death is an evolving tension that emerges over the long course of history. The touchstones I examine here are all a part of Christian theological history, which I believe intensifies the enmities between God and death and embeds them into theological anthropology. I do acknowledge, however, that while this enmity in lifedeath is embedded in powerful articulations of Christian thought, it is never the only Christian perspective. Christian theologians who embrace this enmity remain, at times, conflicted about it. For this reason, even Paul (whose clear articulation of the lifedeath enmity I often cite for the purpose of economy) may not realistically be described as the singular origin of this enmity.

The epistles of Paul do offer a clear articulation of this enmity, more specifically in his first letter to the church in Corinth. Here, Paul assures the community that God has "put all things in subjection under him" (1 Corinthians 15:27). This includes the powers of death. Death may seem powerful, but God subjects death to his own absolute authority. God has the power to defeat death and to make life reign once more, which is what makes the resurrection an important article of faith for Paul. He recognizes that this will test the credibility of these church members. Indeed, one of the motivating factors for writing this letter in the first place appears to have been the fact that some church members considered the resurrection (particularly the resurrection of their *own* bodies after death) to be an optional article of faith. Paul argues against this, and in his critique of their position, he seems to place those disbelievers in a position of enmity in relation to God. "If there is no resurrection of the dead," he chides them, "then Christ has not been raised; and if Christ has not been raised, then our proclamation has been in vain and your faith has been in vain" (1 Corinthians 15:14–15). In other words, if you don't believe God has the power to raise *your* body from the dead, then you simply don't believe in God's power over death. If you don't believe God has power over death, then how could you believe that Jesus was resurrected? If you don't believe in the resurrection, then your faith has been in vain.

Paul does give the Corinthian disbelievers some room for skepticism, however, almost as if Paul understands that such faith in one's own resurrection seems to dismiss the visible facts of reality. Nor does it resonate with other mythical tales, in the way that the resurrection of a heroic figure or spiritual teacher might. It is difficult to imagine oneself, one's own lowly and mortal self, in a grand life beyond death. Perhaps for this reason, Paul casts death as the *last* and final enemy. God has not, yet, put all of his enemies "under his feet" (1 Corinthians 15:25). He has not yet subjected all enemies to his power. But in the time to come, Paul assures the church, he will. Death will not be defeated until the very end of days. This is why death now seems to hold such sway over life in the world.

Paul uses death, nevertheless, to draw a kind of political line. He sets up a boundary between those who believe that God has the power to raise the dead and those who do not. To speak of death as the *last* enemy suggests that those who believe death is the final thing are on the side of the enemy. Those who believe death is absolute are unified with the enemy, who is death itself. Paul does not suggest that death has foot soldiers on earth that his churches must do battle with. Yet there is already the nascent possibility of reading a politicized (martial, militant) form of subjectivity in his words. The contemporary theologian R. C. Sproul, for instance, reads in this passage what he calls a "Champion Christology" that inspires Christians to become "hyper-conquerors" who live without fear because they take comfort in Christ's victory over death. These hyper-conquering Christians can act with bold confidence in life because they know that Christ's victory over death (the enemy) belongs, also, to "those who are beloved of Christ."[21] These mythopoetics can be politically mobilized, in other words. But there is, I think, a distinction between the hyper-conqueror that Sproul calls for and Paul's critique of those who reject resurrection. Paul does seem to articulate a line of distinction between those who believe God's power is supreme and those who disbelieve. But this line of distinction is not yet a matter of theological anthropology—a theologically driven story about being human.

THE HUMAN WHO WAS NOT A CREATURE

In my assessment, a crucial moment for the emergence of a theological anthropology that inhabits (via subjectivity) an enmity toward death was the formation of the Nicene Creed. The Council at Nicaea, summoned by the emperor Constantine I, emerged as a consequence of Christian theology's own evolution as an imperial power. The creed took shape at the council, in response to an imperial demand for ideological uniformity. In it, a new sense of precision and clarity in the determination of insiders and outsiders began to take shape. The Nicene Creed was the work of an empire that had recently begun to understand itself as Christian. It may have taken time for the creed to be fully affirmed. But when it was, it drew new doctrinal maps and boundaries.[22] As with so many quests to reorganize relations between the living, this creed also involved an attempt to change how the living relate to the dead, death, and mortality itself.

This creed began to take shape at the First Council of Nicaea, in 325 CE. At this council the Libyan priest, referred to as Arius of Alexandria, was condemned for his claim that Christ was the firstborn creature of the creator.[23] While it may not appear to be the case in an immediate sense, this debate—which I would argue is integrally about the relationship between mortality (death) and divinity—would come to have a significant impact on subsequent Christian understandings of the relation between life and death.

Prior to this debate, Christian consensus on the divinity of Christ had not yet emerged. There was not widespread agreement among all Christians that both "Christ the Son" and "God the Father" were names for different *persons* of one deity with a singular *nature*. This would eventually become orthodox doctrine. But this orthodoxy would not emerge until it could take shape against the negative figures of heresy. Although Arius's own writings are no longer available to us, a letter from his bishop, Alexander, reports Arius's claim that Christ was the firstborn creature of God. To say that Christ was a creature implied that Christ was a mortal, a created thing. At the First Council of Nicaea it was determined that such a position conflicted with the divinity of Jesus. As this logic went, Christ could not be both a mortal creature who perishes *and* a divine, creating, immortal god. Athanasius of Alexandria—a theologian who was integral to the doctrinal rejection of Arianism—deepened widening fractures between Jews and Christians by claiming that Arian descriptions of the mortality of Jesus were a "Jewish thing." Athanasius encouraged those who wanted to be (or become) Christian to rid and cleanse themselves of the Arian "madness" and to take comfort that "when you cease being Arian you will also cease from the folly of the Jews."[24] So the claim that Christ was a creature, the kind of mortal who could be subject to the powers of death, was condemned as an unchristian heresy.

This emerging Christian position split life from death within the figure of God. Death was extracted from divine subjectivity and placed below it, subjected to it. Life and the divine fused into a pure and seamless whole, and death became alien to them. Christ, as God, was on the side of life eternal. To think of Christ as a simple creature would be to claim that Christ was a killable mortal. And to think of Christ as a creaturely God would be to erode the sharp, binary, either-or distinction between mortals and immortals. It would suggest that death might be blended ambiguously within the divine. If Christ was to be a God who could defeat the enemy that is death, then Christ needed to have absolute power over death—the ability to subjugate it. So Christ, in this emergent frame, would have to exclude death and become sovereign over this enemy alien. In the formation of the Nicene Creed, a great gulf opens up between God and death. And what is said to exist in this gulf is enmity. Christ, in the emergence of this creed, becomes the prototype for the human-above-death.

Surely, many will now be thinking, such an analysis fails to take into account the fact that Christ was *fully human*. To say, as Christian thought affirms, that Christ is both fully human *and* fully divine would seem to suggest that Christ was indeed both mortal and immortal. To be sure, I acknowledge that the hybrid human-divine nature of Christ clearly allows for this figure of Christ the Son to be vulnerable and earthy. Indeed, this idea has held deep theological appeal (even among the most heresiophobic theologians) for centuries, for this very reason. What I am suggesting, however, is that by the logic of the Nicene Creed this vulnerability is not necessarily mortal. It is human. Christ, as it is affirmed at the First Council of Nicaea, is not a creature but is a human. It is this *humanity without creatureliness* that ensures that Christ can be the human-above-death. Christ is not fully creature and fully divine. Christ is fully human and fully divine.

The distinction is crucial. The human becomes a figure that can be considered other to, or different from, the creature.

The human can be different enough from the creature that it can be divinized within this Christian framework. Why? Because the figure of the creature is inherently and intrinsically mortal. The creature dies. While humans must die in one obvious sense, what the emergence of this human-above-death in the Nicene Creed suggests is that the figure of the human nevertheless has some alluring divine potential. The creed does not suggest that all humans are divine immortals. But it does suggest, in its reaction to Arius's theological claims, that what makes humans mortal is their creatureliness rather than their humanity. To suggest that Christ is a creature is to suggest that Christ is mortal and killable. But to suggest that Christ is human is to say something else. The human is now packaged together with divinity and is set against the creaturely. In the figure of Christ, through the human-above-death, the Nicene Creed configures a subjectivity that is human, vulnerable, earthy, and yet still above the level of mere creatureliness. Humans might be mortal, but *humanity* is not where this mortality is embedded. The death and mortality of human life come from another subjective dimension.

This opens up a new subject position for Christians—those who live to follow Christ, who seek to be like Christ. This subject position creates a fracture within the human between its own creaturely (mortal, killable) dimensions and its divine dimensions. To follow Christ was to see one's subjectivity transformed— to become more human and less creaturely. To follow Christ was to set upon the path of becoming like this human-above-death. Those who communed in the name of Christ undertook a weekly ritual in which they ate of Christ's human-divine body and drank Christ's human-divine blood (the eucharist). This ritual rendered these followers not only a community but, more, was said to give them a whole new form of collective existence "in Christ." What would it mean to exist "in Christ"? It would mean, on some level, that these followers sought to inhabit (or ingest) this divine subjectivity. In this ritual consumption, they took Christ's human-divine body into their own. This offered followers a kind of ritual enhancement. What this ritual enhancement actually means has, of course, long been up for debate. Nevertheless, for many Christians across the course of history, it has been understood to be the act of putting a little Christ inside them—an act of incarnating the divine. Like any form of eating, they digest and become what they eat. To metabolize the promise of eternal life, perhaps, is to take a supplement that acts like a laxative to eliminate mortality. To become more like Christ, then, might enable followers to inhabit a mode of being that is closer to Christ's own human-divine nature and less mortal or creaturely. To return to the metaphor of the laxative, as long as one continues to eat the fruits of this created earth, the cleanse is never permanent. But this supplement offers the hope of becoming, like Christ, a human-above-death. And it can be ingested again, on a weekly basis. This is not to say that these followers would ever be able to shake off their mortality. Unlike Christ, they would not fully shake off their creatureliness (though they might try) until the end of days, when God finally defeats death. But in the meantime what emerges for Christians in this frame appears to be a subject position that is nevertheless closer to the divine and less creaturely.

There has been, of course, endless debate among Christian theologians for centuries about the "true" meaning of the eucharistic rites. And the way that Christians describe and narrate this ritual has undergone much change over the centuries. Some of the earliest liturgical descriptions of the eucharist treat it as a simple ritual act of thanksgiving, not unlike Jewish table blessings and prayers. It was not until the third century that the theme of the eucharist as a form of divine sacrifice began to make frequent and notable appearances in prayers.[25] It is also the case that the theme of deification (the transformative process of becoming like God) was developed within Eastern Orthodox theology, marking it as distinct from Western theology in precisely this way. But, despite what has been marked in the officious annals of theological history, there remains a quite literal message in the ritual act of communion. Whatever theological niceties we might use to describe this act, they do not much change the mechanical task of eating what is said to be the body of God. Studies from historians such as Caroline Walker Bynum have illustrated the extent to which the eucharist was—especially for medieval women—a powerful form of mystical communion with God.[26] And, as Angel Méndez-Montoya has succinctly put it, the eucharist is a simple incarnation of God who becomes "food and drink in and through materiality."[27] So the ritual is a method of not only "being touched by God" but "ingesting" God.[28] In eating, as we know, we become what it is that we eat.

It should also be noted that Christian theologians have never, in a uniform or exhaustive way, completely rejected the creatureliness of Christ. Indeed, it is possible (especially prior to, and long after, the Council at Nicaea) to find what appear to be celebrations of it. In the work of Irenaeus of Lyon, who lived and wrote more than a century before the Council at Nicaea, we can see the expression of a Christology that is more creaturely. God, in becoming Christ, was effectively "recapitulating himself in the age-old shaping of the human creature," Irenaeus wrote.[29] In such a musing, Irenaeus comfortably couples humanity and creatureliness in the divine. God, in becoming Christ, becomes both a human and a creature—because humans are mortal creatures. Humanity and mortality are woven together.

In the work of Athanasius, we can see a more decisive struggle against the creatureliness embedded within humans. Athanasius acknowledges the creatureliness of humans. God created man, "as he did all the irrational creatures on the earth," he concedes. But, as he also notes, God made humans "after his own image," which means they were given a little portion of "the power of his own Word." God did this so that humans (unlike other creatures) "might be able to abide ever in blessedness, living the true life which belongs to the saints in paradise."[30] Humans are, by their nature, corruptible (mortal, killable) like all other creatures on earth, concedes Athanasius. But, as humans, they are nevertheless "destined"—by the grace of God alone—to become immortal.[31] Humans have something other than nature within them: the power of being made in God's image, being modeled after the human-above-death. Athanasius departed from Irenaeus who affirmed the creatureliness of the human. But he did echo another sentiment attributed to Irenaeus: "For he was made man that we might be made God."[32] God made himself into a human (*not* a creature) so that humans (*not* creatures) could be divinized.

The legacy of this rejection of creatureliness does inevitably cast a long shadow over Christian theology. Many theologians were tempted to acknowledge that, if Christ became human, and humans are creatures, it must also be true that Christ became a creature. Almost a thousand years after the Council at Nicaea, for instance, Thomas Aquinas admitted that saying "Christ as he is man" is effectively also saying "Christ, as man, is a creature."[33] But he definitively walks back from such an easy claim, citing the proximity of the claim to an Arian heresy. Thus, says Aquinas, any statement about the creatureliness of Christ (logical though it may be) must be said only *with qualification*. Any other human, besides Christ, is "a creature without qualification," he says. "But Christ is a subject subsisting, not only in human, but also in divine, nature; and by reason of the latter he is uncreated." So it cannot be said, for Aquinas, that "without qualification" Christ "is a creature."[34] If one must recognize, logically, that Christ as human must have been creaturely, it must also be noted that this was only a temporary assumption of such creatureliness. In a more elemental way, Christ is uncreated. But Aquinas will affirm, without qualification, that in Christ "a man is God and God is a man."[35] The centuries of emerging tension between humanity and creatureliness, in Christ, have created a clear pathway toward the divine for the form of life that is man (human). But creatureliness, even if it is conceded to be logically bound to the human, remains extricable.

This also means that a shadow subjectivity opens up as a point of contrast. To be a non-Christian (to have no Christ in you) was to be more mortal, more creaturely, and less human-divine. Creatureliness becomes a subject position for those who were—for whatever reasons—excluded from this human-divine category of existence. This was, of course, a clear exclusion of nonhuman mortal creatures. This refusal to encompass all humans within the figure of the human-above-death, and the attempt to push these other humans into a category of creaturely mortality, shared not with the fully human but with the nonhuman, would become a source of political tension, and political subjection, for centuries. This distinction between the fully human and the less human would come to include those who were not friends of God (who did not commune, with Christians, in Christ). In the late ancient world this may have meant primarily meant Jews, or gentiles who would not convert. But in time these enemies would also become the others who Christians encountered through imperialism and colonialism. These others, who were not friends but something else, would come to be described as closer to the condition of creaturely mortality—closer to the other (nonhuman) creatures, and so more intimate with the enemy that is death. That they were closer to death—the enemy—meant that they were more killable. Those who had not been ritually enhanced "in Christ" (by eating Christ's human-divine body) were said to remain further from salvation in the eternal life of God and closer to the privative state where sin and death were thought to collapse into one another. The otherness of the non-Christian is collapsed into a vacuous nondivine otherness that is death. These others might be considered human on some level. They might have degrees or drops of humanity within them. But they would not have access to the ritual transformations that would fold them more decidedly into the subjectivity—into the mode of becoming—that is the human-above-death. And it is here that we see, with more clarity, how theological anthropology illuminates the enmities in lifedeath and helps to amplify and extend it. What I am suggesting is that, in the establishment of the Nicene Creed and the rejection of Arius's theological position on Christ, the seeds were sown for the emergence of what Sylvia Wynter calls a "genre" of the human. This is the figure that I am describing as the human-above-death.

LEGACIES

A growing body of work from scholars studying religion and theology traces the shapes of ancient Christian thought in order to illuminate how modern discourses on race operate in a form of continuity with these ancient theological habits of mind. Denise Buell, for instance, acknowledges that "early Christians defined themselves in terms of being able to transcend ethnicity or race."[36] In this spirit, Christianity has long been understood as a movement that operates beyond racial distinctions. But, as Buell demonstrates, early Christians actually used "ethnic reasoning" to define what they believed was the most legitimate and "most authentic manifestation of humanity."[37] We might say that the universalizing mode of human being that early Christians developed (a subjectivity allegedly above ethnic divisions) was itself labeled a superior manifestation, or genre, of the human. Despite presenting itself against ethnic or racial divisions, Christianity has actually always been actively shaped by what we would call today a racializing logic or ethnic reasoning.

Daniel Boyarin has argued that the years between the church councils at Nicaea and Constantinople were crucial for the formation of differences that would become the partition between Judaism and Christianity.[38] So there was something important for emerging narratives about human differences that arose in response to the Nicene Creed. Nicaea founded an emerging set of boundary-drawing exercises that etched—with increasingly aggressive marks—a line between Christian and non-Christian. It is, in other words, a crucial time for the development of the subjective genre of Christian human being, which I argue tends to model itself after the subjective typology of the human-above-death. What emerges in Nicaea on the most obvious level are the outlines of a new orthodoxy: those who follow Christ must adhere to the belief that the Father and the Son are one and the same. Jesus Christ is not simply human but is also fully divine. What you believe, or profess to believe, about this matter will ultimately have an impact on your identity. If you deny it, you are not a Christian but a heretic.

Yet, of course, the power to draw the line between heresy and orthodoxy has never been a matter of individual choice. Boyarin examines the work of St. Jerome ("one of the most zealous defenders of the new orthodoxy")[39] to illuminate the exercise of church authority in this boundary-drawing exercise. More specifically, he looks to Jerome's description of a group of people who believed in the orthodox Nicene Creed yet thought of themselves as Jews (praying in synagogues, keeping the Sabbath, etc.) In order to protect the emerging notion that Christians could, through the creedal articulations of this new orthodoxy, rigorously distinguish themselves from Jews, Jerome took upon himself the liberty of negating this group's claim to either tradition. "Jerome denied them their claim of being Christian, because they claimed to be Jews," but he also "denied them their claim to be Jews, because they claimed to be Christians." Naturally, he "denied them the possibility of being both, because that was an impossibility in Jerome's worldview."[40] In this exercise Jerome (inspired by the Nicene Creed) undertakes an act of subject creation—he begins to storytellingly charter new versions of the human, using the creed itself. In this emerging story, there are Christians (who cannot be Jewish), Jews (who cannot be Christian), and a third category that is essentially neither (those who might claim to be both). Church authority, in essence, uses the creed to cut off certain possibilities for being human and to charter others.[41]

Work in theology and religious studies has come, increasingly, to see in these emerging late ancient divisions between Jews and Christians incipient dimensions of modern racial imaginations. J. Kameron Carter sees the genesis of modernity's racial imagination in "Christianity's quest to sever itself from its Jewish roots." Jews, in this exercise, become another religion and eventually another race. So Christian attempts to assert Christianity as supreme over (superseding) Judaism generate a categorical rejection that resonates with (and gives shape to) antiblackness. Carter sees, in each of these bifurcating enterprises (Jew/

Christian, white/Black) a set of defensive differentiating techniques or patterns that he names "the theological problem of whiteness."[42] These are the differentiating techniques that give shape to Christian identity as such.

Jeannine Hill Fletcher argues that the theology of Christian supremacy (sparked in the differentiating techniques emerging from the partition of Christianity and Judaism) "gave birth to the ideology of white supremacy."[43] In an examination of documents from the Catholic Church specifically, Fletcher notes that there is a common refrain in these documents that invokes "the idea of humanity's oneness" and argues that this oneness is "part of God's singular design." Yet, within the institution of the Catholic Church there is also a clear focus on "a graded diversity" of this humanity, both inside and outside of the church. "In this theological anthropology," writes Fletcher, "although God creates all humans equally, there is another force at work as the gifts of the Holy Spirit are bestowed in different ways." The gifts are bestowed, particularly, to the faithful. Among those faithful, gifts are understood to be bestowed by rank. So, "based on their cooperation with Jesus Christ, humanity is seen now to form a graded diversity." Within the Catholic Church, some representatives of the Church are understood to be closer to God. And all members of the Church itself are understood to be closer to God than "unbelievers."

Fletcher also notes that this form of Christian supremacy is not unique to the Catholic Church and is instead common to all forms of Christianity. "Some theologians argue that *all* Christians claim supremacy through the singularity of Jesus Christ and in his role as savior of humankind," she writes. When God's favor, and blessings of full humanity, are understood to reside with Christians this results in "a sliding scale of humanity, in which persons of other faiths are seen as less than their Christian counterparts." This view of humanity has been spread across the world through "the ascendancy of Christian political powers and the expansion of Christian empires." Fletcher points to the Nicene Creed as the safe harbor or grounding logic for this view of Christian supremacy. While acknowledging an almost infinite number of expressions of Christian faith, she notes that this particular creed has been given a special kind of power and to this day serves to bind Christians "across time and space" to become "as close as we might come to a universal logic shared by Christians." But there is also, says Fletcher, a clear form of exclusion written into this creed, particularly in its claim that Jesus is the "only begotten" son of God, resulting in a structure for salvation that can only be satisfied through Christianity and a hierarchy within humans, indicating who is close enough to God to be saved and who is not.[44] It is through this Christian supremacy and supersessionism, she argues, that the graded hierarchies of white supremacy are born.

What I suggest, here, is that a genre of the human—the human-above-death—emerges in the wake of the Nicene Creed: the story of a human who is a friend of life and an enemy of the dead and those who really die (death's people). This narrative contributes to a form of enmity that is exploited and amplified in the racializing discourses of modernity. Post-Nicene Christology tells a story about a particular sort of human whose enemy is death. Those who are friends of Christ are friends of life. Those who are not become more creaturely, more mortal, more like the nonhuman; they are mortalized. Death is for these others. Death can be dealt to these others with impunity—these mere creatures—because they do not inhabit the political category of friend. As friends of death, they are enemies of the Christian. They exist within a privative state of sin, and death, and can be left to steep within it. Ultimately, this difference takes root in racial imaginations and associates whiteness and Christianity with human life and blackness with creaturely death.

I am not suggesting that the Nicene Creed, and the narratives about humanity that emerge from it, are racialized in the modern sense. What I am suggesting is that they contribute to an unfolding and emerging narrative about what sort of human being a Christian is, what sort of beings the Christian community is comprised of, and how this form of the human is both patterned after the human-above-death and can be seen as superior to other forms of the human who do not follow Christ. Gil Anidjar explores how it is that the figure of blood contributes to Christian "collective self-fashioning" in the medieval time period (especially during the Inquisition) in a manner that would eventually give shape to "the collective bodies of families and classes, ultimately of nations and races."[45] Anidjar's work is a reminder that a concept with meaning for medieval people—such as blood—is not the same as what we mean today when we use the word "race." And yet, Anidjar also points to the way that blood was becoming a mark of collective identity in the Middle Ages. This collective identity—understood to be shared by Christians, and passed through the blood-sharing ritual of the eucharist—serves as a form of communal substance that will later transmit its gathering power into subsequent historical discourses of nation and race.[46] As Christian individuals come to see themselves as part of a "bloodline," says Anidjar, this is also the beginning of "race" in the sense that "race is, historically at least, insistently tied to blood."[47] I am trying to think, in a similar way, about how the narratives of the past are both translated into and yet also partially constitutive of present modes of thought.

Ultimately, as Amaryah Armstrong has put it, "Christians' imaginations of themselves as the people of God is fundamentally a racial narrative."[48] This narrative, says Armstrong, not only imagines Christians replacing or fulfilling Jewish claims to the peoplehood of God but also seeks to give Christians a redeemed status on the stage of history. In the Western Christian expansion into the New World, through settler-colonialism and slavery, the status of the redeemed white people was defined against blackness and Indigeneity, and this order became racialized. Whiteness becomes the condition of the redeemed, and blackness and Indigeneity are collapsed into sin and privation. Although the differentiations of these redemptive mechanisms may not have emerged as explicitly racialized in the modern sense, there is still a supersessionism built into the theological enterprise of redemption that binds it to the supersessionism of white supremacy today. Against claims that Christianity is "a community open to all and therefore beyond race," Terence Keel instead argues that the logic of Christian supersessionism (the understanding that Christianity supersedes Judaism and renders it irrelevant) has fed into and sustained "a long tradition of racial reasoning" in Christian political theology. It is in this tradition of racial reasoning that modern scientific ideas about race found their seed bed.[49]

For Christian theologians who pattern their thinking according to the model of this ancient theological framework, the sense of what it means to be human is thus structured by the racial reasoning that helped to give shape to the human-above-death. In this reasoning, lifedeath is underwritten by enmity. There can be love within this enmity. It is in this spirit, perhaps, that Toby Jennings calls death a "precious enemy."[50] However precious this enemy might be, the most orthodox forms of Western Christian theology also affirm the evisceration or end of this precious thing. The deity who appears, dead on the cross, is a kind of illusion. Because, as this version of Christian faith tends to affirm (against the false limit that is death), this deity is perpetually undead; this deity is a sign of life that eternally persists far above death and cannot be subjected to it. Rather, as the theologian Karl Barth put it (almost in a singsong), "there is a death which is the death of death: and this is the name of the Gospel."[51] While it might be true that all mortals must die in an immediate sense, there is ultimately (more mysteriously) "no sentence of death against those that are in Christ Jesus."[52] Rather, the real death sentence is for those who are *not* in—who are outside of—Christ Jesus. Death becomes a necrotheological tool of sorts that liberates Christians, leaving the corporal punishment to others. Christians can love death, that precious enemy, because God—through the gospel—has given them access to a form of knowledge that will liberate them, as others are subjected to their punishment. This freedom of the gospel, for Christians, is the promised condition of the human-above-death. As he rises up, above what I call the constellated negative (flickering with traces of sin, guilt, death, privation, fleshiness, blackness), the human-above-death watches the world of mere mortals recede in the rearview.

FIGURE 4.1 Krista Dragomer, *Synodic Portal 4*, 2020

4

CONSTELLATED NEGATIVES

"Death is nothing to us," wrote Epicurus, "for what has been dissolved has no sense experience, and what has no sense experience is nothing to us."[1] There is a kind of comfort in the thought that the dissolution of our embodied existence will not be torture but, instead, will be the end of sense experience—nothing at all. There is even, if we choose to read it this way, a kind of mystical comfort in the nothingness of death; in the dissolution of death I might commune with the empty nothing that I can already intimate, all around and within me. I may lose my senses, but something else—something I can sense in the emptiness of things—will be there. Such comfort may come, in part, from the fact that the nothingness of death "relieve[s] us of its threatening character," suggests Todd May.[2] Nothingness annihilates the sting of death; it promises not pain, but nothing.

While I understand that the conflation of death and nothingness can be intuitive, or even comforting, it is nevertheless the case that Western metaphysics have created a space for death in which death's affinity with nothing is part of a dream of subjection. Regarding death as a figure rife with enmity, Western metaphysics have constellated death with a series of other figures—nothingness, sin, blackness, fleshiness, the womb, animality—as the bright stars in a dark sky of negativity. This constellation draws from the negative poles of what Mary-Jane Rubenstein calls the "raced and gendered ontic distinctions" of Western metaphysics. Ontological distinctions are constantly mapped onto a God-World paradigm wherein maleness, light, good, and the human are drawn toward the divine while the female, darkness, evil, and the nonhuman are pooled into the negative nondivine.[3] In what follows I argue that the vision of death emerging from this constellated negative is rife with, and animated by, what Calvin Warren calls "ontological terror"— a metaphysical form of both fascination with, and terror of, the nothing that blackness is said to incarnate. This ontological terror is, says Warren, fundamentally an "anti-nothing" that is also a form of antiblackness.[4] This ontological terror of death is bound up with a terror of (and fascination with) nothingness, blackness, animality, and other points in this constellated negative.

Attempts to destabilize the orbit that maintains this constellated negative are—by this time—old. They are a recurring feature of Western thought in late modernity. Often such attempts exhibit a romance of negativity—gestures to illuminate the positivity of nothingness (or other points in the constellated negative) that have been obscured by ontological terror. In the work of Martin Heidegger, for instance, we witness an attempt to disrupt this constellated negative. He frames a being's orientation toward death as inevitable without being tragic. And nothingness becomes a site that generates what might be described as a form of positivity. Nevertheless, argues Warren, such attempts to find a kind of "emancipatory potential" in nothingness have failed to take blackness into account.[5] And so, even the sort of ontological disruptions that Heidegger performed remain animated by an ontological terror that seeks to subject this constellated negative to a more potent phenomenon that transcends (and triumphs over) it.

In this chapter I explore the way that theologians such as Thomas Aquinas have helped to develop and perpetuate this constellated negative. But I also explore the disruption of its orbit in the work of Heidegger. In conversation with Warren, as well as the work of Zakiyyah Iman Jackson, I seek to illuminate how the failure to consider the questions posed by blackness continues to leave the constellated negative in a fixed state and cast onto it a dream of subjection. I do not pretend to present a solution to this old metaphysical problem. And I do not offer an alternative epistemology that can somehow dissolve the lines that have, for so long, been drawn and redrawn between these points of the constellated negative. In some real and intractable ways, I am living and thinking in the world that this metaphysic built. In this sense, then, I want to acknowledge that from within such an orientation, the fear and horror that death and dying generate can easily bleed into ontological terror.

What I do consider, however, is that there are visions of, descriptions of, death that cannot be collapsed into ontological terror. To that end I explore a figure of lifedeath in the work of Toni Morrison—what she calls an "always" that is neither eternal life nor annihilation. Morrison does not frame death as either a positive or a negative, and so this "always" is ambivalent—it is neither a dimension of pure terror nor of redemption. But, ultimately, Morrison does invoke a profound disruption of the Western metaphysics that produces a constellated negative; she refuses to deprive the dead of life. This is not the creation of an afterlife, which would rescue the dead from death. Rather, it is a refusal of the bifurcations that fracture life from death. It may be the case that it is difficult, within the world that metaphysics built, to think death without descending into ontological terror. But, perhaps, to think differently about the sisterly dimensions of lifedeath is also to generate a different form of attention—one that can witness what else might emerge when the constellated negatives of Western metaphysics come to life.

FORMATIVE PRIVATIONS

If, for the ancient thinker Epicurus, death was essentially *nothing*, this seems to mark a sharp distinction from the position of Aristotle, who understood death to be a terrible thing. For Aristotle, "life is a good by nature."[6] Death, on the other hand, was "the most terrible of all things."[7] For one thinker, death marks nothing. For the other, death is the most terrible form of thingness. "Despite its comforting appeal," James Stacey Taylor has argued, "the Epicurean position has been almost universally rejected by both philosophers and lay persons alike."[8] For Taylor, then, the time has come to embrace the Epicurean nothingness of death. But is the distinction between these positions as sharp as it might appear? What *sort* of a thing was death to Aristotle? It was, he said, "a limit." What makes this *thing*, this limit, so terrifying is that for the dead, "there is nothing beyond [it], either good or bad."[9] In other words, for Aristotle death was a limit-thing that marked the transition into nothingness. Both Aristotle and Epicurus, then, understand death to be constellated or coupled with nothingness. The difference, perhaps, is that Epicurus finds nothingness comforting while for Aristotle it is a terror. I could have written a book about this distinction: the terror versus the comfort of nothing. But for the time being, I am more interested in the constellation that each of these thinkers marks between death and nothing.

This constellation of negatives remains fixed in the development of Christian thought, especially as Christian thinkers engage Greek sources. Indeed, in Christian thought more figures begin to stick to, or congeal, around this constellated negative. Given his active engagement with Aristotle, Thomas Aquinas is a useful thinker to examine. Aquinas retains the Aristotelean terribleness of death and elaborates or develops the constellated points around it. Death, for Aquinas, was not simply terrible but more specifically a form of evil. As Brian Davies has emphasized, *malum*—for Aquinas—did bear a different emphasis than the term "evil" does for us today. *Malum*, for Aquinas, was simply the undesirable. Davies argues that Aquinas's reading of the word is "more inclusive."[10] Aquinas distinguishes between *malum poenae* ("evil of penalty") and *malum culpae* ("evil of fault"), for instance. The *malum poenae* are evils woven into the fabric of creation— what theologians would later refer to as "natural evils."[11] Things like sickness, aging, and death are evil, according to Aquinas. But they are only evil insofar as they exist as the lack, privation, or deficiency of the good within creation. Privation, for Aquinas, is a state of lack to be contrasted with God and all that the figure of the creator does. If God, in creating the world, generates all that is and puts it in order, then privation is what dissolves created things and takes them apart. Privation is the undoing of creation, the lack of created order. Privation is, essentially, the privation *of* "mode, species, and order."[12] Privation is a counter-creative or decreative anti-speciation.

We could argue, then, that Aquinas might actually defuse theological tensions between God and death. If evil is simply "the privation of a particular good,"[13] then perishing and passing away are part of the order of nature.[14] It's natural for humans and animals (mortal creatures) to die. Death is neutral: it's a part of things. Aquinas does acknowledge, however, that "in accord with the Catholic faith" one must also hold "that death and all such ills of our present life are punishment for original sin."[15] And it is here that we see the tensions between God and death resume; we see the political theology of death reemerge. Death is something that separates humans from God, the sign of a fractured relation.

The good news in the wake of this looming privation (as Aquinas sees it) is that human beings have the potential to become humans-above-death. Humans, says Aquinas, "were created for everlasting happiness."[16] By their very nature, humans are supernaturally predetermined "to have been able not to die." Therefore, in an ultimate sense, death and privation are "contrary to [human] nature."[17] Humans are, in his view, naturally supernatural. So death and dissolution, while natural for all other mortals, are contrary to the natural supernature of humans. The only way that humans really die is when they surrender to sin and evil—when they allow themselves to dissolve into the dissolute nothingness of death, evil, and sin. Notably, however, those who are not understood to be human (such as animals) are ultimately destined to be set in the constellation that orbits around death and nothingness. And so, yet another point emerges in this negative constellation—animals, like sin and evil, are woven into the web that hovers just above privation.

Those who, for whatever reason, do not partake of the supernatural grace of God, made available through Christ, are also destined for nothingness. They are themselves not nothingness, but it is their destiny. These non-Christians are kin to animals, for they have deprived themselves of their supernatural nature. They are merely natural beings. As natural beings, they lack life, in an eternal sense. They are destined for death and, in that sense, are already dead: the living dead. Those who do not commune in Christ become the living dead as they await the pure privation that is their destiny.

Aquinas does suggest that privation lingers within the good things of creation. The created things that God made may harbor privation (the ability to age, the penchant to get sick, inevitable death) within them. But he also reads this perishing as part of the broader corrupt apparatus of dissolution that is evil. Life on earth is conditioned by what Aquinas describes as partial privation. This is the fallen world, after all. So the individual deaths, and the sins of individuals, throw off the general balance of God's created order. Each death is like a little rupture of nothingness in the created order—a little reminder of the nothing that could (without God) be our ultimate destiny. But in a larger schematic, these deaths are bound to what Aquinas calls the "pure privation" that looms in a more apocalyptic dimension below the fabric of our earthbound experience. This pure privation is linked to darkness, which belongs to death.[18] This darkness is not, here, explicitly named blackness. But it is easy to see how the darkness of privation will also be read as blackness, in a constellated negative.

These powerful intellectual formations leave a lasting legacy on Christian preaching and theology, and they become increasingly integrated into formulations of Christian (and non-Christian) subjectivity. The constellated negative becomes increasingly *embodied* in a kind of enemy presence. A hyperbolic, but nevertheless illustrative, point of evidence in favor of this accusation can be found centuries later in the work of the popular but controversial seventeenth-century British Baptist preacher Benjamin Keach. His writings (particularly in a book he called *Tropologia*, which was a "key" to using spiritual metaphors) draw out some of these constellations with special economy. What Keach's *Tropologia* indicates, clearly, is the extent to which other people—specified typologies of other mortal beings—are read as embodiments of the constellated negative. In this sense, the people Keach seeks to subject to the will of God are incarnations of death and nothingness—the living dead.

Keach echoes Aquinas's conflation of death and privation. "Life is opposed to death," he writes, noting that death is "either the privation of natural life" in separating the soul from the body in an ultimate manner or "the privation of spiritual and heavenly life" in separating the soul from God through sin. For Keach "unconverted men" are the living dead because, while death has not robbed them of their lives completely, nevertheless they are "spiritually Dead."[19] As living dead bodies, he suggests that they are more like objects or animals than humans. Such living dead humans, Keach argues, are "unlovely object[s] to look upon" because the lack of God's grace within them leaves them "unregenerate." The living dead, he writes, are "void of all sense" if you "cast fire in his face" or "run a sword into his heart"; the unconverted living dead human "will not complain" because he is a "senseless soul."[20]

Keach walks his readers through a long series of spiritual metaphors that draw comparisons between the living dead ("wicked" or "unconverted" people) and all manner of nonhuman figures. Keach compares the living dead to dogs (who, he suggests, are base and ignoble), bulls (who are heathenish), lions (proud), foxes (crafty), and goats (covetous and unclean). The bonds between animals and humans, here, are the bonds of sin—forms of evil that draw them toward the negative constellation of animality, evil, and death. He interrupts his stream of zoological metaphors in order to liken the living dead to criminalized categories such as thieves and nudists. He rounds out these comparisons with metaphors that liken the living dead first to rocks and then to the devil. Such an example may read as absurd. It is certainly both horrific and hyperbolic. Yet, I think it offers a perverse glimpse into the interpretations that are drawn from the constellation that maintains phenomena such as animality in an inevitable coupling with death and nothingness—a theology of privation. It is, you might say, a theology animated by the ontological terror of a nothing that is embodied by the figure of an enemy.

TERRIFIED OF NOTHING

If nothingness, privation, lack, sin, and death have been critically troubling for Western metaphysics, Calvin Warren has underscored the role that antiblackness plays in this metaphysical project. Nothing, and nothingness, "terrifies metaphysics," says Warren. And metaphysical thinkers seek to dominate this terrifying nothing "by turning nothing into an object of knowledge, something that it can dominate, analyze, calculate, and schematize."[21] This is, perhaps, exactly what we see in Aquinas's schematic coupling of sin and the nothingness of privation. To follow the plan of virtue laid out by a life in faith is to discover the key to a domination of nothingness—to living above, or transcending, death and nothingness. But a life of sin, a life outside the communion of Christ, is a descent into the terror of nothing.

Warren argues, further, that in an antiblack world blackness is inextricably a part of this metaphysical problem. Metaphysics is obsessed with both blackness and nothingness, and the two function in modernity as synonyms. In an antiblack world, "the function of black(ness) is to give form to a formless (nothing.)" Blackness "incarnates metaphysical nothing." So it is that, in an attempt to dominate nothingness (to turn it into an object of knowledge, to discover ever newer methods for escaping it), metaphysics seeks to objectify nothingness, as Warren puts it, "though the black Negro." Metaphysics seeks to objectify, dominate, and exterminate Black people in order to, says Warren, "maintain a sense of security and sustain the fantasy of triumph." The terror of nothingness is projected onto blackness and, in this antiblack world, Black people embody the ontological terror of metaphysics. This metaphysical conflation of blackness and nothingness also configures blackness as a puzzle, as a "great abyss," as something that cannot exist within ontology: a phenomenon that cannot be human. This metaphysical void has "something like existence" and yet "it is *nothing*—the nonhuman, equipment, and the mysterious."[22] This is a form of existence without being.

In an antiblack world, argues Warren, nihilism (which faces, rather than erases, nothing) is crucial because "it undermines the metaphysics, which sustains extreme forms of violence and destruction."[23] And yet, Warren is also clear that the function of nihilism is not to purify the world of its antiblackness; it is not a liberation. "The antiblack world," he writes, "is irredeemable." Instead, he argues, the function of nihilism is to discard the metaphysical fantasies (animated by ontological terror) that animate anti-nothingness and antiblackness. This would mean, in essence, facing the void or an abyss. This, Warren suggests, is the terror that must be confronted without evasion or deflection. And part of this terror is informed by the fear of death. Death, after all, is another dimension of the constellated negative. For Black thought, says Warren, the aim is to shift the emphasis of thinking, not to develop a form of thinking that will somehow redeem the world of its antiblackness. Instead, he writes, "let our thinking lead us into the 'valley of the shadow of death,'" and "once there we can begin to imagine an existence anew."[24]

In the work of Heidegger, of course, there is arguably a form of descent into the valley of death. His project is linked to a descent into the valley of death that other modern critics of

FIGURE 4.2 Krista Dragomer, *Made of Stars*, 2013

metaphysics have also made. In late modern European philosophy there are many distinct attempts to disrupt this constellated negative, rooted in death and nothingness. Modern continental philosophy, which has emerged with varying degrees of angst against the backdrop of this Western metaphysical frame, has often articulated itself in tension with the terms of this constellation. Continental thinkers like Heidegger, in other words, have often pursued critiques and disruptions of this constellated negative.

The work of Heidegger is often held to be synonymous with a twentieth-century philosophical revaluation of death itself. To speak about death philosophically, in the present, one feels almost obligated to pass—in some manner—through him. Warren is, at turns, both appreciative and critical of Heidegger's efforts in this direction. He is, in some sense, inescapable, Warren argues. "His *Destruktion* of Being has left its trace on all our thinking—whether we admit it or not." And yet, Warren writes, Heidegger's work can also be read as "an allegory of antiblackness and black suffering." On the one hand, his work appears to open to the nothing and orient itself toward the valley of death. On the other hand, he also configures a form of thought in which Being (*Dasein*) ultimately "flees the anxiety nothing stimulates and projects it as terror onto blacks."[25] Heidegger remains—in some crucial way, enthralled by the fantasy of dominating or rising above nothing. In this sense, then, while he offers opening gestures toward a critique of metaphysics, he remains both a subject and an agent of an antiblack ontological terror.

NATAL NEGATIVITY

In *Being and Time*, Heidegger declares his intent to "destruct" the history of the Western ontological tradition to make Dasein itself visible on its own terms and the subject of its own history. His "destruction of the history of ontology" sought to loosen up and dissolve the concealments of Dasein that he believed had been in place since Greek ontology became fixed into Christian doctrine in the Middle Ages. Heidegger's move was an attempt to "destroy" the "traditional content of ancient ontology" in order to access something more "primordial" within it. And yet, of course, he also assures his readers that his true intention is not to shake off the tradition so much as it is to "stake out the positive possibility of that tradition."[26] In the end, Heidegger's destruction of Western ontology is more of a rearrangement than a disruption. His own view of death is distinct from, though not a total disruption of, a more ancient Western philosophical and theological imaginary.

Heidegger does take a different view on death than the Western philosophical and theological figures I have been critiquing, to be sure. Death, for him, is not a state of privation, a condition for enmity, or an evil but rather is integral to thinking and being as such. Dasein is notoriously, for him, being-toward-death, which seems to suggest an intimate complicity between being and death. Dasein is revealed to itself, and illuminated, in death. Here, death is so far from privation that it has become a condition of that which confounds privation—the formation of being itself. There is something decidedly positive, for Heidegger, in the negativity of death. Dasein, he says, "reaches its wholeness in death."[27] Its dimension of possibility (the fact that it is always "not yet," not quite actual and only possible) is rooted in the futurity of death as a phenomenon that is anticipated but not yet here.[28]

In what follows I suggest that Heidegger's theorization of Dasein illuminates a natal dimension in death that casts death in a glow that it would not have, were it to be confined to pure mortality. In the end, though, even the natal dimensions of death do not seem to generate a disruption of the negativity of Western metaphysics. This is because birth (with its conceptual links to that philosophically abject space of the womb) has also been a part of this ancient constellated negative. Despite the conceptual revision of philosophies of natality in the work of twentieth-century thinkers such as Hannah Arendt, birth is bound to the fleshiness, the animality, and the darkness of the constellated negative. In this way, the natality of Heidegger's negative functions to fold death back into the constellated negative and he is driven to articulate Dasein against and above it.

It may seem odd, perhaps, to present Heidegger as a thinker of natality. Because of his infamous coupling of death and Dasein, he has often been read (to use a term from the feminist philosopher Grace Jantzen) as a necrophiliac—just another Western philosophical lover of death. Indeed, Heidegger is often read as the paradigmatic counterpoint to Arendt's philosophy of natality, which is read as a radical turn against the androcentric death obsession in Western thought.[29] His fixation on being-toward-death is read as diametrically opposed to Arendt's being-toward-birth. In critiques of him, he tends to be framed as a thinker who is obsessed with mortality *rather than* (indeed, at the expense of) natality. But Anne O'Byrne has noted that while Heidegger *explicitly* privileges mortality in *Being and Time*, and perhaps even obscures natality with this fixation, he is nevertheless deeply dependent upon natality for thinking Dasein.

As O'Byrne notes, natality tends to appear in *Being and Time* under the guise of either "thrownness" or as historicity. Early in the book, natality is linked with thrownness or novelty, and it serves as a figure that is unsettling but nevertheless "richly disruptive" for Heidegger.[30] Indeed, O'Byrne argues that Heidegger's assessment of natality as thrownness is "one of the best-sustained considerations of natality we have."[31] Late in the text of *Being and Time*, he seems to stumble upon the need for natality in order to acknowledge the betweenness of Dasein—the fact that its temporality can be reduced to neither future nor past, death nor birth. Dasein has no betweenness if it is pure mortality or directed merely toward death. As he puts it, Dasein instead "stretches along" between birth and death, and so facilitates "the connectedness of life."[32] It is this sense of connectedness that Heidegger names the "historicizing" dimension of Dasein,[33] and it is only by acknowledging the extent to which it is both a being-toward-birth *and yet* also equally a being-toward-death that this dimension of Dasein is able to come to light. So it is, for Heidegger, that natality becomes key.

In what sense, then, is Heidegger's explication of death natal? To see this, we have to keep in view his description of Dasein as the betweenness that illuminates connections between birth and death. This betweenness becomes an unbreakable bond, a relational dimension between birth and death that casts a deathly shadow on birth and a natal glimmer on death. While he may privilege the futural dimensions of Dasein (its being-toward-death) in what he theorizes explicitly, the betweenness of Dasein is also its inability to be reducible to the pure future—or to death in any reductive sense. It is by being stretched back toward natality that Dasein resists such a reduction. This resistance changes the nature of what death is, for Heidegger. Because natality for him is thrownness, O'Byrne notes that natal anxiety underscores the "groundlessness of our finite existence." It is through natality and natal anxiety that Dasein is not only thrown *toward* death but also how we acknowledge that "*this* Dasein did not always exist."[34] Without natality, Dasein would not be thrown toward (or conscious of) death in the first place because it would not experience this thrownness. The natal dimensions of Dasein pull it away from its mortal drive in order to take perspective—to think about, frame, or understand death in a particular manner.

Mortality forces an acknowledgment of our own contingency, in the sense that our bodies will ultimately cease to live. But natality forces an acknowledgement of our contingency as it reminds us that we did not make ourselves. It is only through a full sense of our contingency (informed by both dimensions) that we are able to understand that we will die. Heidegger does argue, vociferously, that we do not really experience being-toward-death when we live through the death of *others* (rather than our own death).[35] This would appear to indicate that our experience of death is consequently individual and non-relational.[36] But, whether he openly states it or not, the natality of Dasein ensures that we cannot understand death at all without "grasping the past" that throws us toward death.[37] That past is not our own, or own-most, but entirely other—it is ancestral and inherited. Death, for Heidegger, is not biological (that kind of death, he says, is perishing). Instead, death is existential. He does attempt to militate against the way that others seek to publicly interpret the meaning of death, which threatens to encroach on our own individual existential assessment of it.[38] Nevertheless, what Heidegger does not acknowledge or comment on (indeed, seems barely aware of) is that a child is not born knowing how to sleep for more than an hour at a time, let alone knowing that she will die. In the same way that behaviors, including elemental ones such as nursing for basic sustenance, may seem intuitive, they are learned. And the knowledge that there is death, that those we love will die, and that we too will die, is something that children learn—with great difficulty—over time. Children learn through others, by watching others, and by witnessing the deaths of others, that death is part of their own future, too.

We cannot understand the experience of futurity that is being-toward-death without the historicity facilitated by our natality: the natality that binds us to other generations and creates our sense of groundless thrownness. That is to say, it is our natality that facilitates any comprehension of mortality in the first place. While we are always free to reencounter and reshape the existential meaning of this death on our own terms, it is through encounters with the death of others, through social teachings about death that resonate through generations, and rituals and rites of burial or memorial, that natality will always continue to craft our being-toward-death. Indeed, Heidegger himself undertakes this natal labor. In his attempt to craft a social and intellectual understanding of death that not only individualizes its meaning but also seeks to weave death into the fabric of being itself (rather than render it an evil deprivation), he is engaging and performing the care of Dasein. He attempts to mitigate the traumatic effects of being-toward-death. He seeks to illuminate something in death by pulling from the novelty of natality. Heidegger does not make this explicit, but death and birth, natality and mortality, are integrally related in his thinking.

What does this show us? It indicates, to begin with, that his reflections on death are not simple, isolated reflections on death alone, as they might at first appear. He may not be the deathbound necrophiliac that critics have made him out to be. There are natal dimensions not only to his thought but to his death work as well. In this sense, I understand Heidegger to be making an attempt to "destruct" and reshape philosophical discourses on death. There is, then, a subtly disruptive dimension to his reflections on death. He stages a natal disruption of metaphysical death discourses. This generative disruptiveness is tied to a disruption that, I think, he seeks to stir up more broadly within the Western metaphysics of negativity.

Heidegger sees himself in line with Hegel in this task. In Hegel's philosophy, Heidegger finds an implicit (unmarked but nevertheless remarkable) dimension of negativity that confounds our expectation of nothing. Hegel, says Heidegger, presents us with a creative nothing—a nothing that is not privative but is instead generative. Heidegger describes what he calls the "ordinary opinion" that negativity is a kind of fixed set: "saying no, negation, negatedness, not, nothing, and nullity."[39] This is set up as a contrast with negativity in the work of Hegel. For Hegel, Heidegger argues, "nothing" is not simply the "not of beings." Instead, negativity is "the first true thing." Being is not contrasted with negativity, in Hegel, but is instead "the same as the nothing."[40] Hegel tarries with the negative rather than "looking away."[41] Negativity in Hegel, Heidegger argues, is consciousness as such—the very energy of "unconditioned thinking."[42] Negativity in Hegel is a kind of horizon from which things rise. And yet, Heidegger also argues that Hegel himself does not see this negativity as remarkable. Instead, negativity in Hegel remains something "questionless." Negativity, like thinking itself, is seen as self-evident and therefore is unremarkable.[43] Heidegger understands it as his task to mark out the functions of negativity in Hegel in order to illuminate this "concealed ground" of thought.[44] In his commentary on negativity in Hegel, Heidegger unsettles the metaphysical bifurcation of something and nothing, or creation and annihilation. Heidegger does not suggest that negativity is, in any simple sense, positivity. Yet he does highlight generative or productive dimensions of the negative. Heidegger is, in a sense, illuminating the thrownness of both somethingness and nothingness and gesturing toward their productive and mutual co-constitutions. If death, in Heidegger's own philosophy, takes on a kind of glow (as it is subtly shadowed by birth), he seems to see a similar phenomenon unfolding within Hegel's negativity. In this way, I think, Heidegger is highlighting a natal dimension in Hegel's negative. Hegel seems to lift the negative above its privation in the constelled negative of Western metaphysics.

Ultimately, however, the constellated negative remains intact in Heidegger's own work. While he may illuminate the natal dimensions of the constellated negative, it does not shatter or disrupt the constellation itself. In *Language and Death*, Giorgio Agamben explores the contours of negativity in both Hegel and Heidegger. While it may appear, says Agamben, that these thinkers are disrupting or disturbing the negative, it may actually be more accurate to say that they are rearticulating and reaffirming the "originary negativity"[45] that founds metaphysics. This originary negativity is not a disruption of metaphysics but its mystical ground and foundation. It gives metaphysics something to stand on. In this sense, then, while Hegel and Heidegger think, in a concerted way, *about* the constellated negative and while they even seek to find an emancipatory potential in this negative, the liberation they ultimately find can actually be likened to a *return to metaphysics* in the sense that this liberation transcends, triumphs, or rises above the constellated negative. They inhabit the constellated negative in order to appropriate something from it that will help them rise, differently but again, above it.

Agamben explores how it is that the negative serves as the foundation of metaphysics by isolating, more specifically, the function of silence (the lack or privation of sound). Silence is a form of the negative, a lack or privation that serves to ground metaphysics. He points to what he calls the ancient "mythogeme" of the silent voice that appears, already, in late ancient Christian and Gnostic texts. The silent voice as a mystical voice—that site where the otherwise inaudible voice of the divine is revealed, outside of sound—becomes the "ontological foundation of language."[46] It is the other to language, and the ungrounded ground of the Word of God. God as word, language, *gramma*, emerges out of the mystical negativity of the silent voice. Here, then, the negative dimension of silence "is simply the negative foundation of *logos*,"[47] an ungrounded ground in which the theologics of Western metaphysics is rooted. Language itself finds its ungrounded ground in the negativity of the silent voice. This negativity, this nothingness, is actually an originary site against which Western metaphysics articulates itself, against which it founds itself as other. So it is that "negativity is inseparable from metaphysics."[48] Agamben sees, in this problematic, "the limitations" of "critiques of metaphysics" such as Heidegger's. The problem with such critiques tends to be, he argues, that "they hope to surpass the horizon of metaphysics by radicalizing the problem of negativity and ungroundedness, as if a pure and simple repetition of its fundamental problem could lead to a surpassing of metaphysics."[49] Instead, in an attempt to appropriate the negative, they repeat metaphysics' most elemental gesture.

The repetition of the ontology of Western metaphysics—within the negative—becomes most obvious in Agamben's critique of the figure of the human in Hegel and Heidegger. While the human for both Hegel and Heidegger is not articulated in positive ontological terms, the human's constitutive negativity is what continues to reignite its relationship to the metaphysical. The negativity of the human (its total lack of a positive ontological structure) indicates that the human continues to find its tap roots where Western ontological concepts have always sourced their nutrients: mystical negativity. The negativity of the human is not counter-metaphysical but itself a metaphysical figuration. Agamben illustrates this in the emergence of the human, in Hegel and Heidegger, out of the negative mythogeme of the silent (or *silenced*) voice.

He reflects on Hegel's claim in *Science of Logic* that "the death of the animal is the becoming of consciousness."[50] Agamben translates the becoming of consciousness (in Hegel) into the development of human language. So, then, the death of the animal voice (the silencing of the animal voice) creates and gives life to human language. The indeterminacy of the human (its consciousness, its language) borrows its indeterminate shape and form from the death of the animal. As the animal dies (as the animal voice is silenced), what emerges is the human (constituted, metaphysically, by consciousness and language). Underlying what Hegel calls the negativity of consciousness is death itself—the death of what was animal, within the human. In this conceptual structure human language bears traces of its emergence out of this deathly negativity and resounds with "the expression and memory of the animal's death."[51] Human language "dwells in the realm of death" because it is the articulation of the "vanishing trace" that is animal death. The birth of what metaphysics has alleged to make the human singular and distinct (language, consciousness) is dependent upon death and the negative—specifically the death of what is said to be animal. Metaphysics kills, or perhaps sacrifices, the animal. As it kills the animal, the death of the animal forms the negative ground for the emergence of the human. The death of the animal is natal; it is what (in Western metaphysics) births the human.

This natal negativity is also, in its way, a form of human violence. In this death of the animal we can see the human-above-death emerging. Unlike Aquinas's human-above-death (who is built for happiness and, when he agrees to fill himself up with Christ, fundamentally supernatural), this human-above-death is filled with nothing but negative content. It is rife with what Aquinas would have named privation. Yet this is a human-above-death, nevertheless, because it articulates itself *against* this negativity and so becomes, in this sense, other to it. This figure of the human is born out of the death of what is said to be animal—it rises above it. It tries to fly away. This is a creation of the human out of a kind of ontological terror of death that flees its two-legged animality.

This correlates with Heidegger's observation that, even though the Dasein that constitutes a human being is a being-toward-death, this Dasein nevertheless still subjects death *to itself* and so rises up out of (above) the death of animal mortality. This is more than a claim that death, for Heidegger, is not biological perishing. Rather, I am making a claim about the existential dimension of death. In what sense? Dasein is a being *toward* death. But it is ultimately more than, and above, death.

Dasein is life. But it is also more than life, and so subjects life to itself. Dasein's potentiality, its "not-yet," is rooted within death. And yet, says Heidegger, Dasein does not find its "end" in death. Death does not stop Dasein but merely serves as a kind of natal negativity that potentiates the transcendence of Dasein into another dimension. "Death is a way to be," says Heidegger, and as soon as Dasein finds itself inhabiting this "way to be," it takes it over and usurps it.[52]

Death is ultimately, for Heidegger, merely "a phenomenon of life."[53] This means that death is subordinate to life. And Dasein is "superordinate" to life.[54] So it is that Heidegger reinforces what are ultimately traditional hierarchies in Western metaphysics, in which death is subordinate to life and biological life is subordinate to something still higher. In Dasein, the human heads toward, but ultimately rises up and above, death. Dasein puts death under its boot, as it were, and takes in its power. In Dasein, the human becomes (metaphysically) the human-above-death. This is the more "primordial" metaphysic that Heidegger was after when he sought to destruct metaphysics itself. Death is not *the enemy*, but it is still subservient to Dasein. And there is still something animal within the negativity of death that Dasein rises above and makes subservient to itself. So it is that the old violence of metaphysics—the violence that creates a condition of and for enmity within the negative, so rising above it—remains at play in Heidegger's thinking, despite the work that he also does to disrupt it. What is animal, creaturely, and mortal serves as an embodiment of the negative. Dasein objectifies this dimension of the negative, in animal mortality, and rises above its perishing. So Dasein transcends the constellated negative, leaving its relation to Western metaphysics fixed in place.

Zakiyyah Iman Jackson critiques not merely the way that Enlightenment humanist discourses have conflated Black humans with animals ("denying" Black people their humanity) but, more, the way that Enlightenment thought has performed a violent appropriation of "black(ened) humanity." Jackson describes how thinkers such as Hegel and Heidegger have sought to make the figure of the human *more plastic*, by experimenting with blackness—by reaching into (yet still also pushing against) the negativity that blackness is conflated with. "The fleshy being of blackness is experimented with as if it were infinitely malleable lexical and biological matter," writes Jackson, "such that blackness is produced as sub/super/human at once, a form where form shall not hold."[55] Against this plasticity, the human defines himself. If Agamben's analysis showed us how Hegel and Heidegger's negatively charged human emerged from their appropriation of the death of the animal, Jackson's analysis illuminates racialized dimensions of this constellated negative that Agamben's did not. When race becomes ontologized, writes Jackson, this "fixes blackness, regardless of 'sex,' in the 'feminine position' as that passivity and stasis ascribed to objecthood and death, or objecthood as a form of living death." In this essentializing constellation, argues Jackson, "blackness, womanhood, female sex, passivity, objecthood, inertia, death, and matter" form "an unbreakable chain and negative telos or declension."[56]

Jackson's project, at large, examines the ways that Enlightenment humanist views on blackness and animality form and shape one another, as the idea of the human forms itself against them. This becomes visible in the work of Hegel, says Jackson, in his reflections on African humanity. For him, "the African peoples qualify as human but only tentatively so." Humanity is "an achievement and teleology." And "black(ened) people are the living border dividing forms of life." There is a sense, for Hegel, that a minimum condition of humanity is met for Africans, but ascension into higher registers of the human form is impossible.

He does not *deny* the humanity of Africans. Rather, he asserts that "Black people are animals occupying the human form."[57] The African is an "animal man" trapped within nature.[58] Lacking the ability to become conscious of themselves as historical beings, Hegel argues that Africans are "barred from universal humanity or spirit."[59] But the key here is that Hegel does not deny Africans humanity, pushing them out of the figure of the human. Rather, he configures the blackness of Africans together with animality in order to assert that there is a kind of primordial form of the human that serves as the negative ground or foundation of spirit. Spirit appropriates this negativity in order to give shape to itself. The spirit that is proper to universal man, or full humanity, appropriates this negativity and rises above it. This resonates with Agamben's more limited claim that the human is founded in the death of the animal. The indeterminate negativity of human consciousness and language relies on, and appropriates, the negativity that is born in the death of the animal or is harbored in blackness.

Blackness and animality are part of the constellated negative of Western metaphysics that serves as the foundation for the universal form of man. This is how, says Jackson, Hegel appropriates and exploits the plasticity of the co-constituted negativity of blackness and animality in order to give a new shape and form to the human. Blackness and animality (co-constitutively) make negativity plastic for thinkers like Hegel—the human approximates this negativity to appropriate and then rise above it. The human is reinvented through this plasticity. By bringing blackness and animality (as icons of the negative) close to the human, and yet ultimately pushing them away, Western thinkers have reformed and reshaped their sense of what the human is and how it functions. The human-above-death configures itself against the plasticity of this other human who is said to be destined for death.

In the same way that Heidegger understands himself to find a negative muse in Hegel, Jackson also senses a lineage in this dimension of their thinking. Given that Hegel's reflections on Africans are also, at the same time, reflections on the nature of the animal, Jackson suggests that Hegel's African gives shape to Heidegger's animal.[60] Jackson gestures, especially, toward Heidegger's famous claim that the stone is "worldless," the animal is "poor in world," and man is "world-forming."[61] Here, in nonhuman life, the relation to the world is not formational but is instead a relation of captivation or fixation.[62] The animal, the nonhuman, is imprisoned by the world. The nonhuman is locked into the world of death, destined to regress back into a form of passive lack and privation. Heidegger is not pulling this theory from biology or zoology, notes Jackson. Rather, it is a philosophical distinction. Heidegger is pulling this distinction, this subjective imprisonment within the negative, from Hegel. Heidegger's model for animal life, its poverty and privation, is Hegel's African. Jackson describes it as an "unmarked Hegelianism."[63] And so the figure of the human, for Heidegger, takes its shape against the poverty, privation, and lack of this racialized animality.

Agamben highlights how the figure of the human (who is ultimately the human-above-death) is generated, for Hegel and Heidegger, in the death of the animal. The human-above-death rises above death as it mortalizes animality. But Jackson illuminates that this is not simply animal death but also blackness and Black death. Heidegger may reshape being, Dasein, by bringing it into a close and intimate form of contact with natal negativity. He makes of it something other than what Western metaphysics has made it. And yet, the plasticity that maintains this intensive form of relationality between dimensions of the constellated negative is what gives Dasein this new shape and form. Dasein comes close to death, approximating the constellated negative.

But Dasein still remains captured by an ontological terror that pushes back against the animality, and the blackness, of this constellated negative. Heidegger still affirms that life stands above death, and Dasein is above both life and death. Death, in all its natal negativity, is still subjected to life as it rises above the constellated negative. Death, for Heidegger, loses its enemy status. But it does not shake free of its subjection. Dasein is revealed to itself and can reinvent itself, in death. But death is still under its boot, and ontological terror still gives shape to this view of death.

LIFE AND DEATH, DISRUPTED (ALWAYS)

Jackson argues that is it within Black feminist thought—not in a thinker like Heidegger—that we see a disruption of the Western metaphysics that forms a constellated negative. Rather than argue that black(ened) femininity be included on the life-giving, vitalizing side of this Western metaphysical framework, Jackson instead turns toward what she describes as the "fundamental indefiniteness and opacity in projections and productions of blackness." This indefinite opacity, says Jackson, has the potential to "trouble the ontological [itself] and its arrangements of the world."[64] In the work of African diaspora writers and artists, Jackson finds what she describes as a "centrifugal and dissident way of being, feeling, and knowing existence"[65] that unsettles and explodes the constellations of Western metaphysics that draw together death, nothingness, blackness, womanhood, objecthood, and animality. Figures such as Wangechi Mutu or Toni Morrison reveal, for Jackson, "a potential (with neither a guarantee nor a manifest horizon of possibility—but a potential nonetheless) for mutation beyond a mode of thought and representation that continually adheres to predefined rules and narratives."⁶⁶ In their work, blackness becomes "a matrix" and "a network of intersections" that is also "an essential enabling condition for something of, but distinguishable from, its source." Connected and yet also disconnected from the figurations of blackness produced by Western metaphysics, the work of women like Mutu and Morrison thus "performs a kind of natality" or "a generative function" rather than serving "as an identity."⁶⁷ This dissident dimension of blackness is what Jackson calls the "specter of the black mater" or the "black *mater*(nal)"⁶⁸ that itself "holds the potential to transform the terms of reality and feeling, therefore rewriting the conditions of possibility and the empirical."⁶⁹ Jackson notes that this potential, while disruptive, is still only a potential. This leaves it resistant to easy co-optation. It is a critical potential to gesture toward or reflect on rather than a critical opportunity to seize.

In what remains of this chapter I look to the work of Morrison to catch sight of a disruption or destabilization of the Western metaphysics of life and death. I read her work as a source for conceptual, philosophical thinking. There are many Morrison novels to source, if we are looking for a destabilization of the lifedeath relation articulated in the political theology of death. *Beloved*, which features a ghostly character who embodies or illuminates the uncertainties of lifedeath, might be an obvious place to look. And *Song of Solomon*, with its Dead family who can communicate with the dead (and includes the complex character Pilate, born to a dead mother and lacking a navel to mark her natality). But I find, in *Sula*, a clear and evocative challenge to the binary distinctions, and the relation of enmity, between life and death that the political theology of death sources in order to fuel its ontological terror.

Juda Bennett argues that *Sula* anticipates *Beloved* in interesting ways. The character Sula, says Bennett, *becomes* a ghost (or an ancestor, perhaps) over the course of the novel and so both prefigures and joins Beloved in transgressing "that ultimate boundary marked by Western dualistic thinking of life and death."[70] Tessa Roynon argues that *Sula* is a novel that, in any number of ways, exposes the "sterility" of these Western "binary oppositions."[71] In *Sula* points of sharp contrast dissolve and unsettle. Jaleel Akhtar notes that Sula herself is treated by other characters as a scapegoat figure, one who transgresses differences and taboos.[72] In this role she also becomes a kind of "sponge" who soaks up "communal impurities" (such as guilt or death) and so becomes a site of communal transformation.[73] Whatever the case may be, Sula is a disruptive, unsettling, and deeply powerful character. Morrison herself has observed that she has always thought of Sula as "quintessentially black, metaphysically black, if you will." This is not, Morrison notes, about "melanin" and "certainly not unquestioning fidelity to the tribe." Instead, Sula is "New World black and New World woman extracting choice from choicelessness, responding inventively to found things. Improvisational. Daring, disruptive, imaginative, modern, out-of-the-house, outlawed, unpolicing, uncontained, and uncontainable. And dangerously female."[74]

Hortense Spillers has argued that Sula, as a character, "inscribes a new dimension of being": a breakthrough (both literal and figurative) into a "new female being."[75] For readers, Sula refuses old literary tropes: "She is not consciousness of the black race personified, nor 'tragic mulatta,' nor for white ones is she 'mammy,' 'Negress,' 'coon,' or 'maid.' She is herself."[76] Sula is not only full of moral ambiguity but she is also "both loved and hated by the reader," both rejected and embraced because of the fact that she confronts the reader with a "corruption of absolutes." What is left in their place is not redemptive but is, instead, "the complex, alienated, transitory gestures of a personality who has no framework or moral reference beyond or other than herself."⁷⁷ But Sula is not an egoist. If the character is provocative precisely because she is *for* herself and *of* herself, she is not especially *about* herself. She is, instead, a charged ambivalence, "an embodiment of a metaphysical chaos in pursuit of an activity both proper and sufficient to herself."⁷⁸ Yet, as Spillers points out, Sula's moral ambiguities are themselves shaped by something entirely other than white society and whiteness. Instead, Morrison seems to suggest, what troubles at Sula is "an idle imagination." She is an artist without a form, and it is in this sense that she is dangerous.⁷⁹ She is not a woman who has been limited by the "evil force" of whiteness, or even by the presence or absence of a man. Rather, she is "a character whose failings are directly traceable to the absence of a discursive/imaginative project—some *thing* to do."⁸⁰

Sula, as a character, becomes an interpretive problem. But Spillers suggests that it is not as a character in a narrative that Sula is most compelling. Rather, although she occupies that position, her position within the story is as a form of "potential being." And as a dimension of potential being, *Sula* suggests that "subversion itself" is "an aspect of liberation that women must confront from its various angles." Her "outlawry" may not be the best variety, says Spillers, but "that she has the will toward rebellion itself *is* the stunning idea." And this idea, Spillers writes, "has no particular dimension in time, yet it is for all time."⁸¹ This idea is always. Sula is a potential being, a new woman, she is anti-metaphysical blackness; Sula is not a character so much as a concept, a figure, a kind of philosophical form that disrupts philosophical forms. She exists neither in time nor outside of it but instead within a kind of *always* that corrupts the lines between here and there, now and then, life and death.⁸²

In *Sula* the funeral scene of a small child—Chicken Little, who falls to his death in the river—directly challenges the binary oppositions that fracture lifedeath. Standing before the coffin of this small child, Morrison writes, those in attendance at the funeral "thought of all that life and death locked into that little closed coffin." There is, here, a clear acknowledgement of the unbreakable lifedeath bond that stirs, perhaps, most acutely in the wake of a tragic death. In response those in attendance "danced and screamed." This was not to protest the will of God, Morrison notes. This was not a scream of complaint. Rather, she says, this was confirmation of "their conviction that the only way to avoid the Hand of God is to get in it."[83] To get into the Hand of God, perhaps, is to inhabit that site where both possibilities are fully at play, where lifedeath builds like a storm that rises in joy and agony.

Later in the novel, the character Nel (who, along with Sula, had been present at and complicit in the accidental death of Chicken Little) reflects on the old grief of these mourners. While, at the time, Nel viewed their mourning displays with disdain and thought of them as "unbecoming," in the discovery of her own acute grief she begins to understand them. They were screaming, she thought, because "they could not let that heart-smashing event pass unrecorded, unidentified." To mourn in "good taste" (to mourn, she implies, in the sterile manner of white people), to "let the dead go with a mere whispering, a slight murmur," was "poisonous, unnatural." Instead, in the presence of a death "there must be much rage and saliva." In the presence of death, "the body must move and throw itself about, the eyes must roll, the hands should have no peace, and the throat should release all the yearning, despair and outrage that accompany the stupidity of loss."[84] Death is not an enemy here. But death does call for a reaction, a counterpoint. One is called to bring something undeniably vital (screams, saliva, rage, despair, eye rolling, dancing) to meet with death. Not as a complaint but simply because this is the sort of antagonism one brings on behalf of the dead and in the wake of death. To inhabit lifedeath is, perhaps, to meet those death-bound moments with much life, fighting for life or with life. To refuse to do this is poison.

The most enigmatic and complex characters in *Sula*—the war veteran Shadrack and Sula herself—also configure, together, a complex relation to lifedeath. Shadrack witnesses death on the battlefield in France in 1917 and is permanently marked by this memory. It introduced him to "the smell of death." What terrified him, subsequently, was not death or dying but instead "the unexpectedness of both." To mitigate this uncertainty, he institutes what he calls National Suicide Day—a day devoted not to the memory of those lost to suicide but to acknowledging the possibility of suicide. The idea, he muses, is that this gets the possibility of death out in the open so that the rest of the year "would be safe and free."[85] In this sense, it is almost like a (fleeting) exorcism of the possibility of death. But Kathryn Nichol has argued that his ritual act is not as much about self-destruction as it is about ritual protest and disruption.[86] Shadrack, a Black veteran who is subjected to the spectacle of death in war and whose service to the nation is both exploited and unacknowledged, stages a yearly ritual protest against the necropolitical order that surrounds him and his community. The possibility of suicide is a reminder that the necropolitical structures of white supremacy do not actually have the ultimate power over life and death.

When Shadrack meets Sula, as a young girl, he seems to sense intuitively that she too understands something about this uncertainty he feels. She stumbles into his cabin to discern whether he can tell that she and her friend Nel have just been implicated in Chicken Little's accidental death. It is unclear what exactly Shadrack knows. But, as he reflects later, he felt a strong desire to offer her an assurance. "When he looked at her face he had also seen the skull beneath" and, thinking that she saw it, too, "he tried to think of something to say to comfort her, something to stop the hurt spilling out of her eyes." What he said to her was simply "always." He said this so that "she would not be afraid of change—the falling away of skin, the drip and slide of blood, and the exposure of bone underneath. He had said 'always' to convince her, assure her, of permanency."[87] The permanency he offers her is nothing more than uncertainty; the continuous endurance of change itself. But in the moment, her face lit up. She discovers this permanent uncertainty, this "always," for herself as she grows.

This "always" is revealed to Sula, perhaps, most clearly and potently in sex. Sula pursues sex as often as she can. It is, Morrison writes, the one place where Sula can find what she's really looking for. While, initially, she thought she was after the joy of lovemaking, Sula later decides it's the "sootiness" or wickedness of sex that she enjoys. After time, however, she realizes that she is bored by those lovers who think of sex as healthy and beautiful. And neither does she actually believe that sex is wicked. Instead, she comes to understand that what she's truly looking for is a "cutting edge" where she can stop cooperating with her body and instead "assert herself in the air, particles of strength gathered in her like steel shavings drawn to a spacious magnetic center, forming a tight cluster." While it seems, for a brief spell, that nothing can break this cluster apart, it does break and she leaps "from the edge into soundlessness" where she goes down "howling in a stinging awareness of the end of things."[88] Through sex, and in finding what she is looking for, Sula finds "not eternity" but instead "the death of time" and "a loneliness so profound the word itself had no meaning." This death of time is a kind of always—a profound and painful solitude. It makes Sula weep. After sex she cries "tears for the deaths of the littlest things: the

FIGURE 4.3 Krista Dragomer, *A Planetary Cross Pollination Event*, 2013

castaway shoes of children, broken stems of marsh grass battered by the sea."[89] And yet, despite the pain this causes her, it reveals something to her that she does not cease to look for. This lonely death of time is not nothing; it is not an annihilation but a cutting edge, a zone of understanding.

Sula does not yet connect this painful solitude, this death of time, with the "always" that Shadrack illuminated for her in her youth. But on her own deathbed, she draws the connection. In the moments before her death she finds herself "completely alone—where she had always wanted to be—free of the possibility of distraction." She inhabits that old solitude she's always sought. And yet in this solitude, she is also profoundly connected to the elements of material reality. She imagines herself pulling her legs into her chest, closing her eyes, and floating "until she met a rain scent and would know the water was near." She launches into this cutting edge where the body meets the end of the body, the edge that she sought out in sex. Once there, she lets the water envelop her, "carry her, and wash her tired flesh away always." She pauses when she strikes upon this word. "Always. Who said that? She tried hard to think. Who was it that had promised her a sleep of water always?" Not a sleep of death but of water. In this deathbed reflection she comes to realize that she is no longer breathing. She is seized with fear, anticipating pain. But she smiles when she realizes that she does not need to smile because she is dead. "Well I'll be damned," she thinks to herself. "It didn't even hurt. Wait'll I tell Nel."[90] Morrison gives Sula voice, past this cutting edge that we tend to think of as the line between life and death. Sula—once dead—is not portrayed as communicating with the living. And yet, the possibility that she *might* is not erased. Morrison does not portray Sula as a figure with power over either life or death. She does not enter into, or rise up into, a space of metaphysical eternity. Rather, she inhabits the death of time itself. But neither is she annihilated in this death. Sula endures, uncertainly, in this lonely and yet shifting, changing, flowing "always," casting a figure—through words—of lifedeath.

If, as Jackson has argued, anxieties about the void tend to nullify blackness or to figure "black(ened) femaleness and/or femininity as baleful, phobogenic, fleshly metaphors of the void,"[91] Morrison seems here to anticipate and confound such anxieties, configuring a mutation of thought that gestures beyond the closures of Western metaphysics. Sula, "metaphysically black," does not exist beyond the void, but neither is she reduced to it, undone by it, or annihilated by it. Jackson points to the ontologizing functions that fix blackness, "regardless of 'sex,' in the 'feminine position' as that passivity and stasis ascribed to objecthood and death, or objecthood as a form of living death." These ontologizing functions render "blackness, womanhood, female sex, passivity, objecthood, inertia, death, and matter" as part of "an unbreakable chain and negative telos or declension."[92] Sula is a figure immersed in the various registers of this position and yet through Sula, Morrison also troubles at the perceived limits of this position and reveals instead a "centrifugal and dissident way of being, feeling, and knowing existence."[93] In Sula, then, Morrison illuminates an uncertain relation between life and death that Heidegger did not manage to contend with. Morrison offers a kind of dissent—a counterpoint to the conflation of death and nothingness, one that allows them each to become untethered. Death becomes, instead, a factor of lifedeath and ultimately other than nothing, without becoming something in itself.

What we see, in Morrison's figuration of Sula, is not a philosophical method to be applied to a metaphysical conundrum in order to redeem it of its difficulties or its violence. What Morrison performs, instead, is a disruption of a metaphysical situation and the performance itself is not available for appropriation. Perhaps, however, to think with the "corruption of absolutes" in Morrison's "always," and to think lifedeath against the bifurcations between life and death that we witness in Western metaphysics, can help to cultivate another form of attention—one that can witness what else might emerge when the constellated negatives of Western metaphysics come to life.

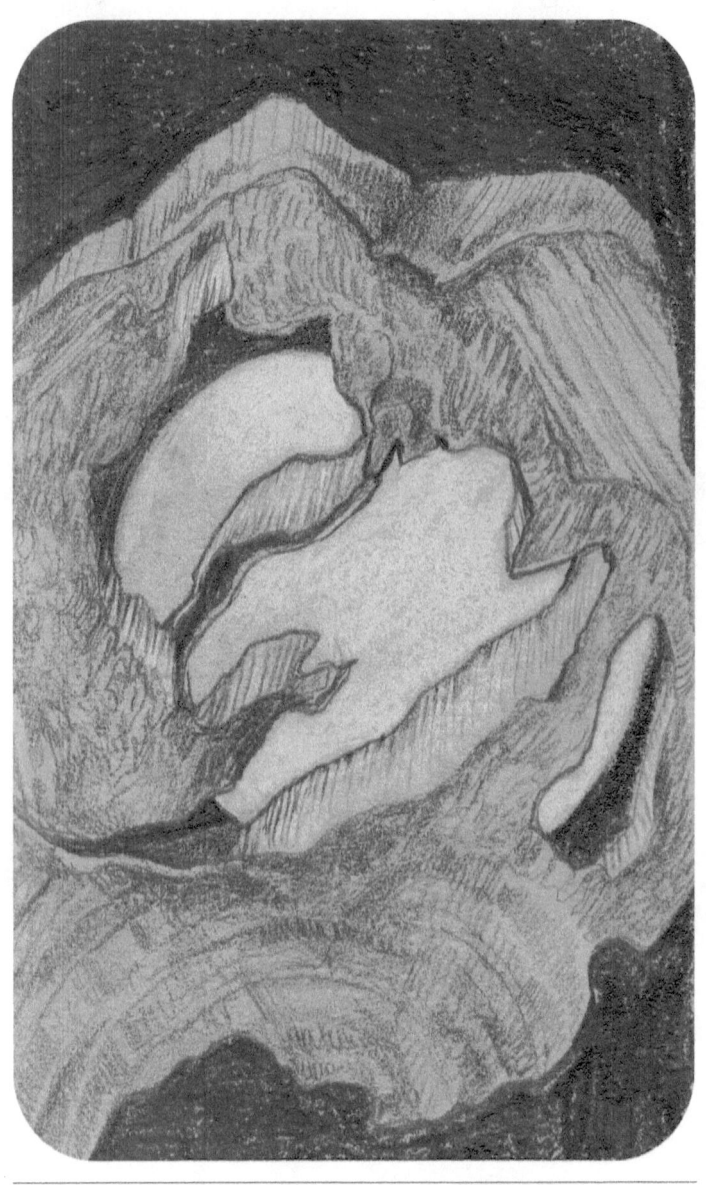

FIGURE 5.1 Krista Dragomer, *Synodic Portal 6*, 2020

5

SISTERHOOD AND ENMITY

In *The Cancer Journals*—essays and reflections on her experience of living through breast cancer and a mastectomy—Audre Lorde describes her struggle with cancer as a battle. But the struggle she describes is not a battle between life and death. Rather, it's a battle against silence and despair, a battle against "this dragon we call america." As a Black woman in America Lorde writes, "We were never meant to survive. Not as human beings."[1] She adds to this, "Neither were most of you here today, Black or not." In this dragon, she writes, we are fighting not to become casualties of the many features of American life that seed cancers: "the cosmic war against radiation, animal fat, air pollution, McDonald's hamburgers and Red Dye No. 2."[2] Cancers leak from the belly of the beast—the dragon. Lorde recognizes that who, and what, we make an enemy of matters. She fights a battle, and she sees enemies on the horizon. But death itself, as death, is not among them.

Neither, to be sure, does Lorde speak of death as a friend. "I carry death around in my body like a condemnation," she writes. "But I do live." Reflecting on this she posits that "there must be some way to integrate death into living, neither ignoring it nor giving in to it."[3] She is struggling to accept death "as

FIGURE 5.2 Krista Dragomer, *Untitled Sketch (cover/bind study)*, 2019

a fact" and yet also not to desire it.[4] She wants to "look death in the face and not shrink from it" and yet also "not ever to embrace it too easily."[5] She is not sure what, exactly, death is. And neither is she very sure how to respond to it. "The only answer to death is the heat and confusion of living," she writes.[6] But she recognizes that there is something potent both in this answer and in the fact of death. "Once I accept the existence of dying, as a life process, who can ever have power over me again?" she muses.[7]

Any living body understands, on a visceral level, that living is a struggle. When this struggle becomes acute—in illness, in accident, in the face of trauma or oppression—this struggle becomes a battle. To be alive, on this planet, is to struggle. Because there are so many potential avenues into, and out of, eventual death, and because death serves as a metaphorical figure to mask other phenomena, it is almost impossible to live without feeling various forms of antagonism toward death. Indeed, as Lorde notes, the heat and confusion of these antagonisms can animate us.

The political theology of death that pits life and death against one another, as enemies, captures these antagonisms effectively. While I have made this political theology a critical target of this book, I also recognize the lure or appeal of it. As long as I remain animated, I will never cease to struggle against death (as it seeps into the most intimate registers of what I call "my" life or the lives of other beings who surround me). This is not, however, to fantasize about the destruction of death itself. Death, too, is a collaborative partner in the enterprises that animate all of us. To conceive of the lifedeath relation as, fundamentally, one of enmity is to suggest that life and death come into opposition in order for—in a more ultimate sense—one to emerge as the ultimate victor while the other is destroyed. Poetically speaking, I think this particular well has run dry. The political theology of death that casts lifedeath in a position of fundamental enmity is itself a life-defeating fantasy. Proponents of the political theology of death might cast their lots with the triumph of life, when it comes to the last things. But life itself, what we call life, is shaped by what we call death. Life—creaturely life, biological life—is incoherent outside of this relation. Why frame this as a relation of pure enmity? Why not articulate and observe this relation in a way that can acknowledge the dimension of mutual care, without eviscerating the antagonisms?

There are many ways to think about opposition, differentiation, and antagonism. But if lifedeath continues to be framed as pure enmity, these antagonisms will always be lured back toward the promise of mutual destruction. To contemplate the enmity in lifedeath is to highlight and amplify the antagonistic tensions that reside in a form of difference. And yet, in the promise of evisceration that resides deep within enmity, particularly when enmity becomes theological, there is a force at work (a kind of strange love) that is also working to facilitate the elimination of this distinction, in the service of destruction. In this chapter I explore the mutually destructive dynamics of this political theology of enmity. And I think with Audre Lorde—who has reflected deeply on death, as well as sisterhood—to illuminate a counterpoetics to this political theology of enmity that is also a theology of death. I explore what it might mean to name the tensions of the lifedeath relation a form of sisterhood. In so doing, I seek to rouse the pluripotent (often antagonistic) relational dynamics in lifedeath. But I also seek to counter or mitigate some of the most destructive effects of the political theology of death.

If the political theology of death illuminates antagonisms in the lifedeath relation, sisterhood does not function to eliminate them. Sisterhood, as I suggest, leaves plenty of space open for antagonisms and forms of radical difference. And yet there is also—in sisterhood—a dimension of companionable challenge, a dimension of care that encourages a moving forward together, as other. This is not a claim that lifedeath is nothing other than sisterhood or that sisterhood is the only possible relational dynamic to read out of lifedeath. Rather, I suggest that sisterhood might be read as a kind of counterpoetic to the political theology of death. Why? Because it is a relational dynamic that sees (and does not erase) the antagonistic or competitive dynamics in lifedeath. And yet, in taking into account the dynamics of mutual support, it can also acknowledge the many ways in which life and death depend upon one another to be the other. It can, in other words, help to navigate around a political theology of death that—in amplifying the enmity in lifedeath—encourages the vision of a life that eviscerates death or a death that eviscerates life.

DEATH-DEALING AND SOFT ENMITY

The political theology of death that pits life and death against one another as enemies is perhaps—in the simplest sense—best described as a political theology built on the friend-enemy distinction. This political theology of enmity was not a conceptual innovation of the German legal theorist Carl Schmitt. But, perhaps, Schmitt's analysis of the political theology of enmity is both comprehensive and simple enough to be a sufficient treatment of the subject. The concept of enmity is at the core of Schmitt's analysis of the political, which was also an analysis of the secularization of theological thought into political theory. His claim was that the unity of a political group was established and maintained through the friend-enemy antithesis. Schmitt argued that the figure of the friend, in political thought, denoted an intense form of union or association while the enemy was a site of dissociation.[8] The enemy is, politically speaking, the other, the stranger—an alien.[9] The enemy is a public figure who serves as an antagonist against which political collectives push, bonding and grouping themselves together as friends. In finding a common enemy, in other words, a political group creates friendly alliances. This rendered the political what Schmitt called "the most intense and extreme antagonism."[10] Schmitt's claim is that this friend-enemy antithesis is universal, and it is the foundation of the political itself. In Schmitt's analysis, "every concrete antagonism" becomes more political as it approaches or approximates the friend-enemy antithesis.[11] An antagonism that is understood to be a relation of intense enmity, in other words, is deeply political or a politicized form of relation.

From this perspective, perhaps, to cast life and death in a position of enmity toward one another is a simple maneuver to politicize the lifedeath relation itself. But it may also be the case that the enmity between life and death was itself a force that was always already structuring Schmitt's own analysis. While he believed that all concrete political antagonisms were structured by the antithesis between friend and enemy, perhaps it was also the case that death hovered in the background of Schmitt's own imagination as the greatest enemy, while God occupied the position of greatest friend. His political analysis, after all, was intended to describe how Western political thought had secularized theological concepts, not merely repeated or reiterated them. This raises a kind of chicken-or-egg question, you might say. Which came first, the friend-enemy distinction or the enmity between life and death? For the time being, it matters little how we answer this. Rather, my point here is to simply underscore the fact that the enmity between life and death (that might, at certain moments, risk flipping over into a strange friendship) is deeply integrated with what Schmitt called political theology—secularized (and politicized) theological concepts. So it is that life and death are figures that are consistently pulled into the friend-enemy distinction in political rhetoric in America, which remains deeply influenced by secularized theological concepts.

This politicization of the lifedeath relation—especially the claim that one's political enemies are weaponizing death against life—sits at the heart of American politics. The political enemies of the American right, for instance, emerge most clearly when they are said to become friends of the greatest enemy (death). Pro-life political activists, for instance, claim to be on the side of (friends with) life. They make a political enemy of those who seek to protect access to (often life-saving) medical procedures such as abortion, casting these political enemies as friends of death who are opposed to the emergence of innocent new life. The position of political virtue becomes symbolically encoded with signs of life. Political enemies are cast as inherently destructive or perverse and are collapsed into the symbolic regime of death. To stand with the enemy is to stand on the side of destruction and chaos, which amplifies the unthinkability of the political alternative.

This previous example may, perhaps, be thick with my own cynicism. And this would seem to suggest that I would distance my own political standpoint from this political theological strategy. So, I should note, there are deployments or rhetorical uses of this strategy that I find myself sympathetic with. Voices on the political left—in the midst of the politicization of the COVID-19 epidemic—frequently labeled Donald Trump and his followers (who belittled the practice of wearing masks to avoid spread of the virus) a "death cult," for instance. Though I may not have leveled this accusation myself, I was sympathetic to the rhetoric. My point here is not that it is somehow misguided or wrong to make use of this rhetorical strategy—to recognize the fact that one's political enemies are (intentionally or not) a cause of death. Rather, my point is that this is a difficult political theology to critique because it remains potent and meaningful—even if in a metaphorical sense—in American politics today. If we hold a particular political position with conviction, and if we know the political alternative to be a potential cause of death, it is essential to bring this to light. And if we believe that our own political position might help to evade forms of tragic and oppressive death, it is inevitable that our position will be poised on the side of life (and, so, against death).

In American political discourse, the codification of political friends as allies for life and political enemies as organizers for death serves as a kind of shorthand. It provides lines in the sand, helping us to decide where we stand. More, it underscores the stakes of political work. Many policies appear, on the surface, to be mundane measures. But the potential implications are matters of life and death for living, breathing people. To help others see this, it is sometimes necessary to amplify these potential stakes. In general, if political actors are either callous about, or sympathetic toward, the death of their constituents, then it should become clear that they are political enemies. In this sense, perhaps, it is a bit of a fool's errand to critique the rhetoric that allies life with political friends and death with political enemies. This rhetoric *does* something; it *illuminates* something.

And yet, of course, this rhetoric can also obscure things. Take, for instance, the earlier example of anti-abortion political rhetoric. While voices on the right might present their anti-abortion politics as pro-life, what these policies actually aim to protect is a form of life that is not yet alive apart from the life who hosts it. These policies create a fracture within the reproductive body, deeming one isolated portion of this living body worthy of political protection while another portion of this same body is determined to be subject to punitive measures under the law. Moreover, under this condition of fracture, the life of this living human being who has undertaken (or been undertaken by) the process of reproduction is not given priority, in the event that the process itself threatens this life. Instead, the reproductive process—which might be death-dealing—is prioritized over the living person. Upon closer analysis, in other words, the clear and simple lines between life and death dissolve in this instance. To claim that a pro-life political position is always, without question, friendly to life is to obscure the complexities of the actual situation.

So, perhaps, it is not entirely out of place to trouble at deployments of this political theology. We might even say that there is a kind of political arrogance at work in the claim to be a friend of life, one who stands opposed to those lovers of death. Life and death work in and through us. Processes that make live, and processes that make die, are at work in our bodies at any given moment. The decisions we make, the political structures we build, might ultimately channel one force or the other. Politics can function to weaponize both life and death. But life and death are forces of inevitability much larger than both us and our political structures. They are not forces we can claim, in effect, to be friends with. We are contingent to forces of life and death in a manner that is not conducive to friendship. We cannot influence either life or death, although we can be (perhaps always are) under their influence. In such instances, perhaps, we are less their friends than their instruments. We can make ourselves and one another more aware of the ways in which our politics instrumentally produce death, conditions of death, or death worlds. Or we can advance political actors and alliances that will enable the living to thrive. But the claim to be either a friend or an enemy to either life or death might be a bit disingenuous.

There are, perhaps, already more nuanced analyses of the political weaponization of life and death circulating in American political discourse. I am thinking, for instance, of Christina Sharpe's analysis of whiteness as death-dealing in the afterlifes of slavery. The whiteness of American political structures produces death, or death worlds, in her analysis. As she describes it, "the ongoing state-sanctioned legal and extralegal murders of Black people are normative and, for this so-called democracy, necessary." Given that this is the "ground layout," she poses, how is it possible "to live in relation to this requirement for our death. What kinds of possibilities might be opened up?"[12] What Sharpe does *not* do, in the wake of these state-sanctioned murders, is to rigorously associate death itself with political enemies and claim an alliance with pure life as a form of resistance or counterpoint. While she critiques these death-dealing politics, and the production of death worlds, a channel for resistance also remains open in conversation with death and the dead. This is what Sharpe calls wake work. Wakes, says Sharpe, "are processes; through them we think about the dead and about our relations to them; they are rituals through which to enact grief and memory. Wakes allow those among the living to mourn the passing of the dead through ritual."[13] While it is clear, in her analysis, that American political structures are death-dealing, for Black communities, it is also clear that death plays a highly complex and ambivalent role in her analysis.

I would suggest, in effect, that Sharpe's analysis takes on death from outside the political theology of death that I have been critiquing; death appears, in her analysis, from an otherwise perspective. To put it another way, I think that Sharpe's political analysis takes death into account in a way that the political theology of death—which pits life and death against one another, as enemies—does not. Sharpe's analysis is not explicitly theological, although the wake, as a ritual, certainly has religious roots, resonances, and undertones. A wake, as she describes it, is "a watching practiced as a religious observance."[14] But to the extent that it poses a kind of challenge, counterpoint, or otherwise to the political theology of death that I have been describing, I would consider wake work a matter of political theology. What this example also indicates are some of the limits of Schmitt's diagnosis. His analysis is useful: it illuminates and describes something. Among other things, perhaps, what it can help us to see are the many ways in which a theologically articulated form of enmity (the enmity between life and death) finds ample and easy homologies in the oppositional dimensions of American politics today. But Sharpe reminds us that it is also possible to think about life and death otherwise. With this in mind, it remains important to question what normative descriptive limits Schmitt's framework might also place on our thinking.

Schmitt's ideas have become a popular diagnostic tool for scholars in the humanities to explore the theological genealogies of modern ideas that appear, on the surface, to be secular. To some extent Schmitt's work serves a primarily descriptive function. Adam Kotsko has reflected on the ways in which Schmitt's interrogation of political theology has itself unfolded into a more general, or widely ranging, conversation about the relationships between theology and politics. What Kotsko sees, in the resurgence of interest in Schmitt's work in recent years, is a building sense of cross-disciplinary curiosity about the "sheer fact of transfer" between politics and theology.[15] Kotsko argues that Schmitt's work on political theology can, itself, give rise to two different modes of doing political theology. On the one hand, Schmitt offers a study of the political itself as grounded within what is essentially "a singular, personal, omnipotent sovereign." On the other hand, Schmitt's work has also offered the occasion for what Kotsko describes as "a nonreductionist analysis of the homologies between political and theological or metaphysical systems."[16] This second form of political theology is more along the lines of what Schmitt himself described as a "sociology of concepts."[17] Kotsko understands this second form of political theology to be something like a "study of systems of legitimacy, of the ways that political, social, economic, and religious orders maintain their explanatory power and justify the loyalty of their adherents."[18] Political theology as a sociology of concepts is inherently genealogical. It understands political ideas to be traceable, via genealogy, to the theological. Because of this, Kotsko suggests, political theology seeks not only to "document the past" but, more, "to make it available as a tool to think with." Genealogies, he suggests, can be "creative attempts to reorder our relationship with the past and present in order to reveal fresh possibilities for the future."[19] Political theological genealogies can look to the past to creatively reorder the future. To some extent, then, part of what Schmitt's thinking offers is a description. And another part of what Schmitt's thinking offers is the illumination of a normative framework for putting life and death in a relation that can be critiqued and resisted. I agree with Tommy Lynch, who argues that even while using Schmitt's analyses (to describe or diagnose political theology) it remains important to question and critique the "simplicity" of some of Schmitt's claims.[20]

Jacob Taubes observed that Schmitt's attempt to render enmity into a concept for political theology may have also been partially responsible for defusing some of the violence embedded within a theological figuration of the enemy. Schmitt, in other words, presents something more like a soft enmity—a more harmless form of enmity—for political thought. In this sense, perhaps, what his analysis does is to tone down or defuse what was once a more violent form of enmity. "Theologians are inclined to define the enemy as something that has to be destroyed," Taubes noted. Relevant here for Taubes, perhaps, is the voice of Paul, who declares death to be the last enemy and proclaims the necessary or inevitable destruction of that enemy (1 Corinthians 15:26). Indeed, Paul was foundational for Taubes's own reading of political theology.[21] Taubes read Paul's letter to the Romans as a "political declaration of war."[22] And it was out of Paul's letters that Taubes appears to have read the figure of the theological enemy—the enemy of God—in the first place.[23] While Paul does not proclaim death to be the enemy, in his letter to the Romans (this declaration was unique to his letter to the Corinthians), Gil Anidjar argues that it is still possible "to follow a significant thread or path in Romans—one could even call it a warpath—whereby the figure of the theological enemy emerges as an uncertain preview or repetition of what Paul elsewhere calls 'the last enemy,' death."[24] The theological enemies—those who oppose God or who have been abandoned by God—are thus destined for destruction. This is not, necessarily, because the enemy must be destroyed by the followers of Jesus themselves (although, of course, for centuries many followers have offered such assistance nevertheless). Rather, the theological enemy is destined for destruction because the enemy of God is allied with death. Indeed, we might even suggest that the enemy of God *can* be loved by Christians precisely because of the fact that this enemy's powers are considered illusory in the face of this inevitable destruction. The certain destruction of the theological enemy facilitates an easier form of pity and love for the enemy, who is destined for annihilation.

Taubes seems to suggest that Schmitt's political theological scheme of enmity emerges with a different dynamic. The secularizing function of political theology, in other words, ultimately softens this enmity. Schmitt's formulation of enmity is not destined, as a theologically articulated enmity like Paul's, to find its central impulse in the drive toward cosmic or divine destruction. Taubes argued that it was one thing to be a theologian and another to be a legal theorist or jurist. Schmitt was the latter, so he was attempting to "find a way of evading the final consequences of this theological definition of the enemy."[25] Schmitt sought to justify the world as it is, said Taubes, not to destroy it.[26] What Taubes articulates in this commentary, argues Mike Grimshaw, is that in political theology the enemy becomes not a figure to destroy but simply one who must be opposed. Taubes makes the observation that, within political discourses on enmity, the enemy remains "central to one's self-identity." So to destroy the enemy is "in the end, to destroy oneself or, at the very least, to lose one's self-identity."[27] Enmity, in political theology, moves out of a theological discourse of divine destruction and into a more ambiguous sphere of opposition. Schmitt's political theology, in secularizing a theological form of enmity, seems to soften the destructive drives embedded within this enmity. So Schmitt explores a view of enmity that is defused, in a critical sense, as it is secularized.

Perhaps, then, Schmitt's political theology of enmity—which places life and death into the friend-enemy distinction—is not as problematic as I have been arguing? Perhaps all it does is introduce a kind of gentle political opposition into the lifedeath relation, toning down what would become (if it were theological) a more inflammatory and destructive form of opposition? I am skeptical that this political theology, which can be described and articulated as a Schmittian frame, is really so protected from the cosmic destruction of a theologically informed enmity. One claim that Lynch urges particular caution with is the relative ease with which Schmitt converts the theological into the political. Such a smooth conversion, Lynch says, "too readily accepts an easy division between the theological and the political—a division which is itself both theological and political."[28] That is to say, the distinction between what is to be considered religious, and what is not, is a distinction internal to the development of Christian theology itself. Perhaps, then, the political theology of death—articulated as a dimension of the politics of enmity—is more aimed at or oriented toward destruction and annihilation than it would seem.

What is it, exactly, that prevents Schmitt's political theological opposition from becoming destructive? If the relation of enmity that gives shape to Schmitt's political theology of the enemy is a theological one, and if it is fundamentally oriented around destruction (grounded in the hope of the enemy's divine destruction), then what *ends* this destructiveness? *Can* it be ended? Or does it simply appear more distant, perhaps temporally? Even if Schmitt's political theology of the enemy defuses this enmity by snipping some of its ties to the figure of God, it does not end the theopolitics of enmity. This theopolitical form of enmity continues to operate in other registers and discourses of the political. In this sense, then, even a defused political theology of enmity (that feeds opposition rather than destruction) is always hovering on the edge of destruction. In American politics, particularly among actors on the political right, the figure of God frequently reappears to grant authority to the right's claim to occupy the position of "friend of life." When do these symbolic appearances also signal a return to a more fundamentally destructive form of enmity? Is there ever such a moment of "return" that can be marked? Or is the return always immanent within the political theology of the enemy? Is the oppositionality of a political theology of the enemy always latently stirring with destructive tension?

I am inclined to read the antagonistic, oppositional tensions of enmity as bound (even if loosely) to latent forms of destruction. In relations of enmity, then, I read a fundamental orientation toward destruction. But what I am not interested in, at present, is a wholesale dismissal of the concept of enmity. Nor am I making the argument that all forms of destruction, or all attempts at destruction, are bad and should be ended. I am not

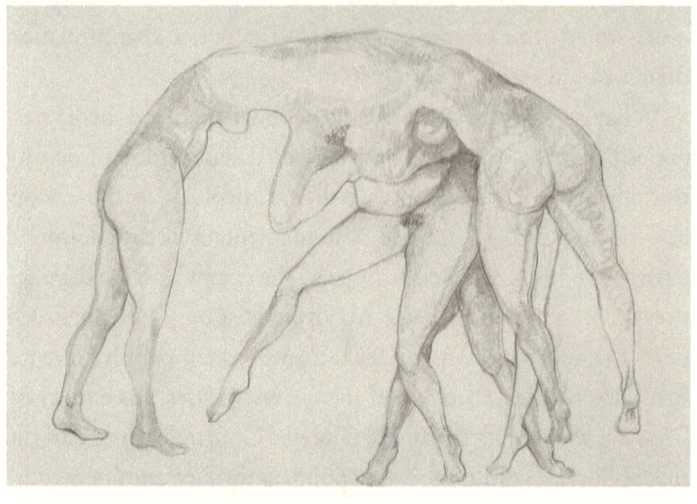

FIGURE 5.3 Krista Dragomer, *Untitled Sketch (group movement)*, 2019

unfurling a pacifistic political diatribe (although, I would also note, neither am I declaring myself to be opposed to pacifism). As I have already intimated, I am skeptical of attempts to do away with enmity as such. But neither is enmity my target. Rather, I am interested in the fact that the lifedeath relation has come to be, over many centuries in Western thought, predominantly configured as a relation of enmity. And what I would like to argue for is the poetic, practical, and political inappropriateness of this model of relation for lifedeath. At least at present.

THE BIOMYTHICAL POETICS OF SISTERHOOD

I was trained, intellectually, in the field of constructive theology. What this means is that I have been trained to understand the critical functions of theology in a particular manner. There are many debates, internal to constructive theology, about what exactly constructive theology is or does. For my purposes here, I would simply point out that part of what I understand to be inherent to constructive theology is a particular kind of speculative enterprise. Constructive theology is critical. Indeed, as a field it was founded by such figures as the feminist theologian Sallie McFague, who sought to dissemble the Christian figure of an omnipotent patriarchal God. But for McFague and other constructive theologians, this critical enterprise always included a form of thinking otherwise. McFague's interest was in a kind of critical decimation, and yet she was also interested in thinking about, as she put it, different models for God.[29] What sort of divinity is left behind, when the patriarchal form crumbles? In this sense, then, the critical functions of constructive theology are accompanied by dimensions of constructive elaboration.

Theology is, more often than not, a discourse about power or a conversation about the nature of power. Typically, in Christian thought, theology has been a discourse on power in its most absolute sense. But we might also qualify theology as a conversation about forms of power that remain inescapably more than human or more than creaturely (forms of power that will forever elude and escape us, such as the powers of life and death). So thinking about theology means thinking about the more than human shapes of power that leave their marks on human life, without ceasing to be radically differentiated from it. And it also means thinking about where those power dynamics have become corrosive or damaging: critique. But constructive theology also involves configuring speculative models for thinking otherwise—models that not only point to the places where things have begun to rust and corrode but that sand off the rust and prime it. Or that pour salt on the rust and then live in the clearings left behind. In constructive theology, part of critique is counterpoetics. To use a different metaphor, in constructive theology the point is not to simply stand before a canvas and speak about the problem of the image. Rather, the point is to stick a knife into the canvas, cut something out, and create another way of seeing the form itself: another dimension of illumination, another poetics.

Audre Lorde argued that poetry and poetics were not simply an artistic practice (a kind of social luxury) but instead a necessary form of thinking. Poetry, wrote Lorde, is "a revelatory distillation of experience, not the sterile word play that, too often, the white fathers distorted the word *poetry* to mean."[30] Poetry offers another mode of thinking apart from what the "white fathers" offered, said Lorde (the philosophical pattern informing us that we think, therefore we are). Instead, wrote Lorde, "the Black mother within each of us—the poet—whispers in our dreams: I feel, therefore I can be free."[31] Poetics, said Lorde, is not about creating another way of thinking but instead about mapping another way of feeling. "There are no new ideas. There are only new ways of making them felt—of examining what these ideas feel like being lived on Sunday morning at 7 A.M., after brunch, during wild love, making war, giving birth, mourning our dead—while we suffer the old longings, battle the old warnings and fears of being silent and impotent and alone, while we taste new possibilities and strengths."[32] Poetry is ultimately, for Lorde, another way of illuminating the worlds we are working through. "The quality of light by which we scrutinize our lives has direct bearing upon the product which we live, and upon the changes we hope to bring about through those lives," she writes. And so, "it is within this light that we form those ideas by which we pursue our magic and make it realized. This is poetry as illumination, for it is through poetry that we give name to those ideas which are—until the poem—nameless and formless, about to be birthed, but already felt."[33]

By gesturing toward the sisterhood relation in lifedeath, I have been attempting to call up a counterpoetics to the political theology of death that is structured on enmity. I want to create a kind of perceptible absence, perhaps, a hole or a vacuum in the political theology of death. I want to, if only for an instant, destabilize this political theology. And I want to help illuminate another possible way of feeling through it. I want to disturb and disrupt the logic that it's founded on. I do not deny the antagonism that structures the lifedeath relation in the political theology of death. It is, instead, to speak about it, to speak differently about it. I do not imagine that this interruption will *purify* discourses on lifedeath. But perhaps I can toss a little rosewater on them, to provide a fresh tonic. Perhaps, in disrupting the political theology of death with another logic—a counterpoetics—it might be possible to disrupt this political theology just long enough to unsettle the antagonism in lifedeath that has been rendered as enmity. And perhaps this disruption will be just disturbing enough that this antagonism might be differently rendered, or differently understood. Perhaps the complex antagonisms and affinities of the lifedeath relation can be understood as bonds of sisterhood rather than a form of enmity that seeks to destroy a precious enemy.

Discourses on life and death tend, often, to traffic in the biomythical. They offer us glimpses into what are, in one sense, simple biological phenomena. From another angle, they are biological phenomena that structure every aspect of our cultural and political lives. Because of this, we cannot help but describe such phenomena with rhetorical and discursive flourishes. In this sense, perhaps, sisterhood is an apt description of the lifedeath relation. Lifedeath is—itself—a deeply biomythical form of relation. Sisterhood, too, is biomythical. Sisterhood describes actual relations between bodies—it describes a form of kinship that one might reduce to blood ties or biology. But it is also a form of relation that extends far beyond these blood bonds and functions without them.

Sisterhood, Christine Downing observed in a reflection on the troubled discourse of sisterhood in the second-wave feminist movement, is a dimension of relational experience that serves to both "challenge and nurture us," even as "we sometimes disappoint and betray one another."[34] Sisterhood is "a deeply interdependent relationship" that "sustains us even as we fail one another."[35] Sisterhood is a source of uplift, even though it is also ambivalent (often a source of disappointment or betrayal). Sisterhood is not a source of redemption or salvation. But it can become a dimension of mutual empowerment. The feminist movement (particularly in its second wave), Downing argues, clearly highlighted the importance of sisterhood. But more often than not, the bond was conceived by the movement in "highly idealized terms." Willfully dismissive of its antagonistic dimensions, this made feminist forms of sisterhood even more subject to "intense feelings of disillusionment."[36] Downing contends, then, that conceiving of sisterhood as a relation that is not only metaphorical but actual and biological might offer a more "resilient and complex sense of what sisterhood might mean."[37] Reflecting on her relationship with her own biological sister, Downing argues that a sister is "the other most like ourselves of any creature in the world." And yet, a sister is also "ineluctably, *other*." In sisterhood there is a simultaneous and paradoxical sense of "likeness and difference, intimacy and otherness."[38] Notably, sisterhood is not a chosen relationship but instead one that is ascribed. There is something in this ascription that renders it safe for expressing forms of hostility and aggression.[39] I would contrast this antagonism with enmity, which is a form of opposition that (especially when it becomes theological, argued

FIGURE 5.4 Krista Dragomer, *Untitled Sketch (conversation companion)*, 2019

Taubes) seems inevitably drawn toward destruction. In sisterhood there is an intimacy that can hold hostility and aggression without being destroyed or undone by it.

Downing also maintains that discourses on sisterhood tend to traffic in death and mortality. This is true for biological sisters, of course, who are mortal companions. But Downing also argues that in myth, one can encounter the sort of complex and ambivalent form of sisterhood that we see among biological sisters. Myths of sisterhood seem to remain bound to death and mortality, as well. One of the reasons Downing makes this claim is that when she set out to look for myths of sisterhood among divine figures in the Ancient Greek tradition, she found none. She did, however, encounter many tales about mortal sisters in Greek myth. Part of this, perhaps, was simply due to the fact that the sisterhood relation is one between women, which was "more invisible to the Greeks than the maternal or fraternal one."[40] But many of the Greek tragedies were oriented around sisterhood. The frequent appearance of sisters in the tragic genre is undoubtedly due, in part, to the many ways in which women were also oppressed. Women are often dealt death. As characters, as in life, women were "betrayed, raped, rendered voiceless" and "previously restricted in their capacity to retaliate." Yet, in defiance of this, many of these tragic sisters often remain "utterly committed to each other" and "able to find a way of communicating."[41] Often the communications of sisterhood occur in these difficult spaces where intimate tragedy hovers just above the world of the dead. Antigone, for instance, is a paradigmatic Greek sister figure. And she pulls the bonds of sisterhood deeper into the ambivalent and ambiguous zones of lifedeath in her own failure to find a home with either the living or the dead.

In the commingling of death, mortality, and sisterhood in these figures of myth, Downing argues that we see another model of sisterhood that the second-wave feminist movement did not clearly evoke. Feminist discourses on sisterhood, she says, often sound "thin and unconvincing" because they "have little prepared us for the ambivalences that seem inevitably to intrude when women bond deeply with women."[42] But in myths of sisterhood we see something that resembles, more nearly, the function of sisterhood as a living bond. Sisterhood, says Downing, teaches us "our limits." It teaches us "that we are contingent, finite, and mortal beings. Sisters teach us that someday we will die—and that this is simply a part of having been here at all."[43]

Sisterhood, as both a biological phenomenon and a mythology, is a lesson on limits, limitations, and limit conditions. Sisterhood provides an acknowledgment of absolute otherness as a form of limit. But within this otherness there is not only antagonism but also a bond of mutual feeling, of care, and of commonality that stretches even across this unbridgeable distance. This is a form of care that encourages growth—it makes you stretch. In this sense, then, a sisterhood dynamic can provide both a fundamental limit or boundary line and yet also a structure of mutual growth and support. Sisterhood is a reminder of the limit on life that is death, but it is also a reminder of the ways in which life limits death and exceeds it. These limits are both nurturing and antagonistic. And these limit discourses are, in their way, also theological.

In Lorde's work, perhaps, we see a clear evocation of the resilient and complex form of sisterhood that Downing is searching for. Lorde also understood the dynamics of sisterhood in a different manner than Downing. Not only would Lorde have experienced the limits of sisterhood in a feminist movement that oscillated around the concerns of white women, but as a Black woman Lorde would have understood sisterhood itself (as a form of relation between Black women) differently. Sisterhood, for Lorde, is deeply paradoxical and riven with both intimacy and otherness. Lorde clearly articulates the possibilities of sisterhood and the many forms of dream work that emerge from it. And yet, neither does Lorde lose sight of how deeply difficult and fraught sisterhood can be. In her work, sisterhood may be celebrated but it is not idealized. Lorde's sense of sisterhood is tactile and complex. Speaking, particularly, of the sense of sisterhood she experiences with other Black women, Lorde acknowledges its power. "We have the stories of Black women who healed each other's wounds, raised each other's children, fought

FIGURE 5.5 Krista Dragomer, *Biopolitical Propositions*, 2019

each other's battles, tilled each other's earth, and eased each other's passages into life and death," Lorde writes. "We know the possibilities of support and connection for which we all yearn, and about which we dream." And yet despite this, Lorde writes, "connections between Black women are not automatic by virtue of our similarities, and the possibilities of genuine connection between us are not easily achieved."[44] The experience of sisterhood is no guarantee of rich connection, even if it does generate dreams about such connective possibility.

Lorde speaks, especially, about the anger that she sometimes directs toward other Black women or that other Black women direct toward her because of her sexuality. "The anger with which I meet another Black woman's slightest deviation from my immediate need or desire or concept of a proper response is a deep and hurtful anger, chosen only in the sense of a choice of desperation—reckless through despair." This is a pain, says Lorde, "that we are so separate who should be most together."[45] There is a deep sense of conflict in Lorde's experience of sisterhood. "I cannot shut you out the way I shut the others out so maybe I can destroy you," she writes. The experience of this separation, writes Lorde, is a consequence of (is fed by) the white hatred that Black women have coped with: a mode of experience so mundane that it becomes an experience of the self. In it, commonality serves to set sisters against one another rather than bind them together.[46] "We learned to savor the taste of our own flesh before any other because that was all that was allowed us," Lorde writes. "And we have become to each other unmentionably dear and immeasurably dangerous."[47]

In spite of, or simply in the midst of, this sense of danger Lorde also writes about a hunger for this sisterhood. "I am hungry for Black women who will not turn from me in anger and contempt even before they know me or hear what I have to say," she writes. "We are, after all, talking about different combinations of the same borrowed sounds."[48] This longing endures within the antagonisms of sisterhood: "Oh sister, where is that dark rich land we wanted to wander through together?"[49] Sisterhood, as Lorde describes it, is a paradoxical inner conflict, one that is driven by both "a strong and ancient tradition of bonding and mutual support, and the memorized threads of that tradition that exist within each of us," as well as "the anger and suspicion engendered by self-hate."[50]

For both Downing and Lorde, of course, these reflections on sisterhood are a reflection on the relations between women. I am turning to them for articulations of, descriptions of, evocations of sisterhood. And yet I do not—here—intend to say anything in particular about relationships between women. Instead, I want to think about sisterhood as something that functions on the level of a sign or a symbol, sisterhood as a vehicle for communicating information—sisterhood as a kind of biomythical poetics. What Downing and Lorde help me to see or understand is sisterhood as a coded pattern of relation—one that is both actual and imagined, both biological and mythical. I am interested in what this pattern of relation might help us to see, or to say, about lifedeath. It is not incidental, however, that sisterhood describes a relation between women. In the political theology of death, which feeds and foments the enmity between life and death, life has become locked to the figure of God—traditionally considered a divine patriarch. And in the long history of the West, as thinkers like Beauvoir have argued, women have been consistently co-implicated with death. Life, then, becomes masculinized in proximity to God. And death, the beloved enemy, is often the feminized force destined for divine destruction or annihilation. We see this, even, in Francis's description of death as a sister. But if life and death are invoked as figures in a sisterly relation, this recodes the relational dynamics in a number of ways.

To describe the lifedeath relation as one of sisterhood is to invoke the absolute otherness, as well as the inevitable intimacies, of life and death. It is to see, in the relation between life and death, forms of mutual support and uplift, as well as competition and antagonism. If the political theology of death has cast life and death as enemies, then a counterpoetics of sisterhood advances a view that is both more complex and less determinate. If the political theology of death seems to hold forth the promise that those friends of life (those friends of God) will be rescued from the grip of death, the biomythical poetics of sisterhood offers no such redemptive promise. If there is a form of sisterhood in lifedeath, then it is a profoundly intimate bond that endures in the midst of what also feels like danger. This is not a bond of mutual destruction (which is not to say that destructive impulses do not arise, from time to time, within it), but something that is both more nurturing and yet also more ambivalent. In this bond of sisterhood there is disappointment and betrayal, as well as mutual empowerment.

If, as Lorde has put it, we sometimes find it difficult to discern where one sister begins and the other ends, we can also say the same thing about life and death. Indeed, this is precisely what the term lifedeath marks. We often have difficulty understanding where it is that life ends and death begins (or vice versa)—even *if* we also understand that they are ineluctably other and not the same at all. Perhaps life and death work, to use Lorde's phrasing, with different combinations of the same borrowed sounds. Perhaps we feel betrayed by the many ways in which life and death betray one another, and we are terrified of the many ways in which they are unspeakably dangerous to one another. And when we ritualize practices for grief and mourning that performatively weave life and death back together again, what we hope to illuminate are not those betrayals or dangers but instead those dimensions of rich resonance where life and death are most together, helping one another through the difficult passages.

FIGURE 6.1 Krista Dragomer, *Synodic Portal 8*, 2020

6

NATAL DISTURBANCE

All theology, as Marcella Althaus-Reid has made potently clear, is sexual theology. Every theology implies, or implicates, a particular sexual position. "Based on sexual categories and heterosexual binary systems, obsessed with sexual behavior and orders, every theological discourse is implicitly a sexual discourse,"[1] Althaus-Reid explained. Grace Jantzen seemed to be acknowledging this in her claim that Western theology and philosophy—dominated by men—has always been "necrophilic." That is to say, Western thinking exhibits a "pathological erotic attraction to corpses or things associated with dead bodies."[2] The sexual position of Western philosophy and theology, Jantzen suggests, is necrophilic. We see this, Jantzen argued, in the cultural fascination with death and violence that characterizes Western modernity. Western culture is violent and deadly because Western minds (or the minds of the men who have claimed to know the mind) have been perversely obsessed with death.

Jantzen contended (echoing Beauvoir's claim that the fear of death is a fear of women) that this necrophilia is gendered—fed by a misogynistic fear of both birth and bodies that birth. But Jantzen also argued that this resentment of birth fed a love of death, as if to hide from birth is to take shelter in death. Those who live in the modern West, said Jantzen, are confronted with a "joyless habitus" that is now "acting out a long history of gendered violence and death."[3] Western philosophy has sought to illuminate a universal bond between all subjects through the claim that (as Socrates notoriously put it) "all men are mortal." Jantzen cautioned that this was not a simple statement of fact but, instead, an attempt to construct a sense of human subjectivity.[4] To claim that our fundamental bond is our mortality is to suggest that we find our human truth only in death. The remedy for this, Jantzen argued, is to focus on our bonds in birth or natality rather than death or mortality. Only in this way, only by countering and so "resolving the obsession with death," can there be "hope for life," she maintained.[5] The symbolic of birth was, for Jantzen, a therapeutic resource to disrupt the gloomy "imaginary of death" haunting an androcentric Western intellectual culture.[6] Birth and natality, she said, promote a "symbolic of flourishing, of growth and fruition."[7]

Jantzen, we might say, seeks to flip the script on what she considers the sexual theology of Western philosophy and theology. If the sexual position of this tradition has been a misogyny that drives a perverse erotic attraction to violence and death, then Jantzen wanted to advance a different position—one that was biophilic rather than necrophilic. In natality Jantzen saw a counterpoint to this misogyny. Birth, she suggests, points toward something life-positive that is inherently biophilic. Natality, read primarily out of the work of Hannah Arendt, is not the same as birth. Indeed, Arendt distinguished natality from birth more rigorously than did Jantzen. Nevertheless, Arendt does not own the figure of natality and, despite philosophical efforts to cordon natality off from birth, such efforts fall apart in the everydayness of life and language. Medically, obstetrically, the language of biological birth continues to be natal. This language fuses with experiences of birth, and it effectively casts a natal dimension on the process. I appreciate Jantzen's critique, especially her demand that birth (the sticky emergence of life) be taken as seriously—in a philosophical sense—as the speculative and futuristic end of life.[8] I would agree that, in fracturing life from death and assuming a relation of pure enmity between the two, Western philosophers and theologians have tended to focus myopically and resentfully on the deathbound limits of embodiment. Natality and birth do generate a different locus of attention; they illuminate particular dimensions and intensities in life processes. But I also think that Jantzen's critical project remains structured by—rather than disruptive of—a set of binary distinctions.

Jantzen is, to begin with, still deeply beholden to the binary distinctions structured by the political theology of death. In her analysis, life and death remain bifurcated and in a state of war. She seeks to destabilize the dominance of death, and she argues that the way to do this is by advancing the powers of life over and against death. But, in this way, Jantzen's analysis continues to weaponize one against the other. She is still beholden, furthermore, to the binary distinction between man and woman. If the history of Western philosophy and theology has been dominated by men, she is perhaps pushing for an imaginary that is dominated by women. But the figures that she rouses in this association—birth, natality—are essential to the imaginary of women only in an essentialist sense. Only, that is to say, by a logic that associates women with biological reproduction. This sexual position is reproductive. There are ambivalent and troubling dimensions of natality—non-biophilic and death-dealing dimensions of natality, we might even say—that Jantzen's analysis does not explore.

In this chapter I argue that conceptual celebrations of birth and natality, such as Jantzen's, often tend to harbor the political theology of death within them. When Jantzen, for instance, sharply bifurcates birth (as a force of life) from death she deepens the ancient enmity between life and death. She did clarify that her aim was not to set up a binary (natality versus mortality) but was instead to argue that there has historically been a "fundamental imbalance of attention" in Western thinking.[9] Ultimately, however, Jantzen's accusation that those who contemplate death are necrophilic does, in its way, harbor a form of enmity toward death and those who think it. More, to lift up birth as a force on the side of life, *rather than* the side of death, only serves to feed this enmity. Birth and natality are presented as a domain of positivity and uplift. But this is a sanitized view of birth. Embodied birthing processes are not free of death but are riven within it in complicated and problematic ways. With this in mind, I reflect on a set of natal disruptions or disturbances. Black feminist critiques of reproductive discourses and psychoanalysis help me, especially, in this chapter to highlight the deep ambivalence of birth and natality. Birth itself has always been death-laden. The outcome of a birth is, often, not more life but death. On a long enough timeline, death is the outcome of all birth. Natality bears death within it, just as mortality is full of the forces of life and rife with novelty. There are burdens in being born, and abilities that emerge only in the face of, or wake of, death. In the idea—endemic especially to Western intellectual history—that life is "bookmarked" by birth and death, one comes to be associated with beginnings and the other with endings. But our lives, as we live through and into them, are not contained by these phenomena as if we were living through a linear narrative that begins clearly in the birth chapter and ends with death. Our lives are constantly interrupted and newly informed by births and deaths. Natality and mortality are phenomena of lifedeath. What emerges, when life emerges, are livingdying entities: natalmortals.

NATAL SECRETS

Jantzen's reading of natality is, of course, founded on Arendt's philosophy of natality. When we examine the emergence of natality, as a concept, what I find both fascinating and illuminating is how much its own emergence is founded on a set of constitutive elisions—a set of secrets. Natality seems to emerge as a concept that is ready to solve a set of philosophical problems: issues derived from (and in tension with) the metaphysical heritage of Western theology and philosophy. But in order to solve these problems, natality needs to harbor a set of secrets. Natality needs to disguise its own processes of emergence, and it needs to keep its deeper alliances and histories hidden or obscured.

I have already written, in an earlier chapter, about Heidegger's natal negative. One dimension of his attempt to destruct the history of Western ontology was to strategically lift natality up from what I described as the constellated negative shaped by Western metaphysics. Heidegger recognized the enmity toward death, in the history of Western metaphysics, and believed that part of resisting this ontological legacy was to think death differently. He troubled at the constellated negative of Western metaphysics. But Calvin Warren and Zakiyyah Iman Jackson illuminate Heidegger's failure to see the fuller dimensions of this constellated negative in his failure to think blackness. Heidegger did appear to be aware, on some level, of the co-implicated negative dimensions of both death and birth in Western metaphysics. In this sense, then, he saw the disruptive potential of bringing them together or illuminating their proximities. To think of Heidegger as a philosopher of natality is, perhaps, counterintuitive in that many more familiar genealogies of natality tend to read his fixation on being-toward-death in diametric opposition to Arendt's being-toward-birth. Thinkers such as Jantzen, for instance, critique Heidegger's morbid fixation on death and read natality as a kind of tonic to counteract this fixation. But as Anne O'Byrne has noted, while Heidegger *explicitly* privileges mortality in *Being and Time*, and perhaps even obscures natality with this fixation, he is nevertheless deeply dependent upon natality for thinking Dasein.

In *Being and Time*, natality tends to appear under the guise of either thrownness or historicity, argues O'Byrne. And it is through its connectedness to both birth *and* death that Dasein is able to come clearly to light, for Heidegger. Because natality is, for him, thrownness, O'Byrne notes that natal anxiety functions to underscore the "groundlessness of our finite existence." It is through natality and natal anxiety that Dasein is not only thrown *toward* death but also how we acknowledge that "*this* Dasein did not always exist."[10] So it is that, without natality, Dasein would not be thrown toward (or conscious of) death in the first place.

I also argued that there is a natal dimension to the death work that Heidegger is doing in *Being and Time*. While mortality forces an acknowledgment of our own contingency in the sense that our bodies will ultimately cease to live, natality forces an acknowledgement of our contingency in the sense that we did not make ourselves. It is only through a full sense of our contingency (informed by both dimensions) that we are able to understand that we will die. While Heidegger might argue, vociferously, that we do not really experience being-toward-death when we live through the death of *others* (rather than our own death),[11] and so the experience of death is consequently individual and non-relational,[12] the natality of Dasein ensures that we cannot understand death at all without "grasping the past" that throws us toward death.[13] That past is not our own, or ownmost, but entirely other—it is ancestral and inherited. Death, for Heidegger, is not biological (that kind of death is perishing) but existential. And Heidegger does attempt to militate against the way that others seek to publicly interpret the meaning of death, encroaching on our own individual existential assessment of death.[14] Nevertheless, what he does not acknowledge is that we cannot understand the experience of futurity that is being-toward-death without the historicity facilitated by our natality. This historicity binds us to other generations, and these bonds with the ancestral generate our sense of groundless thrownness. While we are always free to reencounter and reshape the existential meaning of this death on our own terms, it is living through the death of others, through cross-generational social teachings about death and rites of burial, that natality continues to craft our being-toward-death. Heidegger does some of this natal labor himself in crafting a social and intellectual understanding of death. He performs the care of Dasein in an attempt to mitigate the traumatic effects of being-toward-death.

Arendt embraced natality more explicitly than Heidegger. For this reason, she is typically cited in genealogies of the concept. Like Heidegger, her conceptualization of natality was founded in an attempt to resist the legacies of Western metaphysics. But, like Heidegger, she does not seem to be aware of the fact that because she is pulling from the well of Western metaphysics' constellated negative, she is lifting up a concept that will need to keep its own metaphysical origins a secret, in order to play the resistant role she needs it to. The history of Arendt's philosophy of natality illustrates the extent to which this concept actually originated within metaphysics rather than physical processes such as childbirth, or the bodies of children. The original draft of her dissertation on Augustine of Hippo did not include any direct references to the concept of natality. But she returned to this work about thirty years later and added the term in. In other words, while she may not have had a word for it yet, there were already intimations of natality in her earliest intellectual work. It would appear, at least on one level, that Arendt was formulating her theory of natality as a counterpoint to Augustine's metaphysical theology. Her philosophy of natality was, in other words, born out of Western metaphysics and not the physical experience of a birth event.

For Arendt, however, the philosophy of natality was also a *critique* of Western metaphysics. In her published revisions to this text, she argued that Augustine—like so many other thinkers in the Western metaphysical tradition—was obsessed with death. Augustine, she argued, believed that the future of life on Earth was nothing other than death. For him, life was "determined by death" and might even "more properly be called death."[15] He was awaiting the next stage, after life. But to Arendt what this effectively meant (from a standpoint within the world) was nothing but death. In *Life of the Mind*, Arendt again lamented Augustine's fixation on death, arguing that while he himself clearly saw that "every man, being created in the singular, is a new beginning by virtue of his birth," he failed to draw the necessary conclusion that this made us *natals* instead of *mortals*.[16]

Here, Arendt is both sourcing and turning away from Augustine's metaphysical theology. She borrows from him the dimension of novelty and the symbolic of a new beginning but seeks to excise the negative pulse of death. She makes it clear that natality should be viewed as a disruptive and oppositional concept—an alternative to the notion that we are mortals. Natality seems to stand in opposition to mortality, as if a thinker must choose a singular mode for thinking subjectivity. Natality is a concept to be contrasted with mortality, not to think alongside it. We are either living or we are dying. We must choose a power with which to align; we are either on the side of life or on the side of death. This sort of false choice rings with the enmity of the political theology of death. In other words, although natality presents itself to Arendt as disruptive, natality also appears to be a theory that contributes to the bifurcation of life and death rather than unsettling such bifurcations. This lends to what I believe is the obfuscating and disembodied view that birth bears no inherent relation to death—as if birth and life could be optimistically sanitized of death. Natality, then, is marked as a site of hope while mortality is pessimistic. And this form of natality is not explicitly about the child but about life itself.

For Arendt the symbolic figure of the child and the future that the child represents were nevertheless at the heart of the notion of natality—if only implicitly. Her natality was not to be thought of as biological birth. In spite of this, it was an ontological principle of action laden with the novelty that comes with birth, with "the new beginning inherent in birth."[17] Adriana Cavarero has argued that in developing her philosophy of natality alongside Augustine's theological metaphysics, Arendt found a way to speak abstractly about birth, informed by and yet discursively "freed from the embarrassing figure of the newborn."[18] For a Christian thinker like Augustine, the baby child of the nativity scene was arguably implicit in his theologic. But the vulnerable, screaming, and imperiously dependent figure of the newborn did not need to be conceptually invoked. It was simply one of the symbolic, scriptural icons of the divine. A theologian like Augustine could, instead, borrow ontologically from such a figure while muting the biological dimensions (less relevant, in a platonic view, to metaphysical reflections). In a theologic like Augustine's there is no diaper to change, only the novelty of life incarnated in another bright star.

Augustine's abstractions enable Arendt's abstractions, leaving her representation of natality, as Cavarero puts it, "quite abstract and cold" as if it were "an homage to the old philosophical vice of sacrificing the real world's complexity to the purity of the concept."[19] In spite of the fact that Arendt resists invoking the figure of the newborn, Cavarero argues that for Arendt, the newborn was still "the undisputed star of the theater of birth," which is to say that "he steals the scene on the stage where life begins."[20] This is not because Arendt celebrates the child explicitly so much as it is that she effaces the figure of the mother (whose body births) from natality. If, for Augustine, the power of the mother who birthed the divine child was contingent (not itself the power of a divinity), she is also contingent to Arendt's analysis. Cavarero's critique of Arendt's erasure of the mother is that it renders what might otherwise be a relational concept (birth or natality) into an "auto-referential" fixation on a singular figure:[21] the novelty of the child.

Arendt seeks to disconnect natality from biological birth. But her philosophy of natality nevertheless seems animated by a sentimental perspective on birth and childhood. This view is severed from the blood, the wounds, the screams, and the scars of birth. It is focused, instead, on the novel emergence of a new human life. This sentimental dimension of natality has, I think, influenced the way that Jantzen theorizes birth and natality. She is not concerned with lifedeath as such or with exploring the role of phenomena such as fermentation or decay in the germination of beauty. Indeed, in passages of Jantzen's work a form of life seems to emerge that has been sanitized of the germination and fermentation of those deaths that have long disgusted the men of Western philosophy. Robin May Schott has argued that because Jantzen's symbolic of death is "wholly negative" she seems to conclude that the "symbolic of natality must be wholly positive."[22]

There is a deceptive and sanitizing sort of optimism in this life-ascendant or life-triumphant reading of natality. Natality reads as a positive construct that can counteract the fearsome or dangerous negativities of our contemporary political moment. If we live in a world dominated by death, and death-driven violence, natality or birth seems to offer refuge, shelter, or perhaps even salvation. If we remove birth from a death-laden frame, this would seem to lift some cloud on the horizon. But a conceptual erasure of death does not make it disappear. Rather than contribute to the infinite repetition of this illusory bifurcation of lifedeath, I think it is crucial to attend to the fact that natality has always (as I argued in an earlier chapter) been bound to the metaphysical negative. Perhaps, in this way, the shifting uncertainties of lifedeath can come into clearer view. Indeed, this may even help to clarify that the positive, uprising dimensions of life are always and already interlaced with death (and other varieties of the negative).

The fact that we find ourselves in the midst of so many death-worlds, in these early decades of the twenty-first century, has inspired direct critiques not only of Arendt's philosophy of natality but of birth and reproduction itself. Natality as a conceptual *and* a biological phenomenon has been targeted for its optimism. David Benatar has argued that, given the current conditions of life on the planet, antinatalism is not misanthropic but philanthropic. Benatar's own position is that "coming into existence is always a serious harm." He suggests that "powerful biological dispositions towards optimism" prevent such a conclusion from resonating with most people. Nevertheless, he insists that natality "always constitutes a net harm."[23] No one alive, he says, "is lucky enough never to have come into existence."[24] Those who procreate are not making noble contributions to humankind but instead are "occupying the tip of a generational iceberg of suffering."[25] Benatar does not argue that joy, happiness, or forms of the good are nonexistent. He acknowledges that both good and bad things happen to those who emerge into existence. But he also argues for a "crucial asymmetry between the good and the bad things." What he means, he elaborates, is that "the absence of bad things, such as pain, is good even if there is nobody to enjoy that good." On the other hand, "the absence of good things, such as pleasure, is bad only if there is somebody who is deprived of these good things." In the absence of entities to experience the bad, what exists is predominantly the good. Therefore, there is more good than bad if there are no existents. His implication is that it is always damaging to bring someone into existence, subjecting them to the suffering of life. For Benatar, "the avoidance of the bad by never existing is a real advantage over existence."[26] Speaking to the possibility of total human extinction (and to the fact that his argument seems to indicate his approval of this possibility) he notes that extinction "may be bad for those who precede it, particularly those who immediately precede it," but in his mind, "the state of human extinction itself is not bad." He argues that it would probably be better "if human extinction happens earlier rather than later."[27]

Perhaps unsurprisingly Benatar's arguments have been met with both approval and total indignation. They rarely fail to cause a reaction. There is some indication that, even for him, this antinatalist position is simply a logical exercise. He seems to harbor an abiding conviction that a biological impulse toward optimism is embedded so deeply in humans that such arguments will forever fail to be more than logical exercises.[28] I am less optimistic about optimism. But I am also less interested in logical exercises. Nor do I have much interest in conversations about birth that contemplate it purely as a matter of choice rather than (also) a matter of accident, compulsion, obligation, or trauma. But I bring up Benatar's position neither to critique nor commend it. Rather, I think it offers a clear illustration of how it is that—in this bleak present—natality as a conceptual icon not only fails to inspire or create hope but also can be read as actively damaging. If Jantzen found a curative, a therapeutic resource, or a source of hope in natality, then antinatalists such as Benatar might argue that this hope is coercive—not a source of thriving but an imposition of suffering. Natality seems to cast a kind of sugar glaze over painful contingencies and attempts to render the future sunny and bright.

Birth itself can be a process full of agony, rife with a sense of the presence of death. This is not to say that it is not beautiful. But the beauty of birth is never without agony. Indeed, it has always been an incredibly dangerous process and many millions of people—largely women—have not lived through to its end or have been killed by the process itself. It is not uncommon (indeed, it is commonplace) to wonder, on the verge or in the midst of labor, if one will see through to its other side. The long and intensifying pain of labor can be mitigated by a flickering but merciful erasure of the senses that might be described as little moments of death. This is a kind of nothing that is also warm, dark, and calm. Birth is full of various forms of agony—why should natality be free of it? Birth is a process that is, in flashes, indistinguishable from death. Why should the concept of natality be read as a counterpoint to this mortality?

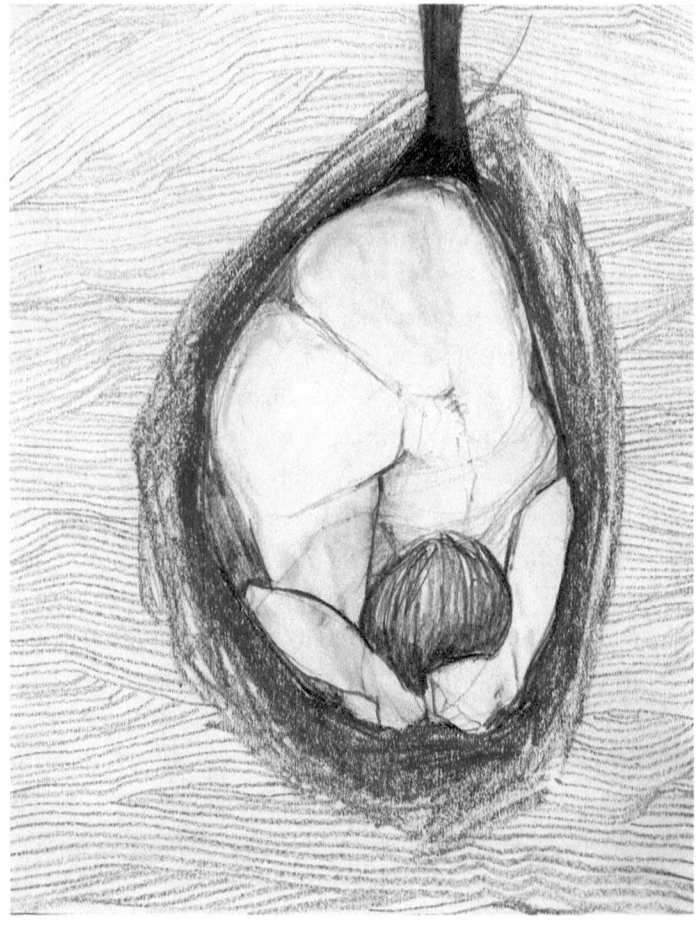

FIGURE 6.2 Krista Dragomer, *Untitled Sketch (growth)*, 2019

Indeed, when we look again at the genealogy of natality—its roots in Western metaphysical theology and philosophy—the lifedeath of natality becomes even more explicit. Just as Arendt's philosophy of natality was not explicitly about birth, or children, it has no apparent relation to God or the theological. But it may also be the case that, when we examine the theological genealogy of natality, we see why the figure remains bound to the constellated negative and why natality might disrupt death but can never become disconnected from it. In order to explore this genealogy of natality, I want to turn back to the work of Arendt, more specifically her reading of Augustine's theologics. There are, arguably, some marks that Augustine's metaphysically driven work may have made on Arendt, despite her resistance. There are shadows haunting the figure of natality. As Julia Lupton has noted, the concept of natality—inspired as it was (at least in part) by Arendt's reading of Augustine—bears the "unremarked marks" of both sexuality and scripture.[29] We have, already, examined some of the disruptive marks that sex, sexuality, birth, and bodies have left on natality. Let us now examine this other dimension.

It is in Arendt's reading of Augustine's formulation of the powerful dimensions of the creature-creator relation that she discovers this focus on birth, novelty, and newness. Lupton observes that Arendt's natality is, in essence, "creatureliness deprived of its divine reference." Natality is creatureliness, secularized. As each new creature was said to have been created, ex nihilo, by the creating God of life, natality, too, is a radical new beginning "beyond any script, testament or dowry that might be laid out for us by family, church, or state."[30] The dimension of futurity, in natality, seems to be borrowed from creatureliness. While the figure of the creature seems to present us with the image of a made, formed, fashioned, or subjected thing, Lupton reminds us that the Latin term *creatura* contained the verbal suffix *-ura*, which indicates that something is about to occur (also present in *futura*, *natura*, and *figura*.) Creatureliness also indicates a form of life "with the sense of continued or potential process, action, or emergence."[31] For this reason, the action and dimension of a process embedded within creatureliness also becomes visible in natality.

What Arendt does not borrow, overtly, from creatureliness is its mortality. In secularizing creatureliness, she seeks to cleanse it of these traces of death. The question is, of course, whether she has effectively discarded it. I have pointed out that, in the development of Christian metaphysics, the creatureliness of Christ is rejected in favor of his divinity. For thinkers like Augustine, creatureliness falls decidedly on the side of mortality. If natality is creatureliness, secularized, then Arendt leaves unremarked that inextricable mark of mortality that is left on natality, even as the most obvious theological residues are wiped away. As is often the case with processes of secularization, she seems to imagine that a figure can be pulled from its ancient context and reinvented without bearing any traces of its ancient heritage. Natality is creatureliness, secularized and reinvented. But the unremarked traces of mortality haunt it like a shadow or a remnant. The marks of mortality endure within natality when we examine its life as a concept. Ultimately, I would argue, to set natality against mortality would be to set natality against itself. It cannot, effectively, be done.

Cavarero has critiqued Arendt's attempted erasure of the mother from the philosophy of birth. This is, she suggests, an attempt to render a relational process into one that is auto-referential. But birth itself is fundamentally relational—it is the process of one literally emerging from another. To think natality as a counterpoint to mortality is, I would argue, a similar attempt to render natality non-relational. Natality becomes an icon for thinking life against death rather than a window through which the sisterhood dimensions of lifedeath become more visible. We see, in examining the theological genealogy of creatureliness, this inextricable dimension of relationality at work within it. The figure of the creature is, after all, inherently relational and cannot be thought without its relational counterpart. Indeed, despite all conceptual assertions of its power, neither does the figure of a creator make sense outside of the relational creature-creator paradigm. What would a creator be without a creation? The creature depends on the creator. But so, too, is the creator inclined toward, or dependent upon, the creature for its own coherence. Theological reflections on creatureliness have focused on different dimensions of the figure. Some, like Nicholas of Cusa, have emphasized the processual elements within creatureliness—what Lupton has identified as the -*ura* of creatures—that drive action. Cusa's suggestion that creatures are "finite infinities" or little "created gods"[32] seems to place a sharper point on these powerful uprising dimensions of creatureliness. Indeed, the creature's close proximity to the figure of the creator seems to instill creatureliness with this power—as if, by pulling so close to the infinite, creatures not only bask in its glow but also begin to radiate its light and heat themselves. Other theologians, such as Augustine, have placed more emphasis on the death-bound mortality of creatures by illustrating a sharper contrast between creature and creator. The creature is distinct from the creator because its life expires and is not eternal. But taken as a figure with its own complex history, creatureliness contains both of these dimensions—power and action as well as vulnerability (with its dependent contingencies).

When we remark on some of the unremarked shadows of natality, the contours of what might be a more complex and ambivalent figure of natality emerge. It may be the case, of course, that natality has accrued value as a concept precisely because of its sharp opposition to its own unremarked marks. Because natality is not a concept directly tied to the birthing body of the mother, its unmarked abstractions may have generated and inspired its conceptual deployment in biopolitical discourses. Miguel Vatter, for instance, has read natality not so much as a theory that makes reference to birth but as a theory that can affirm life in the face of thanatopolitics. As Vatter has put it, natality is a biopolitical concept that offers a direct counter to the thanatopolitical and "a response to the politics of death," which he argues are "implicit in modern biopolitics."[33] Natality, in other words, is a kind of generic life-infused tonic to counteract the death drives of biopolitics. But I wonder if this quest to demonize death isn't a distraction from a more pressing problem in biopolitics—that living, breathing political actors and networks wield death as a political tool of destruction and domination.

Natality, in my analysis, is incapable of offering an infusion of pure life into thanatopolitics because natality is a thinly veiled secularization of creatureliness. This means that natality has always had death and mortality embedded within it. Natality, as creatureliness secularized, has never been a channel or portal to become the human-above-death, though it may have been pulled in that direction. This is why natality has so often been woven into that constellated negative that pulls the darkness of the womb into that set of figures aligned with the negative dimensions of metaphysics. Thinkers like Arendt or Jantzen may have sought to lift natality and birth up into the lighter or more transcendent registers of metaphysics (inspired, perhaps, by the sentimental view of birth that has pervaded Europe and the United States in late modernity). But neither natality nor birth are ever free of the negative, or death.

Ultimately, as Black feminist thinkers help us to see, creatureliness and the natality that it generates might be better understood as sites of disturbance. Creatureliness articulates a form of finitude that explodes powerfully out of, and into, life—it is a process of emergence and a dimension of potency, as if it were the production of a little created god. But it is also a form that expires and decays. Natality, as creatureliness secularized, bears both of these elements within it. But discourses of natality have sought to obscure one of these poles of experience. To set natality against the backdrop of its theological genealogy allows us to disturb or disrupt this way of thinking natality. This theological point of reference highlights natality as a pole of finitude and a figure of lifedeath. Birth is not a triumph over death but a phenomenon that pulses with death and ushers in various forms of death. Birth is like a window through which lifedeath becomes more visible. Birth turns lifedeath inside out, and then inside out again and again, until the relation has been twisted into the shape of a new helix. Natality is not shorn of death, or abstracted from mortality, but a crucial site where the tensions of lifedeath are intensified, made visible, and struggled with. Natality and mortality are different sides of the Möbius strip of lifedeath.

ANOTHER GENERATIONALITY

For those working in Black studies, discussions of birth and natality have never been without dimensions of anguish. Orlando Patterson has famously argued that the institution of slavery, and the social death of the slave, was predicated on natal alienation. Social death, says Patterson, was a process of "social negation" in which a person was "desocialized and depersonalized."[34] It is, in this sense, a kind of living death—a foundational dimension of life is negated or annihilated. In his reading slaves were socially negated (subjected to social death) through natal alienation—removing a person's claims to birth family or extended community, thus stripping the person of the ability to pass these kin ties on to subsequent generations.[35] Patterson described social death as the "outward conception" of the slave's natal alienation, "articulated and reinforced."[36] The process of isolation that is social death is initiated by natal alienation. In this context, clearly, natality is ambivalent and also, in its way, a source of death. He does not make any ontological claims about the nature of birth as such. Nevertheless, natality and birth are clearly bound in problematic ways to death. There is lifedeath in this symbolic of natality.

Black feminists have theorized, more explicitly, the complex role that birth and reproduction played in the institution of slavery, illuminating deeper (more ambivalent) dimensions of both natal anguish and natal power to make and unmake kinship. As Dorothy Roberts has succinctly put it, procreation and reproduction have always been central to white supremacy.[37] "Black procreation," she writes, "helped to sustain slavery, giving slave masters an economic incentive to govern Black women's lives."[38] This laid the groundwork for centuries of reproductive regulation that have permanently shaped American life and politics. "The American legal system is rooted in this monstrous combination of racial and gender domination," says Roberts.[39] Slavery "forced its victims to perpetuate the very institution that subjugated them by bearing children who were the property of their masters."[40] There is, then, a clear sense in which birth and natality bear within them the seeds of suffering, subjugation, and death in this analysis.

Birth does not remain, however, a simple dimension of subjection. "Black women's labors have not been easy to reckon with conceptually," writes Saidiya Hartman. Given that "the future of slavery" in North America "depended upon black women's reproductive capacity," subjection itself is anchored into "black women's reproductive capacities."[41] So Hartman, like Roberts, articulates reproduction not only as a source of, but a continuation of, the violent legacies of slavery. To the extent that slavery "conscripted the womb,"[42] Black women's role as "provider of care" unfolds alongside "her exploitation and use by the world, a world blind to her gifts, her intellect, her talents." Hartman calls it a "brilliant and formidable labor of care," one that has also "been produced through violent structures of slavery, anti-black racism, virulent sexism, and disposability." And yet, despite this, Hartman also notes that this form of care, while it may be "exploited by racial capitalism," cannot be "reducible to or exhausted by it." There is something in it that nourishes, instead, "the latent text of the fugitive," which enables those "who were never meant to survive" to instead "sometimes do just that." This labor of care is freely given; Hartman calls it "the black heart of our social poiesis, of making and relation."[43] Black women's labor can also make apparent, she says, "the gender non-conformity of the black community, its "extended modes of kinship, its queer domesticity, promiscuous sociality and loose intimacy, and its serial and fluid conjugal relations."[44]

Grace Kyungwon Hong highlights the way a disruptive form of temporality in the work of Black feminist thinkers unsettles and disrupts the bifurcation of life and death. The work of Black feminist and queer scholars, argues Hong, is marked by an "insistent refusal to separate life and death." If white liberalism is founded on "the particular disavowal of Black death," Hong argues that Black cultural production is an explicit refusal of this disavowal.[45] It is also a disruption of white discourses on both life and death. Hong illuminates the way that both Black feminist and queer scholars have explored blackness as, "a complex, violent, and violated relationship to normative modes of kinship based on procreation."[46] While this experience of being alienated from "generationality" has often been "characterized as death," Hong argues that this critique fails on at least one level. That is to say, Hong argues that if this experience is to be understood as death, then it also becomes crucial to acknowledge the "generative and proliferative" aspects and conditions of death.[47] Death is not simply a form of absence but might also be marked by "presence and possibility."[48]

The generative and proliferative dimensions of death do not highlight some inherent goodness in death. But they do confound and disrupt the Western metaphysics of life and death. Black feminist thinkers do this, says Hong, precisely by decoupling any automatic link between life and reproduction, instead gesturing toward the proliferative capacities of death. Hong points, for instance, to the work of Hortense Spillers, who notes that "genetic reproduction is not the elaboration of the life-principle in its cultural overlap" but instead "an extension of the boundaries of proliferating properties."[49] Reproduction is not life, and life itself cannot be reduced to reproduction. Rather, reproduction is a form of proliferation. And reproduction is not the only force to sustain proliferation. In conditions of death, too, there are proliferations. Troubling at Patterson's equivocation of natal alienation and social death, Hong notes that Black feminists remind us of what was—nevertheless—inherited and passed down in the death-laden natal conditions. Even social death, Hong suggests, is a form in itself. So, "it is not so much that the 'socially dead' had no function but rather that they performed the function of representing nothingness itself." What was passed down and inherited, even in natal alienation, was not nothing but instead "the status of *nothingness itself*."[50]

Hong compares this queer temporality to Lee Edelman's critique of reproductive futurity. If, for Edelman, the future is reproductive and structured by procreation, then a queer critique repudiates both reproduction and futurity. But Hong suggests that Edelman might too neatly conflate futurity and procreation. What this futurity cannot account for, she says, is the way that forced procreation—as in the conditions of enslavement—is "as much a foreclosing of futurity and identity as the rejection of procreation."[51] Reproduction under conditions of enslavement was not valuable "because it was organized around the kind of sentimentality and affective investment that Edelman presumes."[52] Rather, "the sentimentalized protection of childhood within European/American bourgeois society was materially dependent on enslavement, with its thoroughly unsentimental, economic attitude to enslaved procreation."[53] In conditions of reproduction enforced and maintained through the institution of slavery, both birth/natality and death/mortality operate simultaneously as foreclosure and possibility. Here we see, perhaps, formations of natality and mortality that each—in their way—illuminate lifedeath.

Is there a whiteness to the natality that thinkers such as Arendt and Jantzen articulate? There is, at least, a dimension of erasure that enables whiteness. And natality is used in their work in an effort to sanitize life of its death. Natality emerges as part of an effort to cleanse birth of its metaphysical roots in the negative—to somehow remove the traces of that constellated negative that remain so difficult for life to shake off, those contingent but ideologically fixed bonds between figures such as death, nothingness, blackness, or the mysterious and almost invisible space of the birthing womb. It seems that in thinking natality, philosophers such as Jantzen and Arendt sought to unplug natality from the negative and plug it, instead, straight into the pure positivity of metaphysical life. Black feminist critiques of reproduction, however, illustrate the failure of such sanitizing gestures. This highlights, we might say, the death drives that nevertheless endure within natality.

NATALITY'S DEATH DRIVE

Psychoanalysis itself echoes the constitutive death drive that Black feminist thought has illuminated in natality. The death drive, in psychoanalysis, highlights a constitutive disturbance that refuses to give way to either life-ascendance or death-ascendance but, instead, confounds the relational dynamics between the two. Death, wrote the psychoanalyst Sabina Spielrein, "is horrible." And yet, she also conceded, it can still be a "salutary blessing." The reason for this paradoxical assessment, she suggested, is that death is the gateway of "a coming into being."[54] Death is, in its way, a sign of regeneration. Spielrein understood death to be caught up within, and something of a condition for, birth. Birth, of course, often ends with death—infant and maternal mortality is, and has always been, a risky and terrifying dimension of the birth experience. But as Spielrein also notes, a birth is a destruction. "One is destroyed during pregnancy," she writes, "through the child that develops as a malevolent growth at the mother's expense."[55] The creation of a mother is a destruction of the person who was not a mother. Spielrein was a mother of two. And while this language (particularly the term "malevolent") may easily offend, Spielrein was simply arguing that death and birth are part of a mutually constitutive process. Birth may be presented simplistically as blessed, affirmative, holy, and pure. But this is a sentimental simplification that effaces the charged negatives within birth. Spielrein is not suggesting that birth is malevolent, but that both birth and death are more ambiguous than their symbolic representations. Moreover, they bleed into one another. In birth there is blood, as well as pain, and risk, and destruction. There is beauty, and joy, and wonder, too, of course. But even in this joy and beauty, birth holds the hands of death.

Spielrein posited that the negative emotions that accompany eroticism and reproductive instincts (disgust or loathing) may be attributed to something "in our depths," something that, "paradoxical as it may sound, wills self-injury while the ego counteracts it with pleasure." This appears, she suggests, as a "wish for self-injury" or a "joy in pain."[56] If her theory sounds much like Freud's theory of the death drive, this would be no mere accident. Her paper "Destruction as the Cause of Coming into Being" was presented to Freud's Vienna circle in 1911—nine years before the publication of Freud's own theory of the death instinct.[57] Although Freud briefly footnotes her theory, he does not acknowledge that her work may have contributed to the structure of the theory itself. Aside from the fact that Freud likely saw no benefit in citing this relatively unknown woman, it may have been that Spielrein saw something at work in the death drive that Freud did not want to illuminate. When we lose sight of this *thing*, however, a dimension of tension and ambiguity in the death drive falls away, and the drive itself appears on the verge of asserting a sovereign authority in death.

Spielrein argued that this intimate relation of life and death—within a reproductive or erotic instinct—was ego-shattering. In the ego-destroying coincidence of lifedeath, she argued that a tendency toward self-dissolution was at work. This was a sign, she suggested, that at the depth of our psyche there is no "I" but instead "only its summation, the 'We.' "[58] In birth and death, and phenomena such as sex, Spielrein suggested that we are involved in a kind of self-dissolution into a "primal substance," that is, ultimately a collective state outside of the ego.[59] This dissolution is both a birth and a death.[60] She illuminates, we might even say, the complex sisterly tensions of lifedeath: a mutually reinforcing form of creation and an antagonistic dissolution.

Simona Forti argues that psychoanalysis, particularly the theory of the death drive, was a watershed moment in the intellectual life of the West. This theory, Forti argues, generated an impetus to rethink the relation between life and death. In the death drive, Forti suggests, there is an "ethics of honesty" that refuses to stage a dualistic battle between life and death. Rather, in the theory of the death drive Forti sees precisely the sort of lifedeath that Western thought sought to mute with what she describes as its grandiose theory of evil (aligning life with the good and death with evil). The theory of the death drive, Forti argues, is "a humble, patient, subjective recognition of ambivalence—a position that forces us to deconstruct, again and again, every purely divisive conception of opposites."[61] More than anything, it forces us to deconstruct the oppositional logic of enmity between life and death.

Theories of the death drive, even in psychoanalysis, can serve to sharply bifurcate life from death, however. This is especially true when death remains untouched by natal disruptions. Although the death instinct was, for Freud, a limitation on the pleasure principle, he also argued that the core impulse of the death drive was to return to the inorganic state (what he called the initial conditions of life on Earth).[62] But if the dead (and the inorganic) is understood to be life's point of origin, then death itself would seem, for Freud, to sit at the heart of biological life. Death acts, if not as a source, then as a reminder of life's most primordial (deathly) origins. This risks subsuming—although does not of necessity subsume—life within the powers of death. Life and death are related, for Freud, but the powers of death can sometimes appear to remain ascendant, as if to trump the powers of life. There is the risk in this iteration of the theory that death might be presented as sovereign or absolute.

I see this risk also at play in the work of Jacques Lacan, who situated the death drive not in the realm of biology but within the historical domain. The death drive, he argued, "can only be defined as a function of the signifying chain."[63] So the theory of the death drive is less a theory about the death of biological bodies than a theory about "human experiences, human interchanges" and "intersubjectivity." The death drive, Lacan notes, is the theory that something in the human "constrains [us] to step out of the limits of life."[64] It is a principle of self-limitation. For Lacan, perhaps the most crucial cultural function of death is its limitation of the ego. Here his theory resonates with Spielrein's. Death reveals that, "beyond the homeostases of the ego, there exists a dimension, another current, another necessity." So the ego becomes motivated by "this compulsion to return to something that has been excluded by the subject or which never entered into it."[65] For Lacan and Spielrein the death drive is a relational force that dissolves the ego. If the life of the ego is to remain self-enclosed, death is a loss and dispossession that propels the ego out of itself. But it is also a site of subjective connection.

This dimension beyond the ego, argued Lacan, is the site of meaning in human life. So death becomes not only a symbol but *the* paradigmatic symbol of limitation that allows for symbolic meaning as such to emerge. The death instinct is "the mask of the symbolic order," which introduces a principle of limitation that orders the plurality of life. The symbolic order, for Lacan, is "in travail" and insists "on being realized." The death instinct provides conditions of limitation that focus and filter this travail into symbolic meaning.[66] Lacan highlights some of the relational and connective powers of death—death facilitates a coming-to-be in the symbolic order and connects the ego to what is beyond the ego. Death becomes connected to something germinational, something that ferments and creates novelty—death becomes, perhaps, more natal.

Despite this resonance with Spielrein, Lacan is also drawn, like Freud, toward a reading of the death drive that would seem to render death in the position of perpetual ascendance. For instance, Lacan argues that life's *only* drive is toward death. "All that life is concerned with is seeking repose as much as possible while awaiting death," he says. So it is that dozing off, for Lacan, is "the most natural of all vital states," indicating that "life is concerned solely with dying."[67] He reads the theory of the death drive as what he calls a "creationist theory." If (as Freud claimed) death is at the primordial origin of life, then life is always pulled (as if toward a source) back to death. Such a view is crucial, says Lacan, because this creationist perspective on death "is the only one that allows us to glimpse the possibility of the radical elimination of God."[68] Lacan seems attuned to the fundamental problem that death has faced in Western metaphysics: it has been presented as the enemy of God. But he does not seek to unsettle or disrupt this metaphysical situation as much as he wants to flip or reverse it. He recruits death, as God's enemy, in order to eliminate God. Only death, Lacan seems to suggest, can occupy the sovereign position that God once did. So he draws all things into a kind of entropic creationism.

In the theory of the death drive, Forti argues, life and death become "part and parcel of one another." But this may not be the case for all instantiations of this theory. In some cases, instead, life becomes an epiphenomenon of death (as death was once a metaphysical epiphenomenon of life). Spielrein's focus on birth as a site of both creation and destruction offers a view of the sisterly dimensions of lifedeath. Death takes on a creative, supportive function. But it also remains destructive and antagonistic (as does birth, in different ways). This is, I would suggest, a more ambivalent reading of the death drive. And this more ambivalent reading may actually *highlight* the theological dimensions of natality rather than subjecting the theological to death's erasure.

OTHER THAN LIFEDEATH

In erasing the traces of creatureliness in natality, and in the attempt to cleanse natality of its associations with other dimensions of the metaphysical negative (to render it a figure of pure positivity or pure biophilia), I think that philosophies of natality perpetuate a set of misunderstandings—not only about natality and birth but about life, death, and lifedeath. When natality becomes dislocated, when it becomes a concept that stands against (rather than in conversation with) the constellated negatives of Western metaphysics, natality serves as a concept that keeps the political theology of death locked in place. Natality, as a figure of pure biophilia (sanitized of death) stands opposed to—in a kind of battle with—the necrophilic powers of death.

We are, if anything, natalmortals. What emerges, when life emerges, are livingdying entities, natalmortals who creep, crawl, roll, limp, and leap to the oscillating rhythms of lifedeath. If we are natalmortals, if we are livingdying entities constituted by the sisterly tensions of lifedeath, then this condition destabilizes any automatic connections or alliances between life and the principle of the absolute, or death and the principle of the absolute. Through a long alliance between God and life (between life and the principle of the absolute, metaphysically speaking), Western thought has maintained a constellated negative that pools together privation, sin, evil, death, animality, the womb, fleshiness, blackness, and woman. But this has never been the only theological reading of the relationship between God and life.

Theologically (rather than metaphysically) speaking,[69] there is no necessary connection between God and biological life, against death. Natality and mortality are both phenomena of creaturely life. If there is a creator of this creaturely life, then this creator is not allied with one side of this life (its birth, its emergence, its life) rather than another (its end or its death), as both phenomena are at play within creation. Rather, the connection between this creator and its creatures is of another sort—it is a connective distinction, an intimate relation of difference. In order to impart a sense of connection, or continuity, into this connective distinction, theologians have often used the term "life" as a mark of continuity.[70] But this leads to easy confusion because the life of God is an eternal, rather than a creaturely, form of life. To speak of life as the site of a connective distinction between creature and creator, in other words, calls for its own elisions and obfuscations. This fails to illuminate the sisterly tensions of lifedeath. And it would suggest that there is only one power—either of life or of death—that can be part of the divine. As we watch ourselves age, or ripen, we watch ourselves fall. And we are aging and ripening from the moment of our birth: falling, and falling, and falling.

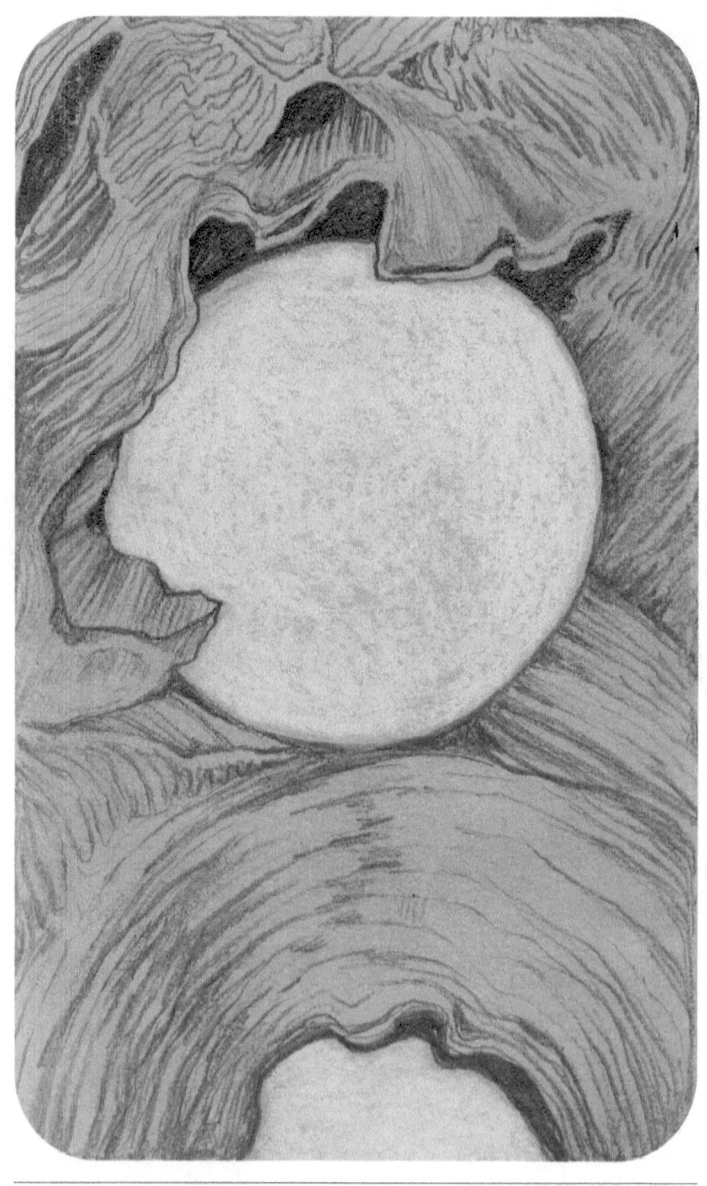

FIGURE CON.1 Krista Dragomer, *Synodic Portal 7*, 2020

CONCLUSION
Into the Dirt

"Shall we descend together into the dust?"

Job 17:15–16

There is a gulf between the living and the dead, but it is not an abyss. Bridges can be built, portals can be opened—cautiously, and sometimes at great risk. Whatever the risks, the living can listen to the dead. This is not a simple act of stupidity or regression, some failure to find our way into the future, some inability to let go and *just live*. Listening for the dead is not an act of getting lost in a historical past from which we should have allegedly emancipated ourselves. To listen for the dead, or to the dead, is also a natal act. It is a recreation, a different form of engagement with historicity, with the ancestral. It is a way to hear the creaking bones of the past differently, to chart a different path toward a different world and a different future. To listen to the dead is to weave a new web, to reconnect the present and the past. It may even—with care—reconnect the living and the dead in a way that does less violence to them both.

Perhaps listening to the dead—listening differently, asking different questions, hearing different modes of response—can offer another way of thinking about who we are and who we come from. Not everyone needs this balm, perhaps, but some of us do. Some of us were taught that the dead of the earth—those doomed to remain in the earth, to become nothing but dirt—are alien creatures, some lesser form of the human. Some of us were taught that there is a special form of the human who may have the power to leave all of this detritus behind. These teachings close off the ears to any lessons from the dead, sealing a person off, rendering them isolated and solipsistic.

In a time of extinctions, we face not simply death (mine or yours), but we reflect—collectively—on our death. We contemplate a scale of death that we may not be able to emotionally process or comprehend. Untethered leaps into the future—the profiteering grasp for a future that might be totally unlike any world of the past—can be a violent gesture in the face of all of this. It can become the quest for a kind of erasure—a quest to be severed from the dead in the dirt. Those descendents of the people who proffered the advance of "progress" do not know what the future has in store for us. We do not know what is coming. We may no longer know how to make sense of things. We may not know how to make meaning, in the face of what is to come. But we can try to listen differently to the past. We can try to pay a different kind of attention to what the dead—especially the dead whose voices have been muted—speak into life. They know things that we do not. They might help us move differently, think differently, understand ourselves differently, breathe differently into what is to come.

To live in a time of extinctions is to live with an awareness of death—mass death—on the horizon. We are told that death is coming. Not just for one, or some, but for unthinkable numbers.

To live in a time of extinctions is to inhabit this unthinkability. It is our starting point. As Ben Ware has put it, living in the wake of the COVID-19 crisis has made it abundantly clear that "the future of recurring disasters linked to climate change and ecological destruction has *already arrived*." With this in mind, says Ware, our task in the present is not "to try and avert the worst" by prophesying the predicted event of extinction but instead "to find ourselves *within* the current moment of crisis and catastrophe, to take the reality of extinction as our starting point."[1] Extinction is not in the future, or about the future; instead, it is about the present (and how we live from this present into whatever future is to come). Extinction, suggests Eugene Thacker, is something like a symptom of the unthinkable nature of the world today. This world, says Thacker, "is increasingly unthinkable—a world of planetary disaster, emerging pandemics, tectonic shifts, strange weather, oil-drenched seascapes, and the furtive, always-looming threat of extinction." And "in spite of our daily concerns, wants, and desires, it is increasingly difficult to comprehend the world in which we live and are a part."[2] We are faced with unthinkable phenomena, and many of us lack the capacity to comprehend them.

Unthinkability, says Thacker, has long been a central concern of the literary genre of horror. But it has also been a central concern of theology. Both of these conceptual fields have been interested in mediating somehow between life and death "at the limits of the thinkable."[3] So it is that the horrific and unthinkable figure of extinction (like the figure of God) "is always speculative."[4] Extinction can "never be adequately thought, since its very possibility presupposes the absolute negation of all thought."[5] Extinction can, however, be *narrated*. Despite the fact that we cannot really think about what extinction is, or what it actually means, we can still tell stories (including philosophical fictions) about extinction. We create, in other words, biomythical stories about extinction in much the same way that we create so many biomythical narratives and theories about death. For Thacker, horror is the most appropriate genre through which to narrate extinction—whatever it is. This is because, he says, horror as a genre is equipped to confront the enigmatic strangeness of a world-without-us. Horror "takes aim at the presuppositions of philosophical inquiry" such as the claim that the world is always for us, or with us, and "makes of those blind spots its central concern, expressing them not in abstract concepts but in a whole bestiary of impossible life forms—mists, ooze, blobs, slime, clouds." Or for someone like Plato, "hair, mud, and dirt."[6] To follow Plato's horror, the possibility of becoming dirt, of being dirt, marks one possible transition into a horrifyingly alien form of life.

Horror pulls us into a dimension in which our sense of how a form of life comes to be, or what a form of life can do, is completely unsettled. Horror confronts us with impossible forms of life and, in so doing, exposes the blind spots and the limitations in our sense of what is proper to life. While it is commonplace to associate horror with fear, Thacker clarifies that horror is not simply or reductively fear-inducing but instead is also about "the enigmatic thought of the unknown."[7] It is perhaps here that we see horror draw closer to theology. In the relation between humans and God that arises in a biblical text like Job there emerges a kind of horror. There is horror in Job's experience of this relationship—in the fear, the awe, and yet also the strange steadfastness that is his response to the enigmatic, unthinkable, and unknown God who he is in relation with. There is, in other words, a kind of horror in the way that theology takes up the contemplation of this enigmatic unknown—the reality of a dimension that is not "us."

There is horror in theology, and theology can also be a genre of horror, even if many theologians have also envisioned the theological as a method of escape from horror. This flight from the horrific has ensured, in its way, that theology becomes more than simply horrific. But it also haunts theology with the horrific. If one goes looking, it does not take long to realize that the speculative dimensions of theology—thoughts and discourse on the divine—often wander into and out of the horrific. This wandering, this relation between theology and horror, can unsettle and shake loose both the fearful elements of horror (exposing some of the awe and wonder within its enigmas) and yet also remind us of the terror and fear embedded within theological thought, from which we may have expected mere comfort.

To think about extinction as a dimension of an enigmatic unknown—caught up, in challenging ways, between horror and theology—highlights the unthinkability of extinction, its failure to be captured by reductive or simplistic metaphors, without softening the figure of extinction into a figure of romance. Extinction is horrifying because it can be horrifying to (among other things) contemplate the nature of a world without "us." But it is not clear what extinction really is, beyond a speculative figure that reminds us of the limits of "our" knowledge. And part of what the horror of extinction can illuminate for "us" are the repressive limits that "we" have often placed around this "us"; violent and horrific limits, for instance, once (and still) presented as a description of all forms of life that supposedly qualify as human.

To narrate extinction as a dimension of horror, as a figure that exists on the other side of thinkability, is arguably also a departure from the narrative of extinction that Ursula Heise describes as an inevitable declension. Heise argues that contemporary cultural discourses on extinction have been predominantly influenced by a secular narrative of the fall that emerged from the modern environmental movement, tapping into the roots of nineteenth-century anti-industrialism. In this framework the declensionist template for thinking extinction is structured by "the idea that humans have corrupted, and become alienated from, nature itself."[8] Mass extinction events in the more than human world are depicted, in "elegiac or tragic modes," as consequences of this corruption.[9] What Heise calls this declensionist "story template" in which "nature in general and biodiversity in particular has done nothing but deteriorate under the impact of modern societies" has become an underlying feature of extinction narratives. The template is taken for granted, "and details that do not fit into this narrative tend to be underemphasized or left out."[10]

She also notes that cultural discourses of extinction tend to function as "powerful tools" that critique or resist forces of modernization and colonization.[11] With this in mind it sounds almost blasphemous, perhaps, to speak about extinction or to tell extinction narratives in any other mode than the elegiac or the tragic. To speak or think about extinction outside of those modes would seem to be a concession to the forces of modernization and colonization that are driving extinction events. It would seem to be a surrender to their inevitability—simply conceding that extinction is coming and throwing up our hands in defeat. But Heise also cautions that declensionist narratives of extinction can make unjustifiably strong claims to inevitability, even when extinction is only "one possible story."[12]

One might, here, make note of the narratives of inevitable extinction that have been applied to enslaved, formerly enslaved, Indigenous, and colonized peoples. In these cases and instances, extinction is only one possible story that emerges from a violent encounter with colonization or enslavement. To imagine that this moment in history—as many of "us" on the planet live into the dismal future that has been prophesied by climate scientists—is the first time that collective mortality has been grappled with is to erase the histories and existential discourses of Indigenous, enslaved, or colonized communities. Indeed, in American history the term "extinction" has been used to dismiss the survival struggles of Indigenous and formerly enslaved communities as a pseudo-natural form of being toward death,[13] a natural consequence of their form of life. These communities have already lived into, against, and through the proclamation of extinction events.

Heise also cautions that the environmentalist mourning that emerges in the wake of these declensionist narratives of extinction can itself be commodified into forms of "ecologically oriented desire, longing, and nostalgia,"[14] which might serve as a potent contrast to critique and resistance. To remain in the elegiac or tragic mode and to presume the fatal inevitability of extinction is, at times, its own form of surrender that disintegrates into misplaced forms of nostalgia. There is, perhaps, also a dimension of resistance in a narrative of extinction that questions the inevitability and elegiac tone of this declentionist narrative pattern.

I want to be absolutely clear about what I am *not* saying here. To resist the narrative of declension is not to suggest that extinction is the opposite of a tragedy—a benefit of some sort. Extinction can still be horrific, even if it is not elegiac. But there is more than simple fear in the horrific. In the figure of extinction (a figure of collective death) the sisterly tensions of the lifedeath relation are also at work. These tensions are both antagonistic and yet, in entirely other ways, also potentially nurturing. I am not troubling at extinction narratives in order to convince people *not to worry* about mass extinction events in human and more than human lifeworlds. We *should* be worried about what is happening to the lifeworlds around us, in the face of manmade mass death. We *should* be working to change the structures that shape these lifeworlds. And we should be tender toward one another. We, whoever we are (we earthlings, perhaps I could say), should be shielding one another from death and extinction. And there should be room, plenty of room, in which to struggle against narratives of inevitable death. There should plenty of room in which to struggle against (to resist, to dissemble) the proliferating death worlds shaped by manmade mass death. But one of the things that I *am* suggesting is that—perhaps—part of the way that this space for struggle and resistance can emerge is through the acknowledgment among particular forms of life that there is wisdom and justice in aging, growing old, and letting go. There may be forms of death, decay, and dissolution that can help us live into horror with a different sense of where we come from, who we come from, and where we are going.

No form of death (whether individual or collective) is without tragedy. And yet, this does not mean that the best or only alternative or outcome is to attempt to preserve individual or collective lives—as they are—in a state of endless physical, material, suspension. The tragedy that is the loss of life (whether individual or collective) is horrific. If we fear this horrific tragedy, it is with good reason. And if we seek to shield one another from it, it is with good reason. But part of this horror is also the realization that the power of living beings is not infinite. And part of this horror is the illumination of an enigmatic unknown that shifts, changes, and challenges us to see more clearly how life and death do weave back together in the wake of this tragedy. Theologians have often suggested that there is a dimension of justice and wisdom in the work we do to respond to this enigmatic (sometimes terrifying) unknown, often invoked under the name of God.

Horror is an affect, a genre, a mode of encounter, a form of brushing up against the unknown. What theology shows us—in the wisdom that oozes from concepts like *fear of the lord*—is that there is both beauty and horror in the unknown. Theology shows us that beauty and horror are not mutually exclusive. How we speak about them, how we narrate them, what we are up against: they all matter. And there is more than one way to narrate the experience of living and dying in a time of extinctions. Elegy is not obligatory. Or, at least, we are not obligated to restrict ourselves to pure elegy.

The political theology of death that I have critiqued in this book tells a different story. It feeds the narrative of a form of pure life that hovers transcendently above the dead in the dirt. The political theology of death that I have critiqued tells us that it is pure horror to become dirt. It means we are caught up in a constellated negative that remains far from God. But there is another story, left to us by the dead, that tells us we *are* dirt. Dust, even. The second account of creation, in Genesis, tells us that the primordial human—the primordial us or primordial we—was formed from the dirt, the ground, the earth—the אדמה. This primordial human was an earth being made of clay into whose nostrils a creator breathed the breath of life. The emergence of human life on earth has been narrated with such incredible distinction and detail, especially in evolutionary accounts of human life, that the Anthropos, the *Homo sapiens*, or Man himself, seems so incredibly distant from, or other to, this being who emerged from a wild and unpredictable amalgamation of inorganic dust, waters bearing the emergence of unicellular life forms, the radiance of the sun, and the breath of wind over the face of that deep. Yet when we take a wider biomythical perspective on the strange path of emergence of this form of life, the dirt returns to its natural history.

FIGURE CON.2 Krista Dragomer, *Underlit Sky*, 2014

This story of the dirt being who was human is, perhaps, only a lost story from the ancient past. It is a story that Man outgrew long ago. A story that Man severed from the lifeworld and subjectivity of his descendents. In the "mythophilosophical" tradition of the West, say Déborah Danowski and Eduardo Viveiros de Castro, dimensions of nature—such as animality—belong to the past of humanity. Animals, in this view, become living "archefossils."[15] The human is understood to have emerged from a past that was nonhuman. Along these lines, then, "humans belong to the future" and "animals belong to the past." Animals become "trapped inside an exiguous world within an immobile present."[16] They contrast this perspective with the "cosmovisions" of several Amerindian worldviews, including the Yawanawá (Pano speakers from the western Amazon) and the Aikewara (Tupian speakers from the other end of Amazonia). In some of these biomythologies, they note, before the emergence of humans there is a dimension of primordial humanity that was created either by a demiurge of some sort or by the work of some substrate of matter. This primordial humanity is not human in the way that (for instance) modern humanism conceives of the human. But it is a primordial form that can be likened to the human in crucial ways, particularly in its incredible plasticity.[17] In these biomythical narratives, after a series of exploits, this primordial form of humanity undergoes fundamental changes. But, nevertheless, the narrative of a primordial humanity that comes before humans (and is present in the more than human world) endures within these cosmovisions so that "humanity is the active principle at the origin of the proliferation of living forms in a rich, plural world."[18] Animals and other species maintain their own form of humanity that is other than, but nevertheless can resonate with, the humanity of human societies.[19]

This cosmovision impacts the way that Amerindian societies narrate explanations of the end of a world. Notably, for Danowski and Viveiros de Castro, what is missing from many of these narratives is the idea of "a final and definitive destruction." Instead, "what seems to be constant in indigenous mythologies concerning the end of the world," they write, "is the unthinkability of a world without people, without humankind of some sort, however different from ours."[20] These cosmovisions unsettle any easy narrative of the end of the human, for they also tell a particular story about where humanity is derived from and who humanity is related to.

For those who are living in the wake of the world of Man—in a postbiblical secular form of modernity still imaginatively captured by thought forms from Christian theology—a return to the dirt might be read as a return to the deep primordial past of the human; a return that retreats into a nature even more unthinkably inhuman than animality. In this sense, it might read as horrific. To be buried in the soils of the earth, to become part of these soils, might seem to be an evisceration of all that "we" have evolved to become at this moment in human history. It would be an erasure of all that "we" consider human about "us." But there may also be those who have discovered that they have been captured by this form of life that seems—militantly, incessantly—to stoke the most fearful dimensions of this horror. There may be, in other words, those who are more ready to let this form of life—this particular genre of the human—face into the horror of its own ends. And, perhaps, in these ends other performative practices of weaving life and death together—of illuminating the dimensions of nurture in the sisterly tensions of lifedeath—arise. Other ways of listening to the dead.

Perhaps rituals themselves (as they change, grow, develop) can reveal to us how this performative weaving is itself changing and evolving. Writing about the work and research of Katrina Spade—who has sought to reform the death care industry through the development of human composting—Caitlin Doughty suggests that the act of decomposition (of becoming soil) can be a radical ritual practice. Spade's organization Recompose speaks of this process not as a decomposition (which sounds, perhaps, like a declension) but instead a recomposition, a remaking. The recomposition process is designed to use the process of natural organic reduction in order to accelerate the transformation of a human corpse into soil. Bodies are laid, for thirty days, into a cradle of wood chips, alfalfa, straw, and other plant materials. At the end of the process, the soil can be used to enrich living environments. The human composting movement was inspired, in part, by the limits of American urban spaces; we are quickly running out of open land below which we might bury more caskets or open spaces where ashes can be freely scattered. But there is also a strong symbolic component to human composting. Spade notes that in places like the contemporary United States we are "so focused on preventing aging and decay—it's become an obsession." Human composting is an embrace of these processes. And while this might simply be a death care practice, it also offers (symbolically) another set of performative ritual practices for thinking about the relationship between life and death, as well as the afterlife. Perhaps even another way of understanding who we are, in conversation with the dead.

For Doughty, the embrace of aging and decay speaks to her experience of being a woman. "Women's bodies are so often under the purview of man," she writes, "whether it's our reproductive organs, our sexuality, our weight, our manner of dress." Because of this, Doughty finds a kind of freedom in recomposition. It is an embrace of our bodies, and their cycles, "chaotic, messy, and wild." In this sense, she says, recomposition is an "attempt to reclaim our corpses," an attempt to "rot and nourish on our own terms."[21] The website for Recompose also notes that the recomposition process offers another model of the afterlife. "The soil created" in this process "returns the nutrients from our bodies to the natural world." And this "restores forests, sequesters carbon, and nourishes new life." It is not simply another form of expressing who we are, and who we celebrate when we memorialize a death, but it is another way of understanding a collective immortality.

FIGURE CON.3 Krista Dragomer, *The Forest Floor Is Always Busy II*, 2016

The recomposition process is, symbolically, beautiful for those who find beauty in compost. But it can also be unsettling, perhaps even horrifying, from other angles. It embraces a form of life that has been considered fundamentally horrific for the form who once believed he was the universally superior pinnacle of humanity. Dirt is a form of life that is, perhaps, as low as Man could have ever imagined himself falling. But in this unsettling, facing into this horror, there is also beauty. It offers the possibility, as Doughty has argued, of thinking differently—right now—about the nature of our bodies, about who we are, and who we become. In the embrace of decomposition and recomposition, we might say, the horror of being a form of life who becomes dirt is being reframed. Perhaps these processes are calling us deeper into the dirt in order to better see how life and death weave together in the intricate composition of the soil—in order to understand, differently, who our dead are, where they are, and how we might listen to them: essentially, what they have to teach us. And to understand this is to see that what might look—from one angle—like the horrific dissolution of a form of life can also be the beauty of a form of life's unsettling and recomposition. Perhaps there is a kind of justice—a human and a more than human form of justice—in the unsettling or dissolution of a form of life who might see, in the soil and the dirt, nothing but the bubbling fermentation of its enemy's damned and privative life. Even in the dirt, even as we go down into the dust and the dirt, we find one another in ways that we were not expecting. We find ourselves enfolded into forms of life and forms of love that are much more than what we believed could be human. A kind of portal opens up, in which we can catch a different glimpse of the dead, and so ourselves.

NOTES

INTRODUCTION: SISTER DEATH

1. Lynn White Jr., "The Historical Roots of Our Ecologic Crisis," *Science*, new series, 155 (1967): 1203–6, 1206.
2. Citations of this hymn come from the translation in Alessandro Vettori, *Poets of Divine Love: Franciscan Mystical Poetry of the Thirteenth Century* (New York: Fordham University Press, 2004).
3. Vincent Lloyd, "Introduction" to *Race and Political Theology*, ed. Vincent W. Lloyd (Stanford: Stanford University Press, 2012), 5.
4. Simone de Beauvoir, *The Second Sex*, trans. Constance Borde and Sheila Malvony-Chevallier (New York: Vintage, 2011), 165.
5. Beauvoir, *The Second Sex*, 183.
6. Beauvoir, *The Second Sex*, 166.
7. Audre Lorde, *The Cancer Journals* (New York: Penguin, 1980, 2020), 5.
8. Lorde, *The Cancer Journals*, 19.
9. Donna Haraway, *Staying with the Trouble: Making Kin in the Chthulucene* (Durham, N.C,: Duke University Press, 2016), 1.
10. Haraway, *Staying with the Trouble*, 130.
11. Order of the Good Death website: orderofthegooddeath.com. Accessed March 14, 2020.
12. Sarah Chavez, "Why the Story of Death Is the Story of Women," *Yes!* 91 (Fall 2019): 18–24.
13. Sarah Chavez, "Death & the Maidens: Why Women Are Working with Death," in *Death and the Maidens* (blog): https://deadmaidens.com/2016/08/15/death-the-maidens-why-women-are-working-with-death/.

14. Cited in an interview with Cymene Howe, Susanna Zaraysky, and Lois Ann Lorentzen, "Devotional Crossings: Transgender Sex Workers, Santisima Muerte, and Spiritual Solidarity in Guadalajara and San Francisco" in *Religion at the Corner of Bliss and Nirvana: Politics, Identity, and Faith in New Migrant Communities*, ed. Lois Ann Lorentzen, Joaquin Jay Gonzalez III, Kevin M. Chun, and Hien Duc Do (Durham, N.C.: Duke University Press, 2009), 29.
15. See, for instance: Evy Johanne Haland (ed.), *Women, Pain, and Death: Rituals and Everyday Life on the Margins of Europe and Beyond* (Newcastle upon Tyne, UK: Cambridge Scholars, 2008); Clare Bielby and Anna Richards (ed.), *Women and Death 3: Women's Representations of Death in German Culture* (Rochester, N.Y.: Camden House, 2010); *Women and the Material Culture of Death*, ed. Maureen Daly Goggin and Beth Fowkes Tobin (New York: Routledge, 2013); and Karl S. Guthke, *The Gender of Death: A Cultural History in Art and Literature* (Cambridge: Cambridge University Press, 1999).
16. Chavez, "Why the Story of Death," 21.
17. Chavez, "Why the Story of Death," 23.
18. Chavez, "Why the Story of Death," 24.
19. See Ruth Penfold-Mounce, *Death, the Dead, and Popular Culture* (Bingley, UK: Emerald, 2018).
20. Lyn H. Lofland, *The Craft of Dying: The Modern Face of Death* (Cambridge, Mass.: MIT Press, 1978, 2019), 56.
21. Lofland, *Craft of Dying*, 56.
22. Benjamin Noys, *The Culture of Death* (Oxford: Berg, 2005), 1.
23. Noys, *Culture of Death*, 3.
24. Lofland, *Craft of Dying*, 75.
25. Brandy Schillace, *Death's Summer Coat: What the History of Death and Dying Teaches Us About Life and Living* (New York: Pegasus, 2015), 225.
26. Ashley Dawson, *Extinction: A Radical History* (New York: OR, 2016), 12.
27. Jessica K. Weir, "Lives in Connection," in *Manifesto for Living in the Anthropocene*, ed. Deborah Bird Rose, Katherine Gibson, and Ruth Fincher (Santa Barbara, Calif.: Punctum, 2015), 17.
28. Sam Mickey, *Coexistentialism and the Unbearable Intimacy of Ecological Emergency* (Lanham, Md.: Lexington, 2016), 193.
29. Deborah Bird Rose, Thom van Dooren, and Matthew Chrulew, "Introduction" to *Extinction Studies: Stories of Time, Death, and Generations*, ed.

Deborah Bird Rose, Thom van Dooren, and Matthew Chrulew (New York: Columbia University Press, 2017).

1. LIFE, DEATH, AND LIFEDEATH

1. As quoted in Jeff Noonan, *Embodiment and the Meaning of Life* (Montreal: McGill-Queen's University Press, 2018), 182.
2. Thomas Aquinas, *Summa Theologica*, Question LXXV, Art. 1, Reply Obj. 1, Pt. 2 (First Part), trans. Fathers of the English Dominican Province (New York: Benziger, 1915), 337.
3. Noonan, *Embodiment*, 11.
4. Noonan, *Embodiment*, 115.
5. Noonan, *Embodiment*, 115.
6. Noonan, *Embodiment*, 41.
7. Noonan, *Embodiment*, 51.
8. Carl Schmitt, *The Concept of the Political*, trans. George Schwab (Chicago: University of Chicago Press, 1996, 2007), 26.
9. Schmitt, *Concept of the Political*, 27.
10. Schmitt, *Concept of the Political*, 29.
11. Schmitt, *Concept of the Political*, 29.
12. Gil Anidjar, *The Jew, the Arab: A History of the Enemy* (Stanford: Stanford University Press, 2003).
13. Anidjar, *The Jew, the Arab*, 18.
14. Anidjar, *The Jew, the Arab*, 70.
15. Michel Foucault, *The Birth of the Clinic: An Archaeology of Medical Perception*, trans. A. M. Sheridan Smith (New York: Vintage, 1973, 1994), 141.
16. Foucault, *Birth of the Clinic*, 125.
17. Foucault, *Birth of the Clinic*, 142.
18. Foucault, *Birth of the Clinic*, 144.
19. Foucault, *Birth of the Clinic*, 146.
20. Foucault, *Birth of the Clinic*, 198.
21. Foucault, *Birth of the Clinic*, 197.
22. Foucault, *Birth of the Clinic*, 198.
23. Foucault, *Birth of the Clinic*, 198.
24. I am in debt to Gil Anidjar for this insight.
25. Jacques Derrida, *Aporias*, trans. Thomas Dutoit (Stanford: Stanford University Press, 1993), 24.

26. Derrida, *Aporias*, 65.
27. Jacques Derrida, *La vie la mort: Séminaire (1975–1976)* (Paris: Seuil, 2019), 19.
28. Jacques Derrida, *Life Death*, trans. Pascale-Anne Brault and Michael Naas (Chicago: University of Chicago Press, 2020), 4.
29. Sigmund Freud, *Beyond the Pleasure Principle*, trans. C. J. M. Hubback (Digireads.com, 2009). Kindle.
30. He writes, for instance, "I might be asked whether I am myself convinced of the views here set forward, and if so how far. My answer would be that I am neither convinced myself, nor am I seeking to arouse conviction in others. More accurately: I do not know how far I believe them." See Freud, *Beyond the Pleasure Principle*.
31. Freud, *Beyond the Pleasure Principle*.
32. Freud, *Beyond the Pleasure Principle*.
33. Derrida, *Life Death*, 283.
34. Derrida, *Life Death*, 290.
35. Derrida, *Life Death*, 290.
36. Derrida, *Life Death*, 292.
37. Derrida, *Life Death*, 295.
38. Citing Rückert's *Maqâmât* of al-Hariri, in Derrida, *Life Death*, 297.
39. A citation of Nietzsche from a fragment in Georges Bataille, *On Nietzsche*, trans. Stuart Kendall (Albany: SUNY Press, 2015), 169, in Derrida, *Life Death*, 298.
40. From Bataille, *On Nietzsche*, 222, in Derrida, *Life Death*, 299.
41. Derrida, *Life Death*, 283.
42. Derrida, *Life Death*, 297.

2. THE WAR WITH DEATH

1. I am grateful to the work of Carol Wayne White, which initially guided me to this passage in Baldwin's work. James Baldwin, *The Price of the Ticket: Collected Nonfiction 1948–1985* (New York: St Martin's, 1985), 343.
2. Baldwin, *Price of the Ticket*, 374.
3. Christina Sharpe, *In the Wake: On Blackness and Being* (Durham, N.C.: Duke University Press, 2016), 7.

4. Carol Wayne White, *Black Lives and Sacred Humanity: Toward an African American Religious Naturalism* (New York: Fordham University Press, 2017), 43.
5. White, *Black Lives and Sacred Humanity*, 40.
6. Baldwin, *Price of the Ticket*, 373.
7. Sharpe, *In the Wake*, 10.
8. Kathryn Tanner, "Eschatology Without a Future?" in *The End of the World and the Ends of God: Science and Theology on Eschatology*, ed. John Polkinghorne and Michael Welker (Harrisburg, Penn.: Trinity, 2000), 232.
9. Tanner, "Eschatology Without a Future?" 227.
10. For this Tanner cites Job 5:25–26, "Eschatology Without a Future?" 227.
11. Tanner, "Eschatology Without a Future?" 227.
12. Tanner, "Eschatology Without a Future?" *228*.
13. Tanner, "Eschatology Without a Future?" 228.
14. Tanner, "Eschatology Without a Future?" 232.
15. Oscar Cullmann, *Immortality of the Soul or Resurrection of the Dead? The Witness of the New Testament* (Eugene: Wipf & Stock, 1964), 20.
16. Cullmann, *Immortality of the Soul*, 22.
17. Cullmann, *Immortality of the Soul*, 23.
18. Cullmann, *Immortality of the Soul*, 28.
19. Cullmann, *Immortality of the Soul*, 28.
20. Gustaf Aulén, *Christus Victor: A Historical Study of the Three Main Types of the Idea of Atonement*, trans. A. G. Hebert (Eugene: Wipf & Stock, 1931), 4.
21. Thanks to An Yountae for pointing me toward this book. Jairus Victor Grove, *Savage Ecology: War and Geopolitics at the End of the World* (Durham, N.C.: Duke University Press, 2019), 5.
22. Grove, *Savage Ecology*, 39.
23. Grove, *Savage Ecology*, 10.
24. Grove, *Savage Ecology*, 48.
25. Grove, *Savage Ecology*, 43.
26. Grove, *Savage Ecology*, 38.
27. Grove, *Savage Ecology*, 2.
28. Grove, *Savage Ecology*, 6.
29. Grove, *Savage Ecology*, 9.
30. Grove, *Savage Ecology*, 49.

31. Grove, *Savage Ecology*, 50.
32. Grove, *Savage Ecology* 54.
33. Thanks to Gil Anidjar for pointing me toward this book. Edith Wyschogrod, *Spirit in Ashes: Hegel, Heidegger, and Man-Made Mass Death* (New Haven, Conn.: Yale University Press, 1985), xi.
34. Wyschogrod, *Spirit in Ashes*, 2.
35. Wyschogrod, *Spirit in Ashes*, 35.
36. Deborah Bird Rose, *Reports from Wild Country: An Ethics for Decolonization* (Sydney: University of New South Wales Press, 2004), 175.
37. Julieta Aranda and Eben Kirksey, "Toward a Glossary of the Oceanic Undead: A(mphibious) through F(utures)" in *e-flux* 112 (October 2020), https://www.e-flux.com/journal/112/354965/toward-a-glossary-of-the-oceanic-undead-a-mphibious-through-f-utures/.
38. Grove, *Savage Ecology*, 38.
39. Norman O. Brown, *Life Against Death: The Psychoanalytical Meaning of History* (Middletown, Conn.: Wesleyan University Press, 1959, 1985), 77.
40. Brown, *Life Against Death*, 80.
41. Brown, *Life Against Death*, 99.
42. Brown, *Life Against Death*, 101.
43. Brown, *Life Against Death*, 93.
44. Brown, *Life Against Death*, 101.
45. Brown, *Life Against Death*, 102.
46. Thinkers, including Brown, spoke of this human using masculine pronouns, so I'm just going to let them have that.
47. Brown, *Life Against Death*, 109.
48. Brown, *Life Against Death*, 27.
49. Brown, *Life Against Death*, 48.
50. Brown, *Life Against Death*, 66.
51. Achille Mbembe, *Necropolitics*, trans. Steven Corcoran (Durham, N.C.: Duke University Press, 2019), 38.
52. Mbembe, *Necropolitics*, 92.
53. Mbembe, *Necropolitics*, 38.
54. Mbembe, *Necropolitics*, 6.
55. Mbembe, *Necropolitics*, 7.
56. Mbembe, *Necropolitics*, 1.
57. Mbembe, *Necropolitics*, 1.

3. THE HUMAN-ABOVE-DEATH

1. Friedrich Nietzsche, "The Anti-Christ: A Curse on Christianity," in *The Anti-Christ, Ecce Homo, Twilight of the Idols, and Other Writings*, trans. Judith Norman (Cambridge: Cambridge University Press, 2005), 50.
2. Thanks to Virginia Burris for introducing me to this text. See Virginia Burris, *Ancient Christian Ecopoetics: Cosmologies, Saints, Things* (Philadelphia: University of Pennsylvania Press, 2019).
3. Pseudo-Athanasius, *The Life and Regimen of the Blessed and Holy Syncletica*, Part I: The Translation, trans. Elizabeth Bryson Bongie (Eugene: Wipf & Stock, 2003), 13.
4. Pseudo-Athanasius, *Life and Regimen of the Blessed and Holy Syncletica*, 38.
5. Pseudo-Athanasius, *Life and Regimen of the Blessed and Holy Syncletica*, 67.
6. Pseudo-Athanasius, *Life and Regimen of the Blessed and Holy Syncletica*, 68.
7. Tiffany Lethabo King, *The Black Shoals: Offshore Formations of Black and Native Studies* (Durham, N.C.: Duke University Press, 2019).
8. Sylvia Wynter and Katherine McKittrick, "Unparalleled Catastrophe for Our Species? Or, to Give Humanness a Different Future: Conversation," in *Sylvia Wynter: On Being Human as Praxis*, ed. Katherine McKittrick (Durham, N.C.: Duke University Press, 2015), 31.
9. Wynter and McKittrick, "Unparalleled Catastrophe for Our Species?" 28.
10. Wynter and McKittrick, "Unparalleled Catastrophe for Our Species?" 10.
11. Achille Mbembe, *Necropolitics*, trans. Steven Corcoran (Durham, N.C.: Duke University Press, 2019), 38.
12. Mbembe, *Necropolitics*, 64.
13. Mbembe, *Necropolitics*, 66.
14. Rosemary Radford Ruether, *Goddesses and the Divine Feminine: A Western Religious History* (Berkeley: University of California Press, 2005), 76.
15. Rachel S. Hallote, *Death, Burial, and Afterlife in the Biblical World: How the Israelites and Their Neighbors Treated the Dead* (Chicago: Ivan R. Dee, 2001), 22.
16. Hallote, *Death, Burial, and Afterlife in the Biblical World*, 61.
17. Hallote, *Death, Burial, and Afterlife in the Biblical World*, 61.
18. Hallote, *Death, Burial, and Afterlife in the Biblical World*, 141.
19. Hallote, *Death, Burial, and Afterlife in the Biblical World*, 55.
20. Hallote, *Death, Burial, and Afterlife in the Biblical World*, 63.

21. R. C. Sproul, "The Last Enemy," *Tabletalk*, April 1, 2000, https://www.ligonier.org/learn/articles/the-last-enemy/.
22. The Arian position was not officially banned until 381 at the Council at Constantinople.
23. The English term *creature* is in this instance a translation of a variation on the Ancient Greek κτίσμα, which is transliterated as *ktisma*.
24. Athanasius, "Orations Against the Arians," in *The Christological Controversy*, ed. and trans. Richard A. Norris Jr. (Philadelphia: Fortress, 1980), 86.
25. William R. Crockett, *Eucharist: Symbol of Transformation* (Collegeville, Minn.: Liturgical Press, 1989), 56.
26. See Caroline Walker Bynum, *Holy Feast and Holy Fast: The Religious Significance of Food to Medieval Women* (Berkeley: University of California Press, 1987).
27. Angel F. Méndez-Montoya, *The Theology of Food: Eating and the Eucharist* (Hoboken, N.J.: Blackwell, 2012), 38.
28. Méndez-Montoya, *Theology of Food*, 69.
29. Irenaeus of Lyon, "Against Heresies," Bk. 3, Chapters 18–19, in *The Christological Controversy*, 55.
30. Athanasius, "On the Incarnation of the Word," in *Christology of the Later Fathers*, Vol. 3, ed. Edward Rochie Hardy (Philadelphia: Westminster, 1954), 58.
31. Athanasius, "On the Incarnation," 59.
32. Athanasius, "On the Incarnation," 107.
33. Thomas Aquinas, *Summa Theologica*, Vol. 50: *The One Mediator*, trans. Colman E. O'Neill (London: Blackfriars, 1965), 39.
34. Aquinas, *Summa Theologica*, 33.
35. Aquinas, *Summa Theologica*, 11.
36. Denise Kimber Buell, *Why This Race? Ethnic Reasoning in Early Christianity* (New York: Columbia University Press, 2005), 1.
37. Buell, *Why This Race?* 2.
38. Daniel Boyarin, *The Jewish Gospels: The Story of the Jewish Christ* (New York: New Press, 2012), 26.
39. Boyarin, *Jewish Gospels*, 26.
40. Boyarin, *Jewish Gospels*, 27.
41. Boyarin, *Jewish Gospels*, 32.
42. J. Kameron Carter, *Race: A Theological Account* (Oxford: Oxford University Press, 2008), 4.

43. Jeannine Hill Fletcher, *The Sin of White Supremacy: Christianity, Racism, and Religious Diversity in America* (Maryknoll, N.Y.: Orbis, 2017), ch. 1.
44. Fletcher, *Sin of White Supremacy*, ch. 1.
45. Gil Anidjar, *Blood: A Critique of Christianity* (New York: Columbia University Press, 2014), 38.
46. Anidjar, *Blood*, 56.
47. Anidjar, *Blood*, 76.
48. Amaryah Shaye Armstrong, "Christian Order and Racial Order: What Cedric Robinson Has to Teach Us Today," *The Bias Magazine: The Voice of the Christian Left*, June 3, 2020, https://christiansocialism.com/cedric-robinson-racial-order-christianity-socialism/.
49. Terence Keel, *Divine Variations: How Christian Thought Became Racial Science* (Stanford: Stanford University Press, 2018), 9.
50. See Toby Jennings, *Precious Enemy: A Biblical Portrait of Death* (Eugene: Pickwick, 2017).
51. Karl Barth, *Epistle to the Romans*, trans. Edwin C. Hoskyns (Oxford: Oxford University Press, 1933, 1968), 166.
52. Barth, *Epistle to the Romans*, 271.

4. CONSTELLATED NEGATIVES

1. From *Principal Doctrines, II*, cited in Todd May, *Death* (Stocksfield, UK: Acumen, 2009), 23.
2. Todd May, *Death* (New York: Routledge, 2009, 2014), 25.
3. Mary-Jane Rubenstein, *Pantheologies: Gods, Worlds, Monsters* (New York: Columbia University Press, 2018), xx.
4. Calvin L. Warren, *Ontological Terror: Blackness, Nihilism, and Emancipation* (Durham, N.C.: Duke University Press, 2018), Project MUSE, doi:10.1353/book.61312, "Coda: Adieu to the Human", 9.
5. Warren, *Ontological Terror: Blackness, Nihilism, and Emancipation* (Durham: Duke University Press, 2018), Project MUSE, doi:10.1353/book.61312, "Coda: Adieu to the Human", 170.
6. Aristotle, *The Nichomachean Ethics*, trans. R. W. Browne (London: George Bell, 1889).
7. Aristotle, *Nichomachean Ethics*, 71.
8. James Stacey Taylor, *Death, Posthumous Harm, and Bioethics* (New York: Routledge, 2012), 1.

9. Aristotle, *Nichomachean Ethics*, 71.
10. Brian Davies, "Introduction," Thomas Aquinas, *On Evil*, trans. Richard Regan and ed. Brian Davies (Oxford: Oxford University Press, 2003), 14.
11. Davies, "Introduction," 21.
12. Thomas Aquinas, *Summa Theologica*, Vol. 2 Pt. 2, First Section, trans. Fathers of the English Dominican Province (New York: Cosimo, 2007), 969.
13. Thomas Aquinas, *On Evil*, trans. Richard Regan and ed. Brian Davies (Oxford: Oxford University Press, 2003), 56.
14. Aquinas, *On Evil*, 56.
15. Aquinas, *On Evil*, 243.
16. Aquinas, *On Evil*, 246.
17. Aquinas, *On Evil*, 246.
18. Aquinas, *On Evil*, 127.
19. Benjamin Keach, *Tropologia: A Key to Open Scripture Metaphors in Four Books* (London: City Press, 1858), 801.
20. Keach, *Tropologia*, 802.
21. Warren, *Ontological Terror*, 6.
22. Warren, *Ontological Terror*, 15.
23. Warren, *Ontological Terror*, 10.
24. Warren, *Ontological Terror*, 172.
25. Warren, *Ontological Terror*, 9.
26. Martin Heidegger, *Being and Time*, trans. John Macquarrie and Edward Robinson (New York: Harper, 1962, 2008), 44.
27. Heidegger, *Being and Time*, 281.
28. Heidegger, *Being and Time*, 286.
29. See, for instance, Grace Jantzen, *Becoming Divine: Towards a Feminist Philosophy of Religion* (Bloomington: Indiana University Press, 1999), 133–34.
30. Anne O'Byrne, *Natality and Finitude* (Bloomington: Indiana University Press, 2010), 4.
31. O'Byrne, *Natality*, 5.
32. Heidegger, *Being and Time*, 425.
33. Heidegger, *Being and Time*, 427.
34. O'Byrne, *Natality*, 26. Italics mine.
35. Heidegger, *Being and Time*, 282.
36. Heidegger, *Being and Time*, 294.
37. O'Byrne, *Natality*, 29.

38. Heidegger, *Being and Time*, 298.
39. Martin Heidegger, *Hegel*, trans. Joseph Are and Niels Feuerhahn (Bloomington: Indiana University Press, 2015), 29.
40. Heidegger, *Hegel*, 13.
41. Heidegger, *Hegel*, 21.
42. Heidegger, *Hegel*, 11.
43. Heidegger, *Hegel*, 30,
44. Heidegger, *Hegel*, xii.
45. Giorgio Agamben, *Language and Death: The Place of Negativity*, trans. Karen E. Pinkus and Michael Hardt (Minneapolis: University of Minnesota Press, 1991), 4.
46. Agamben, *Language and Death*, 62.
47. Agamben, *Language and Death*, 65.
48. Agamben *Language and Death*, 85.
49. Agamben, *Language and Death*, 85.
50. Agamben, *Language and Death*, 47.
51. Agamben, *Language and Death*, 46.
52. Heidegger, *Being and Time*, 289.
53. Heidegger, *Being and Time*, 290.
54. Heidegger, *Being and Time*, 291.
55. Zakiyyah Iman Jackson, *Becoming Human: Matter and Meaning in an Antiblack World* (New York: New York University Press, 2020), 3.
56. Jackson, *Becoming Human*, 116.
57. Jackson, *Becoming Human*, 22.
58. Jackson, *Becoming Human*, 89.
59. Jackson, *Becoming Human*, 29.
60. Jackson, *Becoming Human*, 99.
61. Jackson, *Becoming Human*, 93.
62. Jackson, *Becoming Human*, 94.
63. Jackson, *Becoming Human*, 99.
64. Jackson, *Becoming Human*, 85.
65. Jackson, *Becoming Human*, 44.
66. Jackson, *Becoming Human*, 43.
67. Jackson, *Becoming Human*, 69.
68. Jackson, *Becoming Human*, 92.
69. Jackson, *Becoming Human*, 101.
70. Juda Bennett, *Toni Morrison and the Queer Pleasure of Ghosts* (Albany: SUNY Press, 2014), 19.

71. Tessa Roynon, *The Cambridge Introduction to Toni Morrison* (New York: Cambridge University Press, 2013), 23.
72. Jaleel Akhtar, *Dismemberment in the Fiction of Toni Morrison* (Newcastle Upon Tyne, UK: Cambridge Scholars), 80.
73. Akhtar, *Dismemberment*, 97.
74. Toni Morrison, *The Source of Self-Regard: Selected Essays, Speeches, and Meditations* (New York: Vintage, 2020), 188.
75. Hortense Spillers, "A Hateful Passion, a Lost Love: Three Women's Fiction," in *Black, White, and in Color: Essays on American Literature and Culture* (Chicago: University of Chicago Press, 2003), 93.
76. Spillers, "A Hateful Passion, a Lost Love," 96.
77. Spillers, "A Hateful Passion, a Lost Love," 95.
78. Spillers, "A Hateful Passion, a Lost Love," 96.
79. Spillers, "A Hateful Passion, a Lost Love," 95.
80. Spillers, "A Hateful Passion, a Lost Love," 96.
81. Spillers, "A Hateful Passion, a Lost Love," 118.
82. Biko Mandela Gray has also been working on the figure of an "always" in Morrison's work. Gray presented on the topic at the 2020 Annual Meeting of the American Academy of Religion, conducted virtually, for the Theology & Continental Philosophy Unit. This article is now published, Biko Mandela Gray (2022), "Now it is Always Now" in Political Theology, DOI: 10.1080/1462317X.2022.20993693
83. Toni Morrison, *Sula* (New York: Vintage, 2007).
84. Morrison, *Sula*.
85. Morrison, *Sula*.
86. Kathryn Nichol, "Locating the Front Line: War, Democracy, and the Nation in Toni Morrison's *Sula* and *Song of Solomon*," in *Death in American Texts and Performances: Corpses, Ghosts, and the Reanimated Dead*, ed. Lisa K. Perdigao and Mark Pizzato (Farnham, UK: Ashgate, 2010), 175.
87. Morrison, *Sula*.
88. Morrison, *Sula*.
89. Morrison, *Sula*.
90. Morrison, *Sula*.
91. Jackson, *Becoming Human*, 83.
92. Jackson, *Becoming Human*, 116.
93. Jackson, *Becoming Human*, 44.

5. SISTERHOOD AND ENMITY

1. Audre Lorde, *The Cancer Journals* (New York: Penguin, 1980, 2020), 15.
2. Lorde, *The Cancer Journals*, 53.
3. Lorde, *The Cancer Journals*, 5.
4. Lorde, *The Cancer Journals*, 19.
5. Lorde, *The Cancer Journals*, 39.
6. Lorde, *The Cancer Journals*, 40.
7. Lorde, *The Cancer Journals*, 18.
8. Carl Schmitt, *The Concept of the Political*, trans. George Schwab (Chicago: University of Chicago Press, 1996, 2007), 26.
9. Schmitt, *Concept of the Political*, 27.
10. Schmitt, *Concept of the Political*, 29.
11. Schmitt, *Concept of the Political*, 29.
12. Christina Sharpe, *In the Wake: On Blackness and Being* (Durham, N.C.: Duke University Press, 2016), 7.
13. Sharpe, *In the Wake*, 21.
14. Sharpe, *In the Wake*, 21.
15. Adam Kotsko, *Neoliberalism's Demons: On the Political Theology of Late Capital* (Stanford: Stanford University Press, 2018), 30.
16. Kotsko, *Neoliberalism's Demons*, 32.
17. Schmitt describes, for instance, his analysis of sovereignty as a sociology of the concept of sovereignty. See Carl Schmitt, *Political Theology: Four Chapters on the Concept of Sovereignty*, trans. George Schwab (Chicago: University of Chicago Press, 1985, 2005), 42.
18. Kotsko, *Neoliberalism's Demons*, 8.
19. Kotsko, *Neoliberalism's Demons*, 9.
20. Thomas Lynch, *Apocalyptic Political Theology: Hegel, Taubes, and Malabou* (London: Bloomsbury, 2019), 8.
21. He called Romans 9–11 "the most important political theology, whether Jewish or Christian." See Jacob Taubes, *To Carl Schmitt, Letters and Reflections*, trans. Keith Tribe (New York: Columbia University Press, 2013), 29.
22. Jacob Taubes, *The Political Theology of Paul*, trans. Dana Hollander (Stanford: Stanford University Press, 2004), 16.
23. Gil Anidjar, *The Jew, the Arab: A History of the Enemy* (Stanford: Stanford University Press, 2003), 5.
24. Anidjar, *The Jew, the Arab*, 6.

25. Taubes, *To Carl Schmitt*, 1.
26. Taubes, *The Political Theology of Paul*, 103.
27. Mike Grimshaw, "Introduction" to Taubes, *To Carl Schmitt*, xv.
28. Lynch, *Apocalyptic Political Theology*, 8.
29. See, for instance, Sallie McFague, *Models of God: Theology for an Ecological, Nuclear Age* (Minneapolis: Fortress, 1987).
30. Audre Lorde, "Poetry is Not a Luxury," in *The Selected Works of Audre Lorde*, ed. Roxane Gay (New York: Norton, 2020), 4.
31. Lorde, "Poetry is Not a Luxury," 5.
32. Lorde, "Poetry is Not a Luxury," 7.
33. Lorde, "Poetry is Not a Luxury," 3.
34. Christine Downing, *Psyche's Sisters: Re-Imagining the Meaning of Sisterhood* (New York: Continuum, 1988, 1990), 4.
35. Downing, *Psyche's Sisters*, 170.
36. Downing, *Psyche's Sisters*, 4.
37. Downing, *Psyche's Sisters*, 4.
38. Downing, *Psyche's Sisters*, 11.
39. Downing, *Psyche's Sisters*, 12.
40. Downing, *Psyche's Sisters*, 17.
41. Downing, *Psyche's Sisters*, 78.
42. Downing, *Psyche's Sisters*, 154.
43. Downing, *Psyche's Sisters*, 170.
44. Audre Lorde, *Sister Outsider* (New York: Penguin Random House, 1982, 2020), 146.
45. Lorde, *Sister Outsider*, 147.
46. Lorde, *Sister Outsider*, 147.
47. Lorde, *Sister Outsider*, 150.
48. Lorde, *Sister Outsider*, 158.
49. Lorde, *Sister Outsider*, 148.
50. Lorde, *Sister Outsider*, 159.

6. NATAL DISTURBANCE

1. Marcella Althaus-Reid, *Indecent Theology: Theological Perversions in Sex, Gender, and Politics* (New York: Routledge, 2000), 22.
2. Grace M. Jantzen, *Death and the Displacement of Beauty*, Vol. I: Foundations of Violence (New York: Routledge, 2004), 5.

6. NATAL DISTURBANCE ❧ 249

3. Jantzen, *Death and the Displacement of Beauty*, 10.
4. Jantzen, *Death and the Displacement of Beauty*, 31.
5. Jantzen, *Death and the Displacement of Beauty*, 6.
6. Grace M. Jantzen, *Becoming Divine: Toward a Feminist Philosophy of Religion* (Bloomington and Indianapolis: Indiana University Press, 1999), 137.
7. Jantzen, *Becoming Divine*, 161.
8. Jantzen, *Becoming Divine*, 2.
9. Jantzen, *Death and the Displacement of Beauty*, 6.
10. Anne O'Byrne, *Natality and Finitude* (Bloomington: Indiana University Press, 2010), 26. Italics mine.
11. Martin Heidegger, *Being and Time*, trans. John Macquarrie and Edward Robinson (New York: Harper, 1962, 2008), 282.
12. Heidegger, *Being and Time*, 294.
13. O'Byrne, *Natality*, 29.
14. Heidegger, *Being and Time*, 298.
15. Hannah Arendt, *Love and Saint Augustine*, ed. Joanna Vecchiarelli Scott and Judith Chelius Stark (Chicago: University of Chicago Press, 1996), 11.
16. Hannah Arendt, *The Life of the Mind* (San Diego: Harcourt, 1977, 1978), 109.
17. Hannah Arendt, *The Human Condition* (Chicago: University of Chicago Press, 1958), 9.
18. Adriana Cavarero, *Inclinations: A Critique of Rectitude*, trans. Amanda Minervini and Adam Sitze (Stanford: Stanford University Press, 2016), 118.
19. Cavarero, *Inclinations*, 115.
20. Cavarero, *Inclinations*, 115.
21. Cavarero, *Inclinations*, 102.
22. Robin May Schott, "Introduction," in Robin May Schott (Ed.), *Birth, Death, and Femininity: Philosophies of Embodiment*, ed. Robin May Schott (Bloomington: Indiana University Press, 2010), 9.
23. David Benatar, *Better to Never Have Been: The Harm of Coming into Existence* (Oxford: Clarendon, 2006), 1.
24. Benatar, *Better to Never Have Been*, 5.
25. Benatar, *Better to Never Have Been*, 6.
26. Benatar, *Better to Never Have Been*, 14.
27. Benatar, *Better to Never Have Been*, 15.
28. Benatar, *Better to Never Have Been*, 1.
29. Julia Reinhard Lupton, "Hannah Arendt's Renaissance: Remarks on Natality," *Journal of Cultural and Religious Theory*, no. 2 (Spring 2006): 10.

30. Lupton, "Hannah Arendt's Renaissance," 13.
31. Lupton, "Hannah Arendt's Renaissance," 12.
32. As Cusa puts it, "The infinite form is received only in a finite way; consequently, every creature is, as it were, a finite infinity or a created god, so it exists in the way in which this best could be." See Nicholas of Cusa, "On Learned Ignorance," in *Selected Spiritual Writings*, trans. H. Lawrence Bond (New York: Paulist, 1997), 134.
33. Miguel Vatter, "Natality and Biopolitics in Hannah Arendt," *Revista de Ciencia Politica* 26, no. 2 (2006): 145.
34. Orlando Patterson, *Slavery and Social Death: A Comparative Study* (Cambridge, Mass.: Harvard University Press, 1982), 38.
35. Patterson, *Slavery and Social Death*, 9.
36. Patterson, *Slavery and Social Death*, 8.
37. Dorothy E. Roberts, *Killing the Black Body: Race, Reproduction, and the Meaning of Liberty* (New York: Vintage, 1997, 2016), 23.
38. Roberts, *Killing the Black Body*, 22.
39. Roberts, *Killing the Black Body*, 23.
40. Roberts, *Killing the Black Body*, 25.
41. Saidiya Hartman, "The Belly of the World: A Note on Black Women's Labors," *Souls: A Critical Journal of Black Politics, Culture, and Society* 18, no. 1 (January–March 2016): 166–73.
42. Hartman, "Belly of the World," 169.
43. Hartman, "Belly of the World," 171.
44. Hartman, "Belly of the World," 169.
45. Grace Kyongwon Hong, *Death Beyond Disavowal: The Impossible Politics of Difference* (Minneapolis: University of Minnesota Press, 2015), 95.
46. Hong, *Death Beyond Disavowal*, 96.
47. Hong, *Death Beyond Disavowal*, 97.
48. Hong, *Death Beyond Disavowal*, 96.
49. Hortense J. Spillers, *Black, White, and in Color: Essays on American Literature and Culture* (Chicago: University of Chicago Press, 2003), 220.
50. Hong, *Death Beyond Disavowal*, 103.
51. Hong, *Death Beyond Disavowal*, 105.
52. Hong, *Death Beyond Disavowal*, 105.
53. Hong, *Death Beyond Disavowal*, 106.

54. Sabina Spielrein, "Destruction as the Cause of Coming into Being," *Journal of Analytic Psychology* 39 (1994): 183.
55. Spielrein, "Destruction," 167.
56. Spielrein, "Destruction," 160.
57. Pamela Cooper-White, " 'The Power that Beautifies and Destroys': Sabina Spielrein and 'Destruction as a Cause of Coming Into Being,' " *Pastoral Psychology* 64 (2015): 259.
58. Spielrein, "Destruction," 160.
59. Spielrein, "Destruction," 174.
60. This dimension of Spielrein's paper may have contributed to Jung's theory of the collective unconscious. Brian R. Skea, "Sabina Spielrein: Out from the Shadow of Jung and Freud," *Journal of Analytic Psychology* 51 (2006): 527.
61. Simona Forti, *The New Demons: Rethinking Power and Evil Today*, trans. Zakiya Hanafi (Stanford: Stanford University Press, 2012), 177.
62. Sigmund Freud, *Beyond the Pleasure Principle*, trans. C. J. M. Hubback (Digireads.com, 2009), 32.
63. Jacques Lacan, *The Ethics of Psychoanalysis 1959–1960: The Seminar of Jacques Lacan, Book VII*, trans. Dennis Ported and ed. Jacques-Alain Miller (New York: Routledge, 1992), 211.
64. Jacques Lacan, *The Ego in Freud's Theory and in the Technique of Psychoanalysis 1954–1955: The Seminar of Jacques Lacan, Book II*, trans. Sylvana Tomaselli and ed. Jacques-Alain Miller (New York: Norton, 1991), 80.
65. Lacan, *The Ego*, 171.
66. Lacan, *The Ego*, 326.
67. Lacan, *The Ego*, 233.
68. Lacan, *The Ego*, 213.
69. Theology as an enterprise is deeply shaped by but not reducible to Western metaphysics.
70. John Polkinghorne argues that, when it comes to eschatology, theological discourses on creation (and so the life of creatures) seeks to mark both continuity with this life and yet also a discontinuity (in light of what is still to come). See John Polkinghorne, "Eschatology: Some Questions and Some Insights from Science," in *The End of the World and the Ends of God: Science and Theology on Eschatology*, ed. John Polkinghorne and Michael Wekler (Harrisburg, Penn.: Trinity, 2000), 30–39.

CONCLUSION: INTO THE DIRT

1. Ben Ware, "Nothing but the End to Come? Extinction Fragments," *e-flux* 111 (September 2020), https://www.e-flux.com/journal/111/345009/nothing-but-the-end-to-come-extinction-fragments/.
2. Eugene Thacker, *In the Dust of This Planet*, Vol. I: *Horror of Philosophy* (Winchester, UK: Zero, 2011), 1.
3. Thacker, *In the Dust of This Planet*, 113.
4. Thacker, *In the Dust of This Planet*, 124.
5. Thacker, *In the Dust of This Planet*, 123.
6. Thacker, *In the Dust of This Planet*, 9.
7. Thacker, *In the Dust of This Planet*, 8.
8. Ursula K. Heise, *Imagining Extinction: The Cultural Meanings of Endangered Species* (Chicago: University of Chicago Press, 2016), 6–7.
9. Heise, *Imagining Extinction*, 13.
10. Heise, *Imagining Extinction*, 22.
11. Heise, *Imagining Extinction*, 23.
12. Heise, *Imagining Extinction*, 23.
13. For a discussion of the way that the term "extinction" was deployed, to assert that the spread of epidemic disease among former slaves was a "foregone conclusion" rather than a public health problem that demanded medical resources see, Jim Downs, *Sick from Freedom: African-American Illness and Suffering During the Civil War and Reconstruction* (Oxford: Oxford University Press), 103.
14. Heise, *Imagining Extinction*, 35.
15. Déborah Danowski and Eduardo Viveiros de Castro, *The Ends of the World*, trans. Rodrigo Nunes (Malden, Mass.: Polity, 2017), 65.
16. Danowski and Viveiros de Castro, 65.
17. Danowski and Viveiros de Castro, 66.
18. Danowski and Viveiros de Castro, 67.
19. Danowski and Viveiros de Castro, 68.
20. Danowski and Viveiros de Castro, 75.
21. Caitlin Doughty, *From Here to Eternity: Traveling the World to Find the Good Death* (New York: Norton, 2017, 2018), 136.

BIBLIOGRAPHY

Agamben, Giorgio. *Language and Death: The Place of Negativity*. Trans. Karen E. Pinkus and Michael Hardt. Minneapolis: University of Minnesota Press, 1991.

Akhtar, Jaleel. *Dismemberment in the Fiction of Toni Morrison*. Newcastle Upon Tyne, UK: Cambridge Scholars, 2014.

Althaus-Reid, Marcella. *Indecent Theology: Theological Perversions in Sex, Gender, and Politics*. New York: Routledge, 2000.

Anidjar, Gil. *Blood: A Critique of Christianity*. New York: Columbia University Press, 2014.

Anidjar, Gil. *The Jew, the Arab: A History of the Enemy*. Stanford: Stanford University Press, 2003.

Aquinas, Thomas. *On Evil*. Ed. Brian Davies and trans. Richard Regan. Oxford: Oxford University Press, 2003.

Aquinas, Thomas. *Summa Theologica*, Pt. 2 (First Part). Trans. Fathers of the English Dominican Province. New York: Benziger, 1915.

Aquinas, Thomas. *Summa Theologica*, Vol. 2, Pt. 2, First Section. Trans. Fathers of the English Dominican Province. New York: Cosimo Classics, 2007.

Aquinas, Thomas. *Summa Theologica*, Vol. 50: *The One Mediator*. Trans. Colman E. O'Neill. London: Blackfriars, 1965.

Aranda, Julieta, and Eben Kirksey. "Toward a Glossary of the Oceanic Undead: A(mphibious) through F(utures)" in *e-flux* 112 (October 2020). https://www.e-flux.com/journal/112/354965/toward-a-glossary-of-the-oceanic-undead-a-mphibious-through-f-utures/.

Arendt, Hannah. *The Human Condition*. Chicago: University of Chicago Press, 1958.
Arendt, Hannah. *The Life of the Mind*. San Diego: Harcourt 1978, 1977.
Arendt, Hannah. *Love and Saint Augustine*. Ed. Joanna Vecchiarelli Scott and Judith Chelius Stark. Chicago: University of Chicago Press, 1996.
Aristotle. *The Nichomachean Ethics*. Trans. R. W. Browne. London: George Bell, 1889.
Armstrong, Amaryah Shaye. "Christian Order and Racial Order: What Cedric Robinson Has to Teach Us Today." *The Bias Magazine: The Voice of the Christian Left*, June 3, 2020. https://christiansocialism.com/cedric-robinson-racial-order-christianity-socialism/.
Athanasius. "On the Incarnation of the Word." In *Christology of the Later Fathers*, Vol. 3, ed. Edward Rochie Hardy. Philadelphia: Westminster, 1954.
Athanasius. "Orations Against the Arians." In *The Christological Controversy*, ed. and trans. Richard A. Norris Jr. Philadelphia: Fortress, 1980.
Aulén, Gustaf. *Christus Victor: A Historical Study of the Three Main Types of the Idea of Atonement*. Trans. A. G. Hebert. Eugene, Ore.: Wipf & Stock, 1931.
Baldwin, James. *The Price of the Ticket: Collected Nonfiction 1948–1985*. New York: St. Martin's, 1985.
Barth, Karl. *Epistle to the Romans*. Trans. Edwin C. Hoskyns. Oxford: Oxford University Press, 1933, 1968.
de Beauvoir, Simone. *The Second Sex*. Trans. Constance Borde and Sheila Malvony-Chevallier. New York: Vintage, 2011.
Benatar, David. *Better to Never Have Been: The Harm of Coming Into Existence*. Oxford: Clarendon, 2006.
Bennett, Juda. *Toni Morrison and the Queer Pleasure of Ghosts*. Albany: State University of New York Press, 2014.
Bielby, Clare, and Anna Richards (ed.). *Women and Death 3: Women's Representations of Death in German Culture*. Rochester, N.Y.: Camden House, 2010.
Boyarin, Daniel. *The Jewish Gospels: The Story of the Jewish Christ*. New York: New Press, 2012.
Brown, Norman O. *Life Against Death: The Psychoanalytical Meaning of History*. Middletown, Conn.: Wesleyan University Press, 1959, 1985.
Buell, Denise Kimber. *Why This Race? Ethnic Reasoning in Early Christianity*. New York: Columbia University Press, 2005.
Burrus, Virginia. *Ancient Christian Ecopoetics: Cosmologies, Saints, Things*. Philadelphia: University of Pennsylvania Press, 2019.

Bynum, Caroline Walker. *Holy Feast and Holy Fast: The Religious Significance of Food to Medieval Women*. Berkeley: University of California Press, 1987.

Carter, J. Kameron. *Race: A Theological Account*. Oxford: Oxford University Press, 2008.

Cavarero, Adriana. *Inclinations: A Critique of Rectitude*. Trans. Amanda Minervini and Adam Sitze. Stanford: Stanford University Press, 2016.

Chavez, Sarah. "Death & the Maidens: Why Women Are Working with Death." In *Death and the Maidens* (blog): https://deadmaidens.com/2016/08/15/death-the-maidens-why-women-are-working-with-death/.

Chavez, Sarah. "Why the Story of Death Is the Story of Women." *Yes!* 91 (Fall 2019): 18–24.

Cooper-White, Pamela. " 'The Power That Beautifies and Destroys': Sabina Spielrein and 'Destruction as a Cause of Coming into Being.' " *Pastoral Psychology* 64 (2015): 259–78.

Crockett, William R. *Eucharist: Symbol of Transformation*. Collegeville, Minn.: Liturgical Press, 1989.

Cullmann, Oscar. *Immortality of the Soul or Resurrection of the Dead? The Witness of the New Testament*. Eugene, Ore.: Wipf & Stock, 1964.

Cusanus, Nicholas. "On Learned Ignorance." In *Selected Spiritual Writings*. Trans. H. Lawrence Bond. New York: Paulist, 1997.

Daly Goggin, Maureen, and Beth Fowkes Tobin (ed.). *Women and the Material Culture of Death*. New York: Routledge, 2013.

Danowski, Déborah, and Eduardo Viveiros de Castro. *The Ends of the World*. Trans. Rodrigo Nunes. Malden, Mass.: Polity, 2017.

Davies, Brian. "Introduction." In *On Evil*, trans. Richard Regan and ed. Brian Davies. Oxford: Oxford University Press, 2003.

Dawson, Ashley. *Extinction: A Radical History*. New York: OR, 2016.

Derrida, Jacques. *Aporias*. Trans. Thomas Dutoit. Stanford: Stanford University Press, 1993.

Derrida, Jacques. *La vie la mort: Séminaire (1975–1976)*. Paris: Seuil, 2019.

Derrida, Jacques. *Life Death*. Trans. Pascale-Anne Brault and Michael Naas. Chicago: University of Chicago Press, 2020.

Doughty, Caitlin. *From Here to Eternity: Traveling the World to Find the Good Death*. New York: Norton, 2017, 2018.

Downing, Christine. *Psyche's Sisters: Re-Imagining the Meaning of Sisterhood*. New York: Continuum, 1988, 1990.

Downs, Jim. *Sick from Freedom: African-American Illness and Suffering During the Civil War and Reconstruction.* Oxford: Oxford University Press.

Fletcher, Jeannine Hill. *The Sin of White Supremacy: Christianity, Racism, and Religious Diversity in America.* Maryknoll, N.Y.: Orbis, 2017.

Forti, Simona. *The New Demons: Rethinking Power and Evil Today.* Trans. Zakiya Hanafi. Stanford: Stanford University Press, 2012.

Foucault, Michel. *The Birth of the Clinic: An Archaeology of Medical Perception.* Trans. A. M. Sheridan Smith. New York: Vintage, 1973, 1994.

Freud, Sigmund. *Beyond the Pleasure Principle.* Trans. C. J. M. Hubback. Digireads.com, 2009.

Grove, Jairus Victor. *Savage Ecology: War and Geopolitics at the End of the World.* Durham, N.C.: Duke University Press, 2019.

Guthke, Karl S. *The Gender of Death: A Cultural History in Art and Literature.* Cambridge: Cambridge University Press, 1999.

Haland, Evy Johanne (ed.). *Women, Pain, and Death: Rituals and Everyday Life on the Margins of Europe and Beyond.* Newcastle upon Tyne, UK: Cambridge Scholars, 2008.

Hallote, Rachel S. *Death, Burial, and Afterlife in the Biblical World: How the Israelites and Their Neighbors Treated the Dead.* Chicago: Ivan R. Dee, 2001.

Haraway, Donna. *Staying with the Trouble: Making Kin in the Chthulucene.* Durham, N.C.: Duke University Press, 2016.

Hartman, Saidiya. "The Belly of the World: A Note on Black Women's Labors." *Souls: A Critical Journal of Black Politics, Culture, and Society* 18, no. 1 (January–March 2016): 166–73.

Heidegger, Martin. *Being and Time.* Trans. John Macquarrie and Edward Robinson. New York: Harper, 1962, 2008.

Heidegger, Martin. *Hegel.* Trans. Joseph Are and Niels Feuerhahn. Bloomington: Indiana University Press, 2015.

Heise, Ursula K. *Imagining Extinction: The Cultural Meanings of Endangered Species.* Chicago: University of Chicago Press, 2016.

Hong, Grace Kyongwon. *Death Beyond Disavowal: The Impossible Politics of Difference.* Minneapolis: University of Minnesota Press, 2015.

Howe, Cymene, Susanna Zaraysky, and Lois Ann Lorentzen. "Devotional Crossings: Transgender Sex Workers, Santisima Muerte, and Spiritual Solidarity in Guadalajara and San Francisco." In *Religion at the Corner of Bliss and Nirvana: Politics, Identity, and Faith in New Migrant Communities,* ed. Lois Ann Lorentzen, Joaquin Jay Gonzalez III, Kevin M. Chun, and Hien Duc Do, 29. Durham, N.C.: Duke University Press, 2009.

Irenaeus of Lyon. "Against Heresies." Bk. 3, Chapters 18–19, in *The Christological Controversy*. Ed. and trans. Richard A. Norris Jr. Philadelphia: Fortress, 1980.

Jackson, Zakiyyah Iman. *Becoming Human: Matter and Meaning in an Antiblack World*. New York: New York University Press, 2020.

Jantzen, Grace. *Becoming Divine: Towards a Feminist Philosophy of Religion*. Bloomington: Indiana University Press, 1999.

Jantzen, Grace M. *Death and the Displacement of Beauty*, Vol. I: Foundations of Violence. New York: Routledge, 2004.

Jennings, Toby. *Precious Enemy: A Biblical Portrait of Death*. Eugene, Ore.: Pickwick, 2017.

Keach, Benjamin. *Tropologia: A Key to Open Scripture Metaphors in Four Books*. London: City Press, 1858.

Keel, Terence. *Divine Variations: How Christian Thought Became Racial Science*. Stanford: Stanford University Press, 2018.

King, Tiffany Lethabo. *The Black Shoals: Offshore Formations of Black and Native Studies*. Durham, N.C.: Duke University Press, 2019.

Kotsko, Adam. *Neoliberalism's Demons: On the Political Theology of Late Capital*. Stanford: Stanford University Press, 2018.

Lacan, Jacques. *The Ego in Freud's Theory and in the Technique of Psychoanalysis 1954–1955: The Seminar of Jacques Lacan, Book II*. Trans. Sylvana Tomaselli and ed. Jacques-Alain Miller. London: Norton, 1991.

Lacan, Jacques. *The Ethics of Psychoanalysis 1959–1960: The Seminar of Jacques Lacan, Book VII*. Trans. Dennis Ported and ed. Jacques-Alain Miller. New York: Routledge, 1992.

Lloyd, Vincent W. (ed.). *Race and Political Theology*. Stanford: Stanford University Press, 2012.

Lofland, Lyn H. *The Craft of Dying: The Modern Face of Death*. Cambridge, Mass.: MIT Press, 1978, 2019.

Lorde, Audre. "Poetry Is Not a Luxury." In *The Selected Works of Audre Lorde*. Ed. Roxane Gay. New York: Norton, 2020.

Lorde, Audre. *The Cancer Journals*. New York: Penguin, 1980, 2020.

Lorde, Audre. *Sister Outsider*. New York: Penguin Random House, 1982, 2020.

Lupton, Julia Reinhard. "Hannah Arendt's Renaissance: Remarks on Natality." *Journal of Cultural and Religious Theory* 7, no. 2 (Spring 2006).

Lynch, Thomas. *Apocalyptic Political Theology: Hegel, Taubes, and Malabou.* London: Bloomsbury, 2019.

May, Todd. *Death.* New York: Routledge, 2009, 2014.

Mbembe, Achille. *Necropolitics.* Trans. Steven Corcoran. Durham, N.C.: Duke University Press, 2019.

McFague, Sallie. *Models of God: Theology for an Ecological, Nuclear Age.* Minneapolis: Fortress, 1987.

Méndez-Montoya, Angel F. *The Theology of Food: Eating and the Eucharist.* Hoboken, N.J.: Blackwell, 2012.

Mickey, Sam. *Coexistentialism and the Unbearable Intimacy of Ecological Emergency.* Lanham, Md.: Lexington, 2016.

Morrison, Toni. *The Source of Self-Regard: Selected Essays, Speeches, and Meditations.* New York: Vintage, 2020.

Morrison, Toni. *Sula.* New York: Vintage, 2007.

Nichol, Kathryn. "Locating the Front Line: War, Democracy, and the Nation in Toni Morrison's *Sula* and *Song of Solomon.*" In *Death in American Texts and Performances: Corpses, Ghosts, and the Reanimated Dead*, ed. Lisa K. Perdigao and Mark Pizzato, 175. Farnham, UK: Ashgate, 2010.

Nietzsche, Friedrich. "The Anti-Christ: A Curse on Christianity." In *The Anti-Christ, Ecce Homo, Twilight of the Idols, and Other Writings*, trans. Judith Norman. Cambridge: Cambridge University Press, 2005.

Noonan, Jeff. *Embodiment and the Meaning of Life.* Montreal: McGill-Queen's University Press, 2018.

Noys, Benjamin. *The Culture of Death.* Oxford: Berg, 2005.

O'Byrne, Anne. *Natality and Finitude.* Bloomington: Indiana University Press, 2010.

Patterson, Orlando. *Slavery and Social Death: A Comparative Study.* Cambridge, Mass.: Harvard University Press, 1982.

Penfold-Mounce, Ruth. *Death, the Dead, and Popular Culture.* Bingley, UK: Emerald, 2018.

Polkinghorne, John. "Eschatology: Some Questions and Some Insights from Science." In *The End of the World and the Ends of God: Science and Theology on Eschatology*, ed. John Polkinghorne and Michael Wekler. Harrisburg, Penn.: Trinity, 2000.

Pseudo-Athanasius. *The Life and Regimen of the Blessed and Holy Syncletica*, Part I: The Translation. Trans. Elizabeth Bryson Bongie. Eugene, Ore.: Wipf & Stock, 2003.

Radford Ruether, Rosemary. *Goddesses and the Divine Feminine: A Western Religious History.* Berkeley: University of California Press, 2005.

Roberts, Dorothy E. *Killing the Black Body: Race, Reproduction, and the Meaning of Liberty.* New York: Vintage, 1997, 2016.

Rose, Deborah Bird. *Reports from Wild Country: An Ethics for Decolonization.* Sydney: University of New South Wales Press, 2004.

Rose, Deborah Bird, Thom van Dooren, and Matthew Chrulew (Ed.). *Extinction Studies: Stories of Time, Death, and Generations.* New York: Columbia University Press, 2017.

Roynon, Tessa. *The Cambridge Introduction to Toni Morrison.* New York: Cambridge University Press, 2013.

Rubenstein, Mary-Jane. *Pantheologies: Gods, Worlds, Monsters.* New York: Columbia University Press, 2018.

Ruether, Rosemary Radford. *Goddesses and the Divine Feminine: A Western Religious History.* Berkeley: University of California Press, 2005.

Schillace, Brandy. *Death's Summer Coat: What the History of Death and Dying Teaches Us About Life and Living.* New York: Pegasus, 2015.

Schmitt, Carl. *The Concept of the Political.* Trans. George Schwab. Chicago: University of Chicago Press, 1996, 2007.

Schmitt, Carl. *Political Theology: Four Chapters on the Concept of Sovereignty.* Trans. George Schwab. Chicago: University of Chicago Press, 1985, 2005.

Schott, Robin May. "Introduction" in *Birth, Death, and Femininity: Philosophies of Embodiment,* ed. Robin May Schott, 9. Bloomington: Indiana University Press, 2010.

Sharpe, Christina. *In the Wake: On Blackness and Being.* Durham, N.C.: Duke University Press, 2016.

Skea, Brian R. "Sabina Spielrein: Out from the Shadow of Jung and Freud." *Journal of Analytic Psychology* 51 (2006): 527–52.

Spielrein, Sabina. "Destruction as the Cause of Coming into Being." *Journal of Analytic Psychology* 39 (1994): 155–86.

Spillers, Hortense J. *Black, White, and in Color: Essays on American Literature and Culture.* Chicago: University of Chicago Press, 2003.

Spillers, Hortense. "A Hateful Passion, a Lost Love: Three Women's Fiction," in *Black, White, and in Color: Essays on American Literature and Culture.* Chicago: University of Chicago Press, 2003.

Sproul, R. C. "The Last Enemy." *Tabletalk*, April 1, 2000. https://www.ligonier.org/learn/articles/the-last-enemy/.

Tanner, Kathryn. "Eschatology Without a Future?" In *The End of the World and the Ends of God: Science and Theology on Eschatology*, ed. John Polkinghorne and Michael Welker. Harrisburg, Penn.: Trinity, 2000.

Taubes, Jacob. *The Political Theology of Paul*. Trans. Dana Hollander. Stanford: Stanford University Press, 2004.

Taubes, Jacob. *To Carl Schmitt, Letters and Reflections*. Trans. Keith Tribe. New York: Columbia, 2013.

Taylor, James Stacey. *Death, Posthumous Harm, and Bioethics*. New York: Routledge, 2012.

Thacker, Eugene. *In the Dust of This Planet*, Vol. I: *Horror of Philosophy*. Winchester, UK: Zero, 2011.

Vatter, Miguel. "Natality and Biopolitics in Hannah Arendt." *Revista de Ciencia Politica* 26, no. 2 (2006): 137–59.

Vettori, Alessandro. *Poets of Divine Love: Franciscan Mystical Poetry of the Thirteenth Century*. New York: Fordham University Press, 2004.

Warren, Calvin L. *Ontological Terror: Blackness, Nihilism, and Emancipation*. Durham, N.C.: Duke University Press, 2018. Project MUSE, doi:10.1353/book.61312.

Ware, Ben. "Nothing but the End to Come? Extinction Fragments." *e-flux* 111 (September 2020). https://www.e-flux.com/journal/111/345009/nothing-but-the-end-to-come-extinction-fragments/.

Weir, Jessica K. "Lives in Connection." In *Manifesto for Living in the Anthropocene*, ed. Deborah Bird Rose, Katherine Gibson, and Ruth Fincher. Santa Barbara, Calif.: Punctum, 2015.

White, Carol Wayne. *Black Lives and Sacred Humanity: Toward an African American Religious Naturalism*. New York: Fordham University Press, 2017.

White, Lynn, Jr. "The Historical Roots of Our Ecologic Crisis." *Science*, new series, 155 (1967): 1203–6.

Wynter, Sylvia, and Katherine McKittrick. "Unparalleled Catastrophe for Our Species? Or, to Give Humanness a Different Future: Conversation." In *Sylvia Wynter: On Being Human as Praxis*, ed. Katherine McKittrick, 31. Durham, N.C.: Duke University Press, 2015.

Wyschogrod, Edith. *Spirit in Ashes: Hegel, Heidegger, and Man-Made Mass Death*. New Haven, Conn.: Yale University Press, 1985.

INDEX

abortion, 165–166; pro-life politics, 165–167
abyss, the, xii, 132, 219
afterlife: Christina Sharpe on the afterlives of slavery, 72, 167; as heaven, xiii, 130; the hope for immortality (individual and collective), 39, 231; and human recomposition, 231; as paradise, xiii, xiv, 112; teaching about death and the afterlife, xviii, xxiv; and Toni Morrison's "always", 125
Agamben, Giorgio, xxi; and bare life, 23; on metaphysics and negativity, 140–147. *See also* animals
aging: Caitlin Doughty and Katrina Spade on the human recomposition process, 261; and evil, 10, 127; as intrinsic form of limitation, 39–40; ripening, 216; and wisdom, 226
Akhtar, Jaleel, 150
Althaus-Reid, Marcella, 187

ancestors, 90, 95, 98, 220, 228; ancestral lineages, 99; and Heidegger's view of the past, 193; the past as inherited and ancestral, 138, 219; Rachel Hallote on the Cult of the Dead, 102–103; in Toni Morrison's *Sula*, 150
angels, xiii, 92
Anidjar, Gil, xxii, 43, 119, 171, 237n24, 240n33
animals: animal death as natural, 127; animal fat, 159; as archefossils, 228–229; and the constellated negative, 10, 124, 128, 135, 215; and Francis of Assisi, 1; in Giorgio Agamben's discussion of metaphysics and negativity, 142–144; in Heidegger, 145–148; as inhuman, 91, 230; and the living dead, 130; and metaphysics, xvii; Norman O. Brown and the flight from animality, 76–80; powers in animal bodies, 93; and race, 81

Anthropocene, 68–69. *See also* Eurocene
Antigone, 180
antinatalism, 197–199. *See also* Benatar, David
apocalyptic, xvii, 129
Aquinas, Thomas: and the constellated negative, 125, 127–131; and privation, 33, 143; views on Christ, 112–113
Aranda, Julieta, 72
Arendt, Hannah, xxi, 49, 204, 209; critiqued by Adriana Cavarero, 195–197; dissertation on Augustine of Hippo, 192–194; as interpreted by Grace Jantzen, 188, 191–192; natality as counterpoint to mortality, 135–136; secularization of creatureliness, 200–202
Aristotle, 126–127
Armstrong, Amaryah, xxiii, 119
atonement (ransom theory of), 67
Augustine of Hippo, 194–196, 201–202. *See also* Arendt, Hannah
Aulén, Gustaf, 67. *See also* atonement
autopsy, 45

Baldwin, James, 61–63, 98, 238n1
Barth, Karl, 121
beauty: and birth, 199, 210; and courage, 29; and decay, 196; and horror, xii–xvi, xx, 227, 232–233; and sensuality, 91
de Beauvoir, Simone, xxi, 8, 16, 19, 49, 184, 187

Becker, Ernest 21–22
Benatar, David, 197–199. *See also* antinatalism
Bennett, Juda, 149
Betcher, Sharon, xv, xxiii
Bible: death in the epistles of Paul, 1, 3, 33–34, 60, 64–65, 71, 93, 104–106, 170–171; and depictions of death, 11, 63–64, 71; Genesis, 64, 66, 227; Gospels, 121; Job, 222; Psalms, 64. *See also* Paul (the apostle)
Bichat, Marie Françoise Xavier, 45, 46
biology: and bare life, 23; biological life and eternal life, 10, 161, 216; and birth, 189, 195–198; and decay, 44, 65; embodiment as biological, 15, 39; and Heidegger's view of death, 138, 143–145, 147, 193; and *homo sapiens*, 95; in psychoanalysis, 74, 212–213; and sisterhood, 179, 181, 184. *See also* biomythology
biomythology, 227, 229; death as biomyth, 64–65; and extinction, 222; and form of life, 69; psychoanalysis as biomyth, 74–76; sisterhood as biomyth, 174, 177, 184–185
birth, xi–xiii, 19; in Audre Lorde, 176; connection to death, 56, 199; and the death drive, 209–210; maternal mortality, 16; in metaphysics (birth of the human), 143; and natality, 49, 135–137, 139–140, 187–197,

200–206, 209; and original sin, 34; in Simone de Beauvoir, 8; in the work of Sabina Spielrein, 211, 214–216. *See also* natality

blackness, 10, 124–125, 129, 215; antiblackness in Christianity, 79, 94, 116–117, 119–121; black feminism, 11, 18, 49; black feminist critiques of reproductive politics, 207; and Calvin Warren, 125, 131–132, 134, 191; and James Baldwin, 61; and Toni Morrison, 151, 153; and Zakiyyah Iman Jackson, 144–151, 156

Boyarin, Daniel, 115

Brown, Norman O., 74–80, 82, 84

Buell, Denise, 114–115

burial, 15, 19, 101–102, 138, 193

Burrus, Virginia, 241n2

Bynum, Caroline Walker, 111

Caciola, Nancy, 15

Carter, J. Kameron, 116–117

catastrophe, xxii, 221

Cavarero, Adriana, 195–196, 202

Chavez, Sarah, 14–16, 19–20, 23–24. *See also* death, death positive

Christianity, 1, 5, 10, 65, 77, 83, 97, 115–120; Christian sensibilities, 3, 87–90; Christian theology and thought, xxi, 6, 8, 104, 127–129, 134, 141, 172, 195, 202, 230; and colonization, 94, 97–98; enmity toward death, 7, 33–34, 43, 67–70, 171; and God, 175; and the human-above-death, 106–121; and the political theology of death, 59, 63; subjectivity, 66, 91

Christology, 90, 98, 105, 111

Chrulew, Matthew, 26

colonialism, 67, 72, 79, 95–96, 113, 120

connective distinction, 10, 216

constellated negative, 10, 121–157, 191–201, 204, 209, 215, 227

contingency, 167, 203; contingencies of flesh, 8; and the figure of the human, 81; and finitude, 62, 180; and natality, 137, 192, 196, 199

Cooper, Melissa, 15

corpse: burial of, 20, 102; in clinical settings, 45–46; corpse meditation, 61; in human recomposition, 230–231; of Jesus, 87; and necrophilia, 187

COVID-19, xvii–xviii, 165, 221

creature, xvi–xvii, 29, 72, 178; creature and creator, 1, 201; creaturely, 175; creaturely life as biological, 10, 66, 161; death as a creature, 7, 9; and human-above-death, 90, 98, 106–114, 118–119; the human as creature, 77; *Laudes Creaturarum* ("In Praise of Creatures"), 2–4; as mortal, xi, 144; and natality, 202–205, 215–216; in Nicholas of Cusa, 250n32; as non-human, 92, 127, 202

Crutzen, Paul, 68

Cullman, Oscar, 65–66

Cusa, Nicholas of, 203, 250n32. *See also* creature

Danowski, Déborah, 228
death: and the afterlife, xviii, xxiv; bond with life 34; and children, xi–xiv; contemplation of, 25, 29, 60–61, 71, 190; death-dealing, 118; death denial, 21; death-drive, 51, 55, 210–215; death positive, 13–16, 18, 20–25, 27–29, 56; death worlds, 72–73, 167–168, 226; and decay, xxii, 2, 10, 34, 44, 63–66, 82, 88, 91–93, 196, 205, 226, 231; as enemy, xx, 3–14, 33–35, 41–44, 47, 59–68, 76, 80–84, 93, 103–108, 114, 118, 120–121, 152–164, 214; flight from, 74–84; as friend, 7–10, 12, 34–35, 41–48, 59, 118, 159, 163–167, 185; and gender, 3–4, 8, 16–17, 19, 100, 124, 184, 187, 206–207; as infinitely complex, 11, 24, 44, 59, 63, 66, 82; as limit, xiv, 2, 4, 8, 34, 36–40, 53–66, 120, 126, 180–18, 189, 213; mass death, 13, 71–73, 220, 226; and mortality, xix, 8, 29; and mortal sisters, 179–180; multispecies mortality, 26; Order of the Good Death, 14; relation to beauty and horror, xx, 227, 233; Sister Death, xxi, 2–4, 7–10, 14, 20, 34–35, 40, 56; triumph over or defeat of (in theology), 4–5, 67–68, 92–93, 104–105, 108–110, 121, 161. *See also* constellated negative; extinction; Heidegger, Martin; lifedeath; mortality; natality; necropolitics; privation; psychoanalysis

decay, xiv, xxii, 1–2, 34, 44, 82, 226; and aging, 231; as a divine power, 88, 91–93; as evil, 10, 63–66; and natality, 196, 205. *See also* beauty; biology; death; soil
declension 145, 157, 223–225, 230. *See also* extinction
deification, 111
Derrida, Jacques, xiv, 11, 36, 48–55. *See also* lifedeath
destiny 62, 128–129
divine; child 195–196; conflict, 67; creation, xvi; and death, 16, 103; in defining theology, 223; destruction, 172–175; divinization, 34; illumination, 4; life as, 7; and metaphysics, 101, 124, 141; multiple forms of, 100; and natality, 201–202, 216; nature as, xvii, 2; and patriarchy, 184; powers, 88; and sisterhood, 180; triumph over death, 66; as uncreaturely, 90, 92–94, 98, 107–115; worship of, 102. *See also* God
Doughty, Caitlin, 14, 230–233
Downing, Christine, 178–181, 184
Dragomer, Krista, iv, vi, xvi–xviii
dreams, 78, 123, 125, 176, 181–183

Edelman, Lee, 208–209
elegy, 227
Enlightenment, 45, 144–145
Epicurus, 123, 126
eternity, 34; and creatures, 128, 216; eternal life, 4, 10, 51, 66–67, 88, 93, 108, 110, 114, 121; and Toni Morrison's "always", 125, 154–156

Eucharist (the), 109–111, 119
Eurocene, 68–70, 73, 79. 83. *See also* Grove, Jairus Victor
evil, 92, 151; death and decay as, 2, 10, 12, 33–34, 74, 82; and non-Christians, 67, 94; and privation, 124–130, 135, 139, 215; and Simona Forti, 212
extinction, 226; extinction narratives, 222–225; time of extinctions, 11, 13, 23, 220–221, 227; of humans 80–81, 198; mass extinction events, 26–29, 68–72; in psychoanalysis, 53, 55

fear, xviii, 39, 156, 176; of death, xi, 8, 13, 17, 29, 36, 61, 125, 132, 187; fearlessness, xxiii, 106; and horror, 222–227, 230
feminism 15, 20, 79, 135; black feminism, 11, 49, 148, 204–210; feminist theology, 175; and sisterhood, 18, 178–181
flesh, 156, 183; contingencies of, 8; divine, xvi; exit from, xiii–xiv; fleshiness and the connective distinction, 10, 121, 124, 135, 145, 215
Fletcher, Jeannine Hill, 117–118
form of life, 47, 66, 166, 196, 225; bare life, 23; creatureliness, 201, 216; divine, 10, 93; and horror, 222, 233; human (man as), 113, 227, 230, 232; martial, 30, 67, 69–71, 78–81, 83, 85. *See also* Grove, Jairus Victor
Fornace, Sarah, 15

Forti, Simona, 212–214
Foucault, Michel, 44–47
Francis of Assisi, xxi, 64, 88; and Sister Death 1–5, 7–10, 184
Freud, Sigmund, 46; death drive, 211–214; the pleasure principle, 51–55; theory of the instincts, 74. *See also* psychoanalysis
friendship, xvi, 167; between life and death, 7, 9; in political theology, 35, 41–47, 164
funeral, 19–20, 151–152
future 13, 29, 39, 62, 72, 90, 136–138, 170, 219–221, 228; of life and death, 15, 194; and natality, 195, 199; predictions of, 102; reproductive futurity, 206, 208

genealogy, 68–69, 94–95, 170, 200–202, 205
genocide, 23, 69
ghosts, 99, 149
Gnostic, 141
God: created gods, 203, 205; as creator, 2; and creatureliness, 106–114; as crucified, 87–88; and death, 4, 91–93, 98–106, 127–130; death of, 47–48, 214; as enemy of death, 3, 5, 7–8, 33–34; and hierarchy, 117–121; and horror, xv, 221–222, 226–227; of life, 10–11, 50, 64–67, 215–216; and natality, 201, 203; and nothingness, xvii; and political theology 164, 171–175, 185; in Spinoza, 80; will of, 152; and world, 124; as word, 141; worship of, 1

Gray, Biko Mandela, 246n82
Greek (ancient), 65, 127, 134, 180, 242n23
grief, 22, 27, 61, 152, 168, 185
Grimshaw, Mike, 172
Grove, Jairus Victor, 68–70, 73. *See also* Eurocene

Hallote, Rachel, 101–102
Haraway, Donna, 13–14
Hartman, Saidiya, 49, 206–207
heaven. *See* afterlife
Hegel, G. W., 50, 139–142, 145–147
Heidegger, Martin, 48–49, 124–125, 132–148, 157, 191–193
Heise, Ursula, 223–225
Holocaust, 23; Auschwitz, 71
Hong, Grace Kyungwon, 207–208
hope, xx, 39, 59, 97, 110, 142, 173, 176, 185; as a dimension of natality, 188, 195, 199
horror, xii–xx, 72, 125, 221–227, 230, 232
Howe, Cymene, 16
human-above-death, 89–90, 93–106, 108–115, 118–121, 143–147, 204

Indigenous, 5, 16, 94, 224, 225, 229
Irenaeus (of Lyon), 111–112

Jackson, Zakiyyah Iman, 125, 144–149, 156, 191
Jantzen, Grace, 49, 136, 187–199, 204, 209
Jennings, Toby, 120
Jesus, 65–70, 87–88, 105–107, 115–121, 171

Judaism, 66, 110; burial traditions, 102; Jewish identity, xiv, 113, 116; Jewish thought, 103, 107; relation to Christianity, 65, 115–117, 120

Keach, Benjamin, 129–130
Keel, Terence, 120
Keller, Catherine, xvii, xxii
King, Tiffany Lethabo, 94
Kirksey, Eben, 72
Kotsko, Adam, xxiii, 169–170
Kübler Ross, Elizabeth, 19, 21–22

Lacan, Jacques, 213–214
Lamorisse, Albert, xv
Lee, Jae Rhim, 15
life, xi, xvii, xxiv, 19, 25, 29, 40, 177; bare life, 23; black life, 61–62; and Christian thought, 87–92, 105–110, 112–114, 118–121, 128–131; creaturely life, 2; and the dead, 125–126, 152–157, 220; and death, xiv, 5, 14, 35, 41, 43–44; and death positivity, 20–21; as divine, 7; embodied, xiii; and enmity toward death, 59, 68–71, 96–97, 100, 161–173; eternal life, 4, 93; experiences, 37, 39; form of life, 30, 74–85, 226–227, 230–233; and God, 64–67; and Heidegger, 136–148; and horror, xix, 222–223; human life, 4; intimacy with death, xx, 17, 28, 101; and lifedeath, 44–56; and Audre Lorde, 159–160; and medical knowledge, 45–47; metaphysics of, 149–150; and

natality, 188–191, 195–198, 201–216; and political theology, 42; powers of, xii, 27, 63, 175; and sisterhood, 8–12, 34, 180–185. *See also* death; lifedeath

lifedeath, xiv, xx, 17–19, 21, 25–29, 63–66, 90–93, 215; in the Bible, 63–66; description of, 33–56; as enmity, 161–164; and God, 100, 101, 104; and natality, 191, 196–197, 200, 202, 205–206, 209; and necropolitics, 97–98; and political theology, 172, 174; and psychoanalysis, 211–212, 214; as sisterhood, 11–12, 14, 126, 177, 180, 184–185, 216, 225, 230; and theological anthropology, 114, 120; and Toni Morrison's "always", 125, 149–157; and the war with death, 74, 75, 77, 82–84; as weaving pattern, 88. *See also* death; life

Lloyd, Vincent, 6

Lofland, Lyn, 21–22, 24

loneliness, 154

Lorde, Audre, 9, 159, 161–162, 176, 182–185

Lorentzen, Lois Ann, 16

Lupton, Julia, 201, 203

Lynch, Tommy, xxii, xxiii, 170, 172

magic, xxiv, 176

marxism, xiv

mass death (manmade), 13, 71–73, 220, 226. *See also* Wyschogrod, Edith

May, Todd, 123

Mbembe, Achille, 83–84, 90, 96–97. *See also* necropolitics

McFague, Sallie, xv, 175, 248n29

medicine, 24, 44, 46–47

memory, xii, 20, 29, 143, 153

Méndez-Montoya, Angel, 111

metaphysics, 131–135, 156–157, 202, 214–215; of death and life, 123–126, 208; of God, 100; of negativity, 139–149, 191–195, 204; and theology, 251n69

Mickey, Sam, 26

militancy, 30, 47, 59, 60, 62, 70, 74, 82

misogyny, 8, 188

more than human, xi, 11, 13, 25–27, 81, 92, 175, 224–225, 229, 233

Morrison, Toni, 125, 148–152, 156–157

mortality, 67, 78, 82, 106; and Christian theology, 90, 92, 98, 107–114; collective, 225; control over, 96–97; denial of, 21–22; and finitude, 34, 46; maternal, 16; and Heidegger, 143–144, 147; mortalized, 118; mortal body, xvi–xvii, 93; mortal condition, xix, 61, 66; mortals, 17, 24, 29, 37, 60, 105, 121, 127, 129; multispecies, 26–29; and natality, 8, 56, 135–139, 188–195, 199, 202–205, 209–210, 215–216; and sisterhood, 179–180. *See also* death; natality

mothers, xiii, xxiv, 3, 18, 91, 149, 176, 196, 202–203, 210

multispecies, xvii, 26–27

Mutu, Wangechi, 148

natality: and birth, 8, 34; and the dead, 219; in Grace Jantzen, 188–192; in Hannah Arendt, xxi, 49, 193–205; natal condition, 29; natalmortals, 56, 215–216; and negativity, 134–149; and psychoanalysis, 210–215; and reproductive politics, 204–209. *See also* birth; death; mortality

necrophilia, 49, 136, 139, 187–188, 190, 215

necropolitics, 24, 83–84, 90, 96–98; necrotheology, 60, 90, 96, 121; thanatopolitics, 204. *See also* Mbembe, Achille

negativity, 48–49, 124, 135, 140–148. *See also* constellated negative; metaphysics; nothingness; Warren, Calvin

Nicaea (Council at), 90, 106–108, 111–112, 115

Nichol, Kathryn, 153

Nietzsche, Friedrich, 46, 54–55, 87–88, 238n39

nihilism, 55, 132. *See also* Warren, Calvin

Noonan, Jeff, 36–40

nothingness (nothing), xvii, 33–34, 61, 123–134, 139–141, 148, 157, 199, 208–209. *See also* constellated negative; negativity; privation; Warren, Calvin

Noys, Benjamin, 22–23, 25

O'Byrne, Anne, 136–137, 192

ontology, 95, 141–142, 191, 195, 206; distinctions, 124; ontological terror, 125–126, 131–134, 143, 148–149; and race, 145, 156. *See also* metaphysics; Warren, Calvin

optimism, 197–198

pain, 39, 97, 183, 198–199; and childbirth, 34, 210; and death, 24, 27, 62–63, 123, 154–156; and embodiment, 37; painful emotions, 18; and pleasure, 55, 211; and suffering, 38

palliative care, 20, 82, 90

pandemic, xvii–xx, 13. *See also* COVID-19

paradise. *See* afterlife

Patterson, Orlando, 205–206, 208

Paul (the Apostle), 1, 3, 33–34, 60, 64–65, 71, 93, 104–106, 170–171

Penfold-Mounce, Ruth, 21

pessimism, 39, 195

poetics, 2, 5, 7–8, 51, 54, 63; and Audre Lorde, 176; and Carl Schmitt, 162–174; counterpoetics, 162, 175–177, 185; of death, 5, 9–11, 14, 33, 35–36, 47, 56, 59, 63, 70, 85; definition of, 6–8, 99; destabilization of, 149, 227; and development of monotheism, 103; of the enemy (enmity), 43, 177, 184–185, 195; and the human-above-death, 88–89, 128; mythopoetics (biomythical), 106, 174, 184; and necropolitics, 97; and privation, 128; political theology, xxii, 161, 215; and race, 120

portals, xii, xv, 92, 219, 233

privation, 10, 33, 82, 94, 120–121, 126–131, 135, 139–143, 147, 215. *See also* death; evil

psychoanalysis 74, 77, 80, 190, 210, 212. *See also* Brown, Norman O.; death; Forti, Simona; Freud, Sigmund; Lacan, Jacques; Spielrein, Sabina

race, 145, 150; anti-black racism, 207; and form of life, 69; and gender domination, 206; and necropolitics, 83, 96; racialized/racializing orders, 60, 62, 81, 95–97, 118, 145–147; and theology, 114–120. *See also* blackness; whiteness

redemption, 80–82, 120, 125, 178

refuge, xviii, xix, 197

relics, 6, 93

reproduction, 18, 49, 100, 166, 189, 197, 206–209

resurrection, 66, 88, 103–106

Reuther, Rosemary Radford, 100

Roberts, Dorothy, 208

Rose, Deborah Bird, 26, 72

Roynon, Tessa, 150

Rubenstein, Mary-Jane, xxiii, 124

salvation, 47, 178, 197

Santa Muerte, 16–17

Schmitt, Carl, 6, 42, 163–164, 169–173. *See also* political theology

Schott, Robin May, 197

secrets, xiv–xvi, 44, 46, 98, 191, 193

secular (secularization), xiv, 5, 24, 94, 202–205, 223, 230; and death, 46, 50; and political theology, 6–7, 33, 163–164, 169, 171–172

senses, xix, 123, 199; and perception, xiii, xvi, xix, xx; sensation, xii, xvi, xviii, 20, 37

shadows, xi, xviii, xix, 112–113, 201–203; of the dead; shadow of death, xviii, 21, 27, 60, 132, 137

Sharpe, Christina, 61–62, 72, 167–169

shelter, xx, 82, 188, 197

Sheol, 11, 64

silence, 18, 27, 61, 141–142, 159

Sin, 10, 33–34, 54, 66–67, 82, 89, 114, 120–121, 128–131, 215; state of, 118; sinners, 98. *See also* evil; privation

Sister Death. *See* death

sisterhood, 8–9, 11–12, 17–18, 56, 91, 97, 162, 174–185, 202

Socrates, 65, 188

soil, 2, 65, 82, 84, 87, 97, 230–233; dirt, 220, 227–228, 230, 232–233. *See also* decay

space-time, xiv–xxiv, 6; across time and space, 118

Spade, Katrina, 15, 230

Spielrein, Sabina, 210–214

Spillers, Hortense, 150–151, 208

Spinoza, Baruch, 80

Srnicek, Nick, 39

suffering, 10, 37–38, 44, 55, 63–64, 92, 134, 176, 198–199, 206; through death, 8

symbolism, 95, 173, 184, 188, 194–195, 197, 206, 210, 213; of God, 100–101; and human

symbolism (*continued*)
recomposition, 231–232; symbolic attention, 82; symbolic death, 94; symbolic imaginary, 30; symbolic regime, 60–61, 165

Syncletica, 91–93

Tanner, Kathryn, 63–66
Taubes, Jacob, 170–172, 179
Taylor, James Stacey, 126
Thacker, Eugene, xxi, 221–222
theology, xiv, xv, xii, 67, 95, 99, 103, 131, 200, 221–223, 227, 251n69; Christian theology, 90, 106, 111–120, 129, 230; constructive theology, xxiii; political theology, 6–7, 43, 59, 63, 161–177; political theology of death, 5, 8–11, 14, 33–36, 47, 56, 70, 85, 87–90, 97, 128, 149, 184–195, 215. *See also* God; divine; political theology
Trump, Donald, 165

vaccine, xviii
Van Dooren, Thom, 26
Vatter, Miguel, 204
virus, xx, 82, 165. *See also* COVID-19; pandemic
vitalism (vitalists), 55; anti-vitalism, 78; vital dimensions, 90–91; vital memory, 29; vital or vitalizing powers, 4, 13, 51, 148, 152, 214; vital resistance, 21

Viveiros de Castro, Eduardo, 228–229

wake: in the wake of, xxvi, 4, 43, 48, 69, 71, 96, 100, 118, 128, 221, 225–226, 230; in the wake of death, 29, 41, 152–153, 190; wake work, 61–62, 168. *See also* Sharpe, Christina

war, 159, 171, 176; Civil War, 19; with death, 30, 56, 59–85, 189; gods of, 100; veteran, 153

Ware, Ben, 221
Warren, Calvin, 124–125, 131–134. *See also* ontology
Weil, Simone, xv
Weir, Jessica, 26
White, Carol Wayne, xxiii, 62, 238n1
Whitehead, Alfred North, 80
whiteness, 60, 62, 81, 117–120, 151, 167, 209; white supremacy, 117–120, 153, 206
Wilde, Oscar, xiii
Williams, Alex, 39
Wynter, Sylvia, 89, 93–96, 114
Wyschogrod, Edith, 71–72

Yountae, An, xxii, 239n21

Zaraysky, Susanna, 16

GPSR Authorized Representative: Easy Access System Europe, Mustamäe tee 50, 10621 Tallinn, Estonia, gpsr.requests@easproject.com

www.ingramcontent.com/pod-product-compliance
Lightning Source LLC
Chambersburg PA
CBHW022038290426
44109CB00014B/901